DESIGN FOR KINGSHIP

SOCIETY OF BIBLICAL LITERATURE

DISSERTATION SERIES

Robert R. Wilson, Editor

Number 69
DESIGN FOR KINGSHIP
The Deuteronomistic Narrative Technique
in 1 Kings 3:4–15

Helen A. Kenik

Helen A. Kenik

DESIGN FOR KINGSHIP

The Deuteronomistic Narrative Technique
in 1 Kings 3:4–15

Scholars Press
Chico, California

BS
1335.2
.K46
1983

DESIGN FOR KINGSHIP
The Deuteronomistic Narrative Technique
in 1 Kings 3:4–15

Helen A. Kenik

Ph.D., 1978
Saint Louis University
Saint Louis, Missouri

Advisor:
Walter A. Brueggemann

©1983
The Society of Biblical Literature

Library of Congress Cataloging in Publication Data

Kenik, Helen A.
    Design for kingship.

    (Dissertation series / Society of Biblical Literature ;
no. 69)
    Thesis (Ph.D.)—Saint Louis University, 1978.
    Bibliography: p.
    1. Bible. O.T. Kings, 1st, III, 4–15—Criticism,
interpretation, etc. 2 Bible. O.T. Kings, 1st, III, 4–15—
Language, style. I. Title. II. Series: Dissertation series
(Society of Biblical Literature) ; no. 69.
BS1335.2.K46 1983   222'.53066   82–21504
ISBN 0–89130–605–6

Printed in the United States of America

Contents

Preface

This is an investigation into the methodology used by the Deuteronomistic Historian in the composition of the dream of Solomon, a key deuteronomistic text, and the theological purpose intended by the Deuteronomist in that composition. It was originally submitted to the Faculty of the School of Divinity of St. Louis University in partial fulfillment of requirements for the Ph.D. degree in Biblical Languages and Literature. The manuscript remains essentially unchanged except for quotations from German sources which I have translated into English for this publication. Because of the time lapse since its completion, the need for updating is apparent. This will be done in the continuing development of the research begun here and in subsequent writings.

With this publication, I bring to completion a major phase of my career. This moment demands a word of gratitude to the scholars who accompanied me and to the friends who supported me financially and otherwise.

There is, first of all, Walter A. Brueggemann, of whom I am the first doctoral student. From this biblical man I learned the power of the Word and the meaning of commitment to the Word. He has been untiring with his direction, constant with his encouragement, and always present with friendship. I acknowledge, also, Dennis J. McCarthy, S.J. whose generosity continually overwhelmed me. He challenged me and clarified my thinking and finally had much influence on the direction of my research. I say thank you to all my teachers, especially Keith Nickle, Charles Miller and Hans Walter Wolff.

I owe much of my education to the Adrian Dominican Congregation. Rosemary Ferguson, O.P. gave me the time and the financial assistance I needed to bring my formal studies to completion. After a number of delays, this publication is a reality. I extend gratitude to Professor Robert R. Wilson, editor of the series, for guiding the manuscript through the editorial stages; and to the readers, whose names are unknown to me, for their recommendation of my work for publication. I am grateful to those who assisted me financially to cover the costs of the final preparations of the manuscript. I acknowledge very especially my brother-in-law, Reverend Vincent Mainelli, and Columbia Theological Seminary for their contributions.

Finally, I attribute the success and ultimate completion of this project to my friends and family. There is one friend whose love, understanding, strength and attention made all the difference. This is my husband, Eugene Mainelli, to whom this book is affectionately dedicated.

I

Martin Noth
and the Deuteronomistic History

The epoch-making work, *Überlieferungsgeschichtliche Studien*, of Martin Noth challenged biblical scholars to look afresh at the books of Deuteronomy to 2 Kings.[1] The books--Deuteronomy, Joshua, Judges, 1-2 Samuel, and 1-2 Kings--which had heretofore been appreciated for their individual content must, since Noth's study, be recognized as a contribution toward a continuous historical presentation.

Noth argued for the rhetorical unity of these books based on an analysis of their language, style and content. Noth recognized that the variety of sources which supplied the basic material for the historical work were remarkably joined and integrated. The coherence was effected, Noth demonstrated, by the inclusion of skillfully composed passages at strategic places within the history. These deuteronomistic compositions were fashioned either in the form of speeches placed on the lips of key persons,[2] or in the form of reflections or summaries that served to clarify the course of events within the history.[3] As a result of

---

[1]Martin Noth, *Überlieferungsgeschichtliche Studien: Die Sammelnden und Bearbeitenden Geschichtswerke im Alten Testament* (3rd ed.; Tübingen: Max Niemeyer, 1967). Hereafter designated as *Ü St.*

[2]The speeches isolated by Noth include the words of Moses in Deuteronomy 31 (*Ü St.*, 39); the speeches of Joshua in Josh 1:11-15 and Joshua 23, of Samuel in 1 Samuel 12, and of Solomon in 1 Kgs 8:14-61 (*Ü St.*, 5).

[3]The summarizing narratives are found in Joshua 12, Judg 2:11-23 and 2 Kgs 17:7-23 (*Ü St.*, 5-6).

To this group of passages, Dennis McCarthy ("II Samuel 7 and the Structure of the Deuteronomic History," *JBL* 84 [1965] 131-38), rightly added another text that must be placed in the same category. He noted that the text, 2 Samuel 7 "fills the same function as the key passages

his insight that the sources appropriated by the Dtr[4] were joined together
by creative compositions of the author himself, Noth concluded that

> Dtr was not only the editor but also the author of an histori-
> cal work which gathered material from quite varied traditions
> and arranged it according to a carefully conceived plan. In
> general Dtr simply reproduced the literary sources at his
> disposal and merely joined the individual segments with a
> connecting narrative. In certain places, however, it can be
> demonstrated that he made a deliberate selection from the
> material before him.[5]

The insight of Noth brought attention to texts in the literature
which, Noth argued, were the creative compositions of the Dtr and with
which the sources for the history were joined into a unified literary document.   Dennis McCarthy[6] advanced awareness of the deuteronomistic
technique in composition by outlining the plan upon which the history was
structured.   By considering the position of each deuteronomistic text
within the narrative whole, McCarthy demonstrated that these texts "set
in relief a carefully worked out over-all structure in the deuteronomic
history as a whole."[7]   McCarthy showed that the deuteronomistic texts
focus upon three moments within Israelite history--the event of the land,
the era of the judges and that of the kings. He argued that the Dtr had
provided three programmatic passages in Deuteronomy 31, Joshua 23, and
2 Samuel 7, and that each of these was subsequently followed by two
other deuteronomistic texts that describe the success or failure of each
program.[8]

The present writer acknowledges the unity of composition in the
DtrH and she affirms that the sources for the history were combined with
great precision according to a theologically-motivated plan. The purpose
for the present study then is to analyze one text which is the composition

---

picked out by Noth" (131). Like Noth, McCarthy isolated this text on the
basis of its function as a link for the sources that had been incorporated
by the author.

[4]After Noth, I use "Dtr" as the designation for the deuteronomistic
author and "DtrH" for the deuteronomistic history work. "Deut" will be
used to designate the book of Deuteronomy.

[5]Noth, *Ü St.*, 11; cf. 89-90, 98.

[6]"II Samuel 7."

[7]Ibid., 131.

[8]Ibid., 137-38.

of the Dtr and thereby come to an understanding of the deuteronomistic methodology for composition. It is hoped that by understanding the deuteronomistic method in composition, we might also gain insight into the plan and message which the Dtr intended.

Of necessity, attention will be given to a single deuteronomistic text--the dream of Solomon in 1 Kgs 3:4-15. The dream of Solomon has not been previously recognized to be one of the speeches created by the Dtr. The writer will demonstrate, however, that, in fact, 1 Kgs 3:4-15 must hereafter be numbered among the texts that have already been isolated as deuteronomistic compositions and that function within the history as a transition between sources.

While this study intends to verify that the dream of Solomon was indeed composed by the Dtr, the writer's primary purpose is not simply this verification. The intention in this study is principally to demonstrate the narrative technique of the Dtr in his literary composition. The work will be modest in its analysis of one single narrative, but with this study is the hope that what is learned about the deuteronomistic methodology in the use of traditions will provide a model for approach to other texts to test composition by the Dtr.

1 Kgs 3:4-15 was selected for study because the writer believes that it is the pivotal text in the deuteronomistic interpretation of kingship. In the dream, the Dtr sets forth the peculiar design for kingship that is programmatic for the deuteronomistic attitude toward kings throughout the Book of Kings. The dream narrative was selected, moreover, because this text allows the writer to demonstrate the appropriation of expressions, formularies, technical language and words from tradition and to elucidate the manner of their combination according to a definite theological motivation. The dream text also provides a vivid illustration of an apparent reworking at the hand of a redactor. We will show, however, that what appears to be an addition to the text is, in fact, a carefully selected idea from tradition which has been deliberately structured into the text to articulate the author's perception of kingship. This text is, furthermore, sufficiently significant for the overall theological focus of the history to allow the writer to demonstrate the dynamic of the Dtr-composed text within the historical content.

In regard to the content of the text selected for study, our analysis will indicate

-- that the Dtr employed traditional elements for composition of the literary work

-- that the traditional elements derive from the literary
   sources of early Yahwism and from sources known in
   royal circles

-- that the traditional elements are combined within a rhetorical form and are uniquely structured into a unified
   whole

-- that the motivational force in the combination of the traditional elements was the design for kingship that the Dtr
   intended to make the basis for his interpretation of kingship.

It is the thesis of the writer that the Dtr composed the dream of Solomon
by adapting traditional elements pertinent to the topic of kingship and by
combining these traditional elements so as to portray kingship in Israel
within the ambience of Mosaic law. We will show that the literary form
selected as the mold for the content of the dream as well as the construction of the narrative serve this single purpose.

Before directly assuming the task of this study, and in order that
this study may be viewed in the framework of past and current research,
the following pages are devoted to a survey of the scholarship that has
been introduced in response to various aspects of Noth's hypothesis.
Those studies will be set forth which either directly respond to the proposal of Noth or which are related according to the judgment of the
writer.

The review of scholarship will be handled in three parts centering
on 1) the theme and purpose of the DtrH; 2) the unity of authorship for
the DtrH; and, 3) the sources for the DtrH. In each of the three sections,
the thesis of Noth will be reviewed, then will follow a summary of and a
critique of the works that pertinently address the issue in question.

UNITY IN THEME AND PURPOSE IN THE DtrH

One aspect of Noth's study that has prompted vigorous reaction
concerns the thematic unity and purpose of the history. Noth averred
that the whole of the history carried but one central message. The
sources selected by the Dtr as well as the texts composed by the Dtr were
directed to the one single end.

The guiding factor that bound the story of Israel into a coherent
whole, according to Noth, was the law which had been given to Israel in
the days of Moses.[9] Noth demonstrated that the various periods of
Israel's history were each designed in such a way as to portray the

[9]Noth, *Ü St.*, 92.

repeated departure of Israel from obedience to the law of Yahweh.[10] As
Noth states:

> The history of Israel had been a time of departure from the
> will of God, and thereby had already anticipated that which
> Dtr attempted to demonstrate in detail in his account.[11]

Because of repeated infidelity, the Dtr showed Israel facing the inevitable
consequences of its apostasy all through the long years of its history. As
a climax, the dire tragedy of the exile was but the just and final end of
that continual turning from Yahweh.[12]

According to Noth, the history was not written for political purposes, nor was its intention to awaken the nation to a new hope for the
future. The sole intention of the author was a didactic one,

> to teach the true meaning of the history of Israel from the
> occupation of the land to the destruction of the old order.
> The meaning which he discovered was that God was acting in
> a discernible way by responding to the ever increasing moral
> decline with warnings and punishments and, finally, when
> these proved fruitless, with total destruction.[13]

---

[10]Ibid., 91-95. So also, Peter R. Ackroyd. "The Historians and
Theologians of the Exilic Age, the Deuteronomic History," in *Exile and
Restoration. A Study of Hebrew Thought of the Sixth Century B.C.* (Phil-
adelphia: Westminster, 1968) 62-83.

[11]Ibid., 93.

[12]Ibid., 100-110. Cf. Martin Noth, "Zur deuteronomistischen
Geschichtsauffassung," *Proceedings XXII Congress of Orientalists, II*
(Leiden: E. J. Brill, 1957) 558-66; and "The Jerusalem Catastrophe of 587
B.C., and its Significance for Israel," in *The Laws of the Pentateuch and
Other Studies* (Philadelphia: Fortress, 1969) 260-80.

A similar interpretation of the deuteronomistic message is espoused
by: O. H. Steck, *Israel und das gewaltsame Geschick der Propheten. Zur
Überlieferung des deuteronomistischen Geschichtsbildes im Alten Testa-
ment, Judentum und Urchristentum* (WMANT 23; Neukirchen-Vluyn:
Neukirchener, 1967) 138-39; Lothar Perlitt, *Bundestheologie im Alten
Testament* (WMANT 36; Neukirchen-Vluyn: Neukirchener, 1969) 32;
Georg Christan Malcholz, *Israel und das Land. Vorarbeiten zu einem Ver-
gleich zwischen Priesterschrift und deuteronomistischen Geschichtswerk*
(Heidelberg Theol. Habilitationschrift, 1969), quoted in Peter Diepold,
Israels Land (BWANT 95; Stuttgart: W. Kohlhammer, 1972) 148-49; and
Diepold, *Israels Land*, 147-50.

[13]Noth, *Ü St.*, 100. The question has correctly been raised whether
didacticism could be the motivation for the writing of the history. Why
would anyone go to the trouble of producing such a massive and complex

The present writer is not in accord with Noth in his explanation of the purpose of the history. It is understandable that if one recognizes but one theme in the history, there might be but one single thrust in the focus of the history. Further elaboration is not necessary at this time, since there are numerous responses to the position of Noth that point up the balance between law and grace, between judgment and forgiveness, and thereby set in question Noth's conclusion that the whole of the history revolves about the infidelity of Israel to the law and that it narrates only the consequent punishment of the nation. Those who responded to Noth attempted to identify other elements in the history that functioned as starting points and which would then indicate a conclusion, kerygma, or emphasis alongside the focus upon law and infidelity to law.

Gerhard von Rad promptly responded to Noth; he answered with the corrective that the DtrH must be viewed as "a history of Yahweh's creative word,"[14] which was active in the form of law and also in the form of promise. Yahweh's word was capable of controlling and destroying, but it also had the potential for salvation and forgiveness. Von Rad argued that the Dtr focused upon both aspects of "word" in his message to the exiles; Yahweh's word functioned as both law and gospel.[15]

To offset the force of the law emphasized by Noth, von Rad focused upon the power of the divine word in history by pointing out the plan of promise-fulfillment that structured the history. In this design, historical events could be traced to a self-fulfilling divine word spoken in prophecy.[16] Within this scheme, von Rad stressed the significance of the Davidic promise as the self-fulfilling word which brings salvation and forgiveness.[17] The gracious promise to David was the word that offered

---

piece of literature to describe a catastrophe when the populace is experiencing the situation in a way that could not be learned better?

[14]"The Deuteronomic Theology of History in I and II Kings," in *The Problem of the Hexateuch and Other Essays* (trans. E. W. Trueman Dicken; New York: McGraw-Hill, 1966) 220, which appears also as "The Deuteronomistic Theology of History in the Books of Kings," in *Studies in Deuteronomy* (SBT 9; London: SCM, 1953) 84. This study originally appeared as *Deuteronomium-Studien*, Part B (FRLANT, n.s. 40; Göttingen: Vandenhoeck & Ruprecht, 1947) 52-64. Cf. *Old Testament Theology: The Theology of Israel's Historical Traditions* (trans. D. M. G. Stalker; New York: Harper & Row, 1962) 341-47.

[15]"Deuteronomic Theology of History," 219.

[16]Ibid., 208-14.

[17]Ibid., 216-21.

hope for some future king who would restore peace and justice to the nation that had turned from Yahweh. The proof of the enduring promise, von Rad claimed, could be found in the notice at the end of Kings, 2 Kgs 25:27-31. With the release of Jehoiachin from prison, there was the assurance that the line of David had not come to an irrevocable end. This concluding statement was of tremendous theological significance for the Dtr, according to von Rad, because it provided "a basis upon which Yahweh could build further if he so willed."[18]

In response to Noth's conclusion that the motifs of lawsuit and judgment determine the scheme of the DtrH, von Rad has appropriately argued that the counter theme of grace which is present in the repeated reference to the tradition of the promise to David ought not be ignored as a foundation for future hope.

A further refinement toward understanding the message of the DtrH came from the pen of Hans Walter Wolff.[19] In response to Noth, Wolff made the point that the leitmotiv of judgment and punishment, which pervade the DtrH, served not as a word of final doom, as Noth suggested, but rather as a call to Israel, an imperative for the nation to "return" to its God.

Based on a study of the use of the key word *sûb* (return) in the DtrH, Wolff set out to illustrate the pattern of repeated failure, followed by repentance, and Yahweh's renewed activity for his people that occurs so often. Wolff showed that defection from Yahweh had begun immediately after Joshua's death. During that time, when the people made repentance, Yahweh sent a Judge to save the people from destruction. And at each instance of infidelity, the same sequence followed. The people were inflicted for their sin, but when they turned to Yahweh and called upon him, Yahweh sent another Judge to deliver them. Likewise, when the people demanded a king and thereby proved disloyal to the covenant relationship with their God, Yahweh again heeded the cry of his

---

[18]Ibid., 220. Cf. Erich Zenger, "Die deuteronomistische Interpretation der Rehabilitierung Jojachins," *BZ* 12 (1968) 16-30.

[19]"The Kerygma of the Deuteronomic Historical Work," in *The Vitality of Old Testament Traditions*, by W. A. Brueggemann and H. W. Wolff (Atlanta: John Knox, 1975) 83-100. This article was first presented as a guest lecture to the theological faculty of the University of Göttingen on July 15, 1960. It appeared originally as "Das Kerygma des deuteronomistischen Geschichtswerks," *ZAW* 73 (1961) 171-86, and was reprinted in H. W. Wolff, *Gesammelte Studien zum Alten Testament* (Theologische Bücherei 22; Munich: Chr. Kaiser, 1964) 308-24.

people and he himself established a king for his people.[20] Wolff boldly
averred that "it is not so much the total apostasy which makes the judgment final as the contemptuous disregard of the call to return."[21]

The pattern of Israel's repeated infidelity culminated finally in the
exile. Even in this situation of disaster, the same pattern can be expected
to be operative. Especially the texts 1 Kgs 8:33, 35, 46-53, in which the
word *sûb* appears repeatedly, speak specifically to this hour of the exile.
If the people will only turn to Yahweh in prayer, and listen to his voice
which had been announced by the prophets, Yahweh's compassion can be
expected to break through as it had throughout history.[22] Wolff proposed
that a second Dtr, the deutero-Dtr, reinforced the theme of *sûb* with the
texts, Deut 4:29-31 and 30:1-10, by placing these immediately before and
after the core material of Deuteronomy so that from the very beginning,
the reader would understand the entire DtrH as an imperative to "return."[23] This possibility for returning to Yahweh, Wolff maintains, holds
out the hope for an exiled people who might otherwise succumb to despair
in the anguish of their plight.

As in the case of Noth, Wolff made no reference to the counter
theme of promise in his study. Walter Brueggemann, thereupon, offered a
supplement to the work of Wolff by drawing attention to the key word *tôb*
(good).[24] The word "good" which belongs to covenant terminology,[25] is

---

[20]Ibid., 86-91. The texts around which Wolff developed his arguments are: Judges 2; 1 Samuel 7 and 12; 2 Kings 17 and 23:25.

Cf. Dennis J. McCarthy, "The Wrath of Yahweh and the Structural
Unity of the Deuteronomistic History," in *Essays in Old Testament Ethics*
(eds. J. Crenshaw and J. T. Willis; New York: KTAV, 1974) 97-110. This
study primarily aims to show how the theme of Yahweh's wrath contributes to the well-knit structure of the DtrH. But McCarthy notes that
the rhetoric of wrath itself points to a final hope. The cycle of anger,
punishment, repentance, and salvation, while implying a penalty for
infidelity, also provides an opportunity for the future. Salvation is always
possible upon repentance.

[21]Ibid., 91.

[22]Ibid., 92-93.

[23]Ibid., 93-97. On the grounds of linguistic comparison with texts
from the DtrH and more particularly with Jeremiah, Wolff proposed that
Deut 4:29-31 and 30:1-10 should be attributed to a second deuteronomistic
hand.

[24]"The Kerygma of the Deuteronomistic Historian," *Int* 22 (1968)
387-402.

[25]On the covenant context of the term "good," see: William L.
Moran, "The Ancient Near Eastern Background of the Love of God in Deu-

significant, according to Brueggemann, as a counter theme to *šûb* because it supplies the motivation for Israel to repent. It offers promises and assurances to Israel when it does repent.[26]

Along with von Rad who based his study on the creative word of God in history, Brueggemann argued that the "good" word spoken to David is the promise that can be trusted. Israel had experienced the "goodness" of Yahweh throughout its history.[27] Because of that experience of the graciousness of Yahweh, even in the present circumstance of exile, Israel has reason to be motivated to repent of the infidelity that had turned it from its God. With full confidence in Yahweh's graciousness, Israel can trust in the "good" word when all seems lost.[28]

From an entirely different starting point in the Ark Narrative, Hermann Timm reached the conclusion that the content and the structure of the DtrH were designed to call Israel to hope and repentance.[29] Timm demonstrated that the Ark Narrative, which he believes was an early source available to the Dtr, was used by the author in such a way as to provide an example of hope for the exiles. Timm compared the situation of the loss of the ark with the situation of the loss of land in exile. That the Ark Narrative had a special meaning in the DtrH, Timm contended, is evident from its strategic position in two sections at the end of the period of Judges and at the inauguration of the Davidic reign. The division is important to show continuity in the saving history from Shiloh to Jerusalem and from the era of the Judges to that of the Monarchy.[30]

But the point made by the historian in the positioning of the traditional ark story, so stressed Timm, was to dramatize for the people the fact that the way remains open for continuing hope in Yahweh. At the time of the writing of the history, when the temple had been destroyed, the king removed from power, and the land in the control of foreign

---

teronomy," *CBQ* 25 (1963) 77-87; and "A Note on the Treaty Terminology of the Sefire Stelas," *JNES* 22 (1963) 173-76; Norbert Lohfink, "Hate and Love in Osee, 1, 15," *CBQ* 25 (1963) 417; Delbert Hillers, "A Note on Some Treaty Terminology in the O.T.," *BASOR* 176 (1964) 46-47; and Dennis J. McCarthy, "Notes on Love of God in Deuteronomy and the Father-Son Relationship between Yahweh and Israel," *CBQ* 27 (1965) 144-47.

[26]Brueggemann, "The Kerygma," 388.

[27]Ibid., 397-400.

[28]Ibid., 401-2.

[29]"Die Ladeerzählung (I Sam. 4-6; II Sam 6) und das Kerygma des deuteronomistischen Geschichtswerkes," *EvT* 26 (1966) 509-26.

[30]Ibid., 516-17.

power, the lesson to be learned was that Yahweh remained as surely present with his people as he had been when the ark seemed lost. In the comparison of the Ark Narrative with the situation of the exile, Timm states:

> With the former as with the latter, with the end of the period of the judges as with the end of the monarchy, the existing order which was granted by Yahweh had so thoroughly collapsed that one could not say where a turn for the better might have its origin. No 'holy remnant' had survived on which one could pin one's hope for a future return to the former existence. Hope had been put in Yahweh alone. On the basis of the experience of God which the ancient narrative could recall, could one not hope that Yahweh, as once before, would again find a way out of this catastrophe to a new historical situation?[31]

Timm successfully argues that the Ark Narrative functions to verify that even with the loss of the land, temple, and king, the future was not entirely hopeless, for Yahweh, and he alone, would bring about a new history.

These reactions to Noth's study offer plausible alternatives to the conclusion introduced by Noth that the message of the DtrH was a praise of Yahweh for his justice and an acceptance of the inevitable disaster that had befallen the nation due to its infidelity to law. These studies suggest that, together with a message of judgment and doom, the DtrH as powerfully speaks of the possibility of return to Yahweh. In various ways, it brings to the mind of the readers a renewed awareness of Yahweh's promise and his ability to act in new ways for his chosen people.[32]

---

[31]Ibid., 519-20. Cf. Anthony F. Campbell, *The Ark Narrative (1 Sam 4-6; 2 Sam 6): A Form-Critical and Traditio-Historical Study* (SBLDS 16; Missoula: Scholars, 1975). This recent study on the narrative structure and interpretation of the Ark Narrative is to be recognized because of its insightful and exciting contribution for future study of the use of literary sources by the Dtr for a theological purpose determined by that writer. More recent is the significant study: Patrick D. Miller and J. J. M. Roberts, *The Hand of the Lord: A Reassessment of the "Ark Narrative" of 1 Samuel* (Baltimore/London: Johns Hopkins University, 1977).

[32]The element of hope in the history is affirmed also by: N. Lohfink, "Bilanz nach der Katastrophe: Das deuteronomistische Geschichtswerk," in *Wort und Botschaft: Eine theologische und kritische Einführung in die Probleme des Alten Testaments* (ed. Josef Schreiner; Würzburg: Echter, 1967) 196-208; and A. Soggin, "Deuteronomistische Geschichtaus-

There is a weakness in the conclusions offered thus far in that each focuses upon a single theme which leads to a single message of either disaster or the possibility for salvation. One single kerygmatic thrust is isolated in each case as if the document were simplistic in its content. To the present, scholarship has not successfully accounted for the complexity of content in the DtrH while maintaining the integrity of the document.[33]

THE AUTHORSHIP OF THE DtrH

There are responders to Noth, however, who have set in relief the thematic multiplicity of the DtrH. Needless to say, these argue for a document that has been successively edited or redacted as if the only explanation for the multifaceted content could be a variety of hands in the composition.

Noth, to be sure, insisted that the work was produced in a continuous narrative process, and we agree with that insight.[34] In an attempt to explain how that was accomplished, Noth argued that the history from Joshua 1 to 2 Kings 25, which relates the events from the conquest of the land to the loss of the land, must have been developed into this rhetorical complex according to a carefully controlled plan. Noth suggested that into this account of the gift and loss of the land, the Dtr incorporated the whole collection of the laws that had served as his motivation for the interpretation of history. Noth reasoned that the speech of Moses in Deut 1:1-4:43, a speech which was the composition of the Dtr, introduced the

---

legung während des babylonischen Exils," in *Oikonomia: Heilsgeschichte als Theme der Theologie* (Fs. Oscar Cullmann; ed. Felix Christ; Hamburg-Bergstedt: Herbert Reich, 1967) 11-17.

[33]A witness to the difficulty presented here is found in a recent dissertation which began in support of Noth's hypothesis. So, Richard Nelson, "The Redactional Duality of the Deuteronomistic History" (Diss., Union Theological Seminary in Virginia, 1973) 38. Nelson states that he "intended to disprove any theory of double redaction and thus support Noth, but that the cumulative evidence eventually forced him to take a position diametrically opposed to his original position."

[34]Commentaries that assume the DtrH to be a unified composition are: Johannes Fichtner, *Das erste Buch von den Königen* (Die Botschaft des Alten Testaments 12/1; Stuttgart: Calwer, 1964); Martin Noth, *Könige* (BKAT 9; Neukirchen-Vluyn: Neukirchener, 1968); Peter F. Ellis, "1-2 Kings," in *JBC*, 179-209; and, Walter Wifall, *The Court History of Israel* (St. Louis: Clayton, 1975).

entire DtrH by setting the stage for the historical narrative within Israelite tradition. Thus, Noth explained how the DtrH was fashioned into a
remarkably coherent whole by a single individual at one particular time
when the Israelite people had been exiled from the land.[35]

Noth had so penetrated the historical content that he was able to
compellingly argue that the entire document came from the pen of a
single author.[36] As in the case of his conclusion regarding the unity of
theme and message, the suggestion of single authorship is seriously challenged. Efforts to demonstrate that the document could not possibly be
the product of a single hand have led to detailed delineations to point out
varying themes, moods, and interests, each of which is attributed to a
separate redactor or editor.

One scholar who temporally followed not far behind Noth was
Alfred Jepsen.[37] Jepsen introduced the theory that the Book of Kings
came into existence as the result of three successive redactions. Jepsen
argued that each author who is identifiable by his interest and contribution took up the previous work and expanded it with sources that were
transparent of that author's own interest and position.

Jepsen proposed that the first redactor was a Jerusalem priest.[38]
This redactor used an already available synchronized chronological work
that included information about the kings until the time of Hezekiah,[39]

---

[35]Noth, *Ü St.*, 5-18, 91-95.

[36]Ibid., 110.

[37]*Die Quellen des Königsbuches* (2nd ed. rev.; Halle [Saale]: Max
Niemeyer, 1956).

[38]Ibid., 105. The siglum suggested by Jepsen to identify the work of
the redactor is 'K.' He states: "For the priestly historical work R^I, we
could think 'Pr' or because it is primarily concerned with kingship, K^P (or
only K)."

[39]Ibid., 30-40. Cf. Helga Weippert, "Die 'deuteronomischen' Beurteilung der Könige von Israel und Judah und das Problem der Redaktion
der Königsbucher," *Bib* 53 (1972) 301-39. Weippert studied the various
judgmental formulae which were applied to the kings of Israel and Judah.
She concluded that the Book of Kings had undergone three successive redactions before reaching a final form at the time shortly after the fall of
Jerusalem. This study supports Jepsen's theory that R^I built upon an
already existing document. The evidence set forth by Weippert indicates
that the account of the kings was first edited on the basis of deuteronomic standards prior to 622 B.C.; in the light of the Josian reform after
622 B.C.; and finally after the fall of Jerusalem.

and to this he added annalistic material from the court archives,[40] as well as his own summary of the cult history of the nation.[41] The personality of R^I Jepsen found most apparent in the summary material that was originally his own creation and which focused the perspective of the sources brought together by him. Jepsen states that:

> R^I is a Jerusalem priest who, in the period shortly after the destruction of the temple and the city, presents an outline of the cultic history of Israel and Judah by taking the synchronistic royal chronicles as a basis and by inserting individual excerpts from the annals. He did this to make comprehensible the judgment of Yahweh which had befallen both nations so that Judah might learn to turn again to God and to His temple.[42]

Jepsen associated the second redactor with the prophetic circles.[43] Without disturbing the context or the general form of the work before him, R^{II} made additions to the work of R^I. These additions were not merely appendages but they pervade the work so that the hand of R^{II} is recognizable throughout the book.[44] R^{II} added the prophetic narratives,[45]

Weippert's study is based on the assumption that Deuteronomy underwent a long process of development and was known long before its discovery in the Temple. This fact is undoubtedly correct. Cf. Norbert Lohfink, "Die Bundesurkunde des Königs Josias," Bib 44 (1963) 261-88, 461-98.

With Weippert's compelling and precise delineation of the formulae in Kings along with the work of those who have noted successive redactions to the major historical work, we come to view the DtrH as the product of a series of static reworkings of a written document. Unfortunately, we know little about the process by which written and oral traditions combined into the product in which we find them. Nonetheless, the writer senses that the process was far more fluid and dynamic than the manner of composition outlined thus far, the changes occurring almost imperceptibly over an extended period of years.

[40]Ibid., 54-60.

[41]Ibid., 60-76.

[42]Ibid., 76. It is noteworthy that the purpose of the first redaction, according to Jepsen, is identical to the motivation for the complete work proposed by Noth.

[43]Jepsen reached this conclusion because the second redactor supposedly inserted predominantly prophet-narratives. Ibid., 78.

[44]Ibid., 79-80.

[45]These are the traditions about Ahijah of Shiloh: 1 Kgs 11:29-31; 14:1-6, 12-13a, 17-18; Elijah and Elisha: 1 Kings 17-19; 21; 2 Kings 1; 2-

other traditions which were of interest to him,[46] as well as his own commentary upon the working out of God's word in history.[47]

Jepsen comments that in this stage of his analysis, he is in accord with Noth.[48] This is to say that R^{II} corresponds with the Dtr who had taken up already existing sources, expanded and altered them, and stamped them with a theological interpretation the governing force of which was God's word spoken in his law.[49]

The DtrH, according to Jepsen, underwent yet a third redaction near the end of the sixth century. The notable priestly concern reflected there, the midrashic elaborations, the congruence with the language and viewpoint of the Chronicler, convinced Jepsen that R^{III} was company to the Levitical movement in the late exilic time. Once the temple was rebuilt and the order of sacrifice was established, the Levites were forced into a situation of having to contest their right to the priesthood.[50] Because the last redaction was marked by a preoccupation with such concerns, Jepsen attributed this final reworking to the Levitical circles.

Jepsen offered a valuable support to the hypothesis of Noth with his conclusion that the Book of Kings was the product of the exilic age.[51] Jepsen proposed that each of the successive redactions was accomplished within the sixth century B.C., in the time between the

---

8:15; as well as the stories about purging Baal worship from Samaria and Jerusalem: 2 Kgs 8:28-10:27; and the prophet stories in 1 Kings 20 and 22.

[46]In this category Jepsen included oral traditions that would have preserved such anecdotes as the stories about Solomon: 1 Kgs 3:16-27; 10:1-10a, and 11:14-25; and traditions surviving from circles other than the prophetic. Foremost of these are the reports from the wisdom circles (see p. 79). Jepsen states that the prophets and the wisdom teachers had produced this work hand in hand (pp. 98-99).

This group includes also the written traditions such as the lists in 1 Kgs 4:1-19 and 5:7-8 (p. 79); the Throne Succession Narrative, and the sources for Joshua, Judges, and Samuel (pp. 95-99).

[47]The creative summary contributed by R^{II} contained whatever concerns Yahweh's choice of Israel, God's law to Israel, Israel's apostasy to other gods, and God's anger and judgment upon Israel (Ibid., 87-98).

[48]Ibid., 105; also 100-101.

[49]Ibid., 90-91. Cf. Noth, *Ü St.,* 89, 91-95.

[50]Ibid., 102-4.

[51]It is important to recognize that it is beyond the interest of Jepsen to account for the integrity of Kings with the other books that comprise the DtrH. Jepsen is working only with Kings and not with the DtrH as such.

destruction and the rebuilding of the Temple. In line with this consideration, Jepsen asserted that all of the prominent parties of Israelite culture
had a hand in the composition of the document: the priests, the prophets
and wisdom teachers and the Levitical preachers. This is to say that
Jepsen proposes a process of composition that was far more dynamic than
has heretofore been suggested. But we ask, is it necessary to account for
this dynamic view and complexity of viewpoints by attributing each to a
separate hand whose particular interest is reflected within the document? We are forced, in this case, to envision a writing brought to completion then successively taken up again to be reworked. Is it possible
that the scribes remaining near Jerusalem after the fall of the city could
have been in touch with the diversity of interests and also have available
to them the source materials with which they worked over an extended
period of time to produce the history as we have it?

Jepsen's analysis that brings out the thematic complexity of Kings
is exceedingly appealing. But we remain uncomfortable with a thesis that
explains this complexity exclusively by a diversity of hands which have
successively reworked the history, as if an individual or closely related
group of individuals were not capable of reflecting a diversity of viewpoints and concerns.

Quite another evaluation of the deuteronomistic material was
made by Walter Dietrich.[52] Dietrich, like Jepsen, distinguished three
distinct redactions within the DtrH. Using the prophetic stories and
speeches as the starting point for his study,[53] Dietrich noted that the

---

[52] *Prophetie und Geschichte. Eine redaktionsgeschichtliche Untersuchung zum deuteronomistischen Geschichtswerk* (FRLANT 108; Göttingen: Vandenhoeck & Ruprecht, 1972).

[53] Ibid., 9-46. Dietrich attributed the prophetic material to the
literary hand DtrP on the basis of similarities in word and/or phrase
usage, and according to their formal pattern. The latter is the typical
prophetic *Gattung,* the scheme of *Begründung--Ankündigung,* or, *Schelt-
wort--Drohwort.* These criteria also suggested to Dietrich that DtrP was
quite familiar with a fundamental strata of the Jeremiah book. Like
Jeremiah, DtrP was the spokesman of the harsh word of *Unheil.* (Ibid.,
104-5).

We recognize another work that bases its findings on the *Propheten-
aussage.* This is O. H. Steck, *Israel und das gewaltsame Geschick der
Propheten,* esp. 66-74 and 137-43. Steck demonstrated on the basis of
literary comparisons that the levels of concepts found within the DtrH
correspond with the development in Levitical preaching during the exile.
This is yet another way to attempt to explain the existence of various

prophetic discourses had been combined with what he considered to be an older literary source consisting primarily of historical material.[54]   Thus, the Dtr whom Dietrich identified as DtrP linked prophecy with history by incorporating into the already existing historical account, which Dietrich called DtrG, examples illustrating the role of the prophet in history.[55] Besides prophetic stories and speeches, the DtrP also took up older prophetic narratives, collections of stories, and simple annalistic notices. He altered, expanded, and artfully expressed these for his purposes so that, as Dietrich states, DtrP can be considered "Tradent von Altem und Schöpfer von Neuem zugleich."[56]

To the strata of historical and prophetic material, a third redactor added that which was essentially of a nomistic character.   This revision includes all that concerned the law: the legal sayings, the paranesis on law, and to be sure, the law code itself.   Dietrich also assigned those traditions that focus upon Judah, Jerusalem, the Davidics and the Temple to DtrN, the final deuteronomistic redactor.[57]

Dietrich neatly delineated the redactional steps according to the nature of the content.   The historical material served as the basis (DtrG).   To this was added prophecy (DtrP), and lastly, the law (DtrN).

---

layers in the formative process of the DtrH. Steck dealt only with a few texts from the DtrH, namely: 2 Kgs 17:7ff; 1 Kgs 8:46-53; and Deut 4:25-31; 28:46-68; 30:1-10. Steck's treatment of these as demonstrative of the steps in an evolutionary process adumbrates the function of these texts, for they are not isolated passages that can be handled for their particular content.   These passages are integrally bound within a context of the DtrH and can be correctly interpreted only for their contribution to the overall design and message of the work.

[54]Ibid., 110-34.

[55]Ibid., 107-9, 139.

[56]Ibid., 134.

[57]Ibid., 44, 147. Dietrich, who is a student of Smend, built upon the thesis of his teacher in proposing the late redactor DtrN. The siglum DtrN and the idea of a systematic reworking of the history around the theme of the law is found in the work of his teacher. See Rudolf Smend, "Das Gesetz und die Völker. Ein Beitrag zur deuteronomistichen Redaktionsgeschichte," in *Probleme Biblischer Theologie* (ed. H. W. Wolff; Munich: Chr. Kaiser, 1971) 494-509.   Smend restricted himself to a limited number of passages within Joshua and Judges, notably those that concern law, and particularly the law dealing with foreigners in the land. Smend argued that the last redaction was accomplished at the time when intermingling with people from other nations was a major concern.

All three were deuteronomists, claims Dietrich, because each was governed by the spirit expressed most clearly in Deuteronomy and the Josian reform. DtrG expressed this spirit in his judgment upon the kings; DtrP, in his zeal against the northern kings who maintained cultic and political independence; DtrN in his inclusion of the law code and his preoccupation with the foreigners from whom Israel was to be distinct.[58]   A unified spirit of the law governed the work, yet each redactor applied the law from a unique perspective. Since the code itself was not added to the history until late in its evolution, the law that governed the history, Dietrich claims, was the unwritten law of Yahweh's claim upon Israel.[59]

In his use of the law as a basis for the history, Dietrich is clearly different from Noth. For Noth, the law code is integral to the historical document, contained there as a legal code and pervading the plurality of traditions. For Dietrich, the use of law corresponds with Wellhausen's theory that law influenced Israelite tradition upon an evolutionary plan. Only the law introduced by the last redactor corresponds with the law as it is understood by Noth.

It should be noted that Dietrich's intention was not primarily to show the Dtr's use of the law. The crux of his study verges on the distinction between the deuteronomic and the legalistic, between what belongs to Israel and what belongs to Judaism. There is the assumption in Dietrich's work that causes him to separate the traditions of Yahwism from the royal traditions of Jerusalem. These latter are attributed to the final redactor, thereby setting them apart from the basic history and the prophetic traditions. There is the intimation in this approach that the basic history and the first redaction contain only those sources that have been traditionally associated with the North, whereas, the southern traditions were the last to be incorporated. The relegation of the royal traditions to the final redaction presents problems in view of the importance

---

[58]Ibid., 146-47.

[59]Ibid., 147. In posing a late date for the legal redaction, Dietrich identifies himself among the followers of Julius Wellhausen (*Prolegomena to the History of Ancient Israel* [New York: Meridian Books, 1957]). Wellhausen espouses the view that the first law for ordering human life was an unwritten law; the the second law and the law that was formative for Israel was the ethical teachings of the prophets; and that the written law which was not found until the time of Josiah was the law that set the course for Israel during the exile and after. The sequence in the development of the DtrH, as Dietrich has presented it, follows essentially the pattern of evolution established by Wellhausen.

of the divine promise to David for the structure of the books of Kings. Also problematic is the arbitrariness with which distinctions are made between what reflects the spirit of the unwritten law and what derives from the written code.

We have serious problems with the methodology of this study, with the basic assumptions, and, of course, with the conclusions. We do recognize, however, the attempt to demonstrate that a multiplicity of traditions apart from the Mosaic law functioned toward the evolution of the document.

Both Jepsen and Dietrich agree with Noth that the DtrH was the product of the exile.[60] They, however, deny that the history was composed by one deuteronomist at one specific time with a single message. Both argue for three distinct reworkings, one of which, it should be noted, was completed around 550 B.C., the date suggested by Noth.[61] Jepsen isolated one redaction before this date and the final revision closer to the end of the sixth century when the temple was rebuilt. Dietrich, on the other hand, considered that the entire process of three redactions was completed by ca. 560 B.C.[62]

For a considerable time before Noth, the hypothesis that the major part of the historical books was completed in the pre-exilic time, was broadly accepted.[63] The explanation given was that they came into being in two stages. The first edition, a pre-exilic stratum, consisted of the basic material. The second, an exilic edition, contained revisions and additions that brought the work into harmony with the situation of the exile.[64]

---

[60]Jepsen, having worked solely with the books of Kings, supports Noth's view in a limited way.

[61]Noth, *Ü St.,* 91.

[62]Much the same conclusion in regard to the time of completion was reached by Wolfgang Richter in his analysis of Judges 2-10. See *Die Bearbeitungen des "Retterbuches" in der deuteronomischen Epoche* (BBB 21; Bonn: Peter Hanstein, 1964); and the review article by W. L. Moran, "A Study of the Deuteronomic History," *Bib* 46 (1965) 223-28.

[63]Wellhausen was the framer of the hypothesis of several editions in the books of Judges, Samuel and Kings. He distinguished the sources or original traditions from the accretions added during the exilic and post-exilic periods. See *Prolegomena,* 288-94; and *Die Composition des Hexateuchs und der historischen Bücher des Alten Testaments* (Berlin: Walter de Gruyter, 1963) 208-301.

[64]The theory of pre-exilic work with exilic editions survives in the work of: Otto Eissfeldt, *The Old Testament: An Introduction. The His-*

Since Noth, the two-stage theory has been reintroduced with great impact by Frank Moore Cross.[65] Cross argued that the author, who prepared the work in the seventh century during the Josian era, wrote the deuteronomistic history of kings "as a programmatic document of Josiah's reform and of his revival of the Davidic state."[66] As the basis for his argument, Cross isolated the two themes--the sin of Jeroboam as the cause of Israel's failure and the faithfulness of David as the foundation for the restoration of the Davidic empire in the era of Josiah.[67] Cross main-

---

tory of the Formation of the Old Testament (New York and Evanston: Harper & Row, 1965) 255-56, 266-67, 280-81, 297-301; Georg Fohrer, Introduction to the Old Testament (New York: Abingdon, 1965) 202-5, 212-13, 225-26, 236-37; Hans W. Hertzberg, Die Bücher Josua, Richter, Ruth (ATD 9; Göttingen: Vandenhoeck & Ruprecht, 1965) 8-9; and, Die Samuelbucher (ATD 10; Göttingen: Vandenhoeck & Ruprecht, 1965) 9; John Gray, I & II Kings. A Commentary (2nd ed. rev.; Philadelphia: Westminster, 1970) 6-9; Norman H. Snaith, "I - II Kings," in IB (ed. George Buttrick; New York: Abingdon, 1954) 3. 1-338; S. Szikszai, "Kings, I and II," in IDB (ed. George Buttrick; New York: Abingdon, 1962) 3. 26-35; C. F. Burney, Notes on the Hebrew Text of the Books of Kings (New York: KTAV, 1970) xv-xix; J. Robinson, The First Book of Kings (The Cambridge Bible Commentary; Cambridge: University Press, 1972) 11-14; and George E. Wright, "Israel in the Promised Land: History Interpreted by Covenant Faith," Encounter 35 (1974) 318-34.

[65]"The Themes of the Book of Kings and the Structure of the Deuteronomistic History," in Cannanite Myth and Hebrew Epic: Essays in the History of the Religion of Israel (Cambridge: Harvard University, 1973) 274-87. This essay first appeared under the title, "The Structure of the Deuteronomic History," in Perspectives in Jewish Learning (ed. J. M. Rosenthal; Chicago: College of Jewish Studies, 1967) 9-24.

[66]Ibid., 287.

[67]Ibid., 278, 281-85. Cf. G. E. Wright, "Israel in the Promised Land," which was written in response to Cross. While Wright concurs with Cross that the deuteronomistic work is basically a pre-exilic document with exilic editing, he deplores the notion that the work was politically motivated (pp. 330-32). Wright correctly observes that such motivation is surely not evident in the book of Deuteronomy, nor in Joshua or Judges. Even in Samuel and Kings, the presentation of kingship is not wholly positive. Wright points out the fact that a tension is kept by the Dtr (e.g. 1 Samuel 8 and 2 Samuel 7) between the divine promise to the Davidic dynasty and the severe qualification of that promise in the removal of ten tribes from the Davidic dynasty (1 Kgs 11:32, 34). Wright contends that the divine promise is considered in no different light by the pre-exilic author than it is by the exilic author.

tained that the juxtaposition of the two themes of threat and promise provide the platform for the Josianic reform. As such, the document spoke to Israel calling it to return to Judah under the leadership of a Davidid and to Yahweh's sole legitimate shrine, the national shrine in Jerusalem.[68] The challenge to Israel was that it return to the God of Israel's covenant.

A second hand, whom Cross calls the exilic editor, introduced the sub-theme of Manasseh's apostasy. This editor intended to show that the fall of Judah was like that of Israel.[69] Cross argues, moreover, that the additions and the retouching done by the editor covered over whatever hope of restoration of the state had originally been highlighted in the deuteronomistic document. The revisions, then, transformed the work into a sermon on history addressed to Judean exiles.[70] The resulting work offered only a "muted hope of repentance and possible return,"[71] since the original theme of hope had been overwritten and contradicted.

Cross was able to say that there are no threats and warnings in the deuteronomistic transitional passages in Kings, nor "little or no hint of inevitable disaster in the deuteronomistic historian's framework and transitional passages in Joshua, Judges and Samuel,"[72] because he has purposefully relegated those very texts to the editorial hand.[73]

Cross has rendered a valuable service in his delineation of the thematic structure in the history of Kings. Because of this work our attention is brought to an awareness of the yet to be discovered complexity of theme in the history and to a realization of the precision by

---

[68]Ibid., 279, 284-85, 287-89.

[69]Ibid., 285-87.

[70]Ibid., 287.

[71]Ibid., 288. Cf. Wolff, "The Kerygma," 94-97. Wolff suggests that two texts in particular come from a second Dtr hand and that these speak a word of hope with the invitation to "return." These are 4:29-31 and 30:1-10.

It should be noted that, in regard to the first of these texts, Cross relegates vv 27-31 to the editor and not vv 29-31, as does Wolff. Wolff distinguishes vv 29-31 which are expressed in the singular from vv 25-28 which are written in the plural. Cross ignores this incongruity or mitigates its significance. Such disagreement among scholars on the criteria for determining what texts should be attributed to a specific hand speaks to the unreliability of such divisions.

[72]Ibid., 288.

[73]So, Deut 4:27-31; 28:36f, 63-68; 29:27; 30:1-10, 11-20; Josh 23:11-13, 15f, 1 Sam 12:25; 1 Kgs 2:4; 3:14; 6:11-13; 8:25b, 46-53; 9:4-9; 2 Kgs 17:19; 20:17f; 23:26-25:30. Ibid., 287, and n. 49.

which each theme has been woven into the history to create the remarkable whole of the present text. The attempt to relegate portions of the text to an author or editor on the basis of the mood of the text must be suspect, however. Cross himself says:

> There are a sprinkling of passages in the Deuteronomistic work which threaten defeat and captivity. These need not necessarily stem from an Exilic editor. Captivity and exile were all too familiar fates in the Neo-Assyrian age. More important, the threat of exile or captivity was common in the curses of Ancient Near Eastern treaties and came naturally over into the curses attached to Israel's covenant.[74]

Why then does Cross insist that the threats and warnings are evidence of the exilic editor alone? It is noteworthy that Cross argues for the same authorship for the promise to David and for the sin of Jeroboam, whereas Jepsen and Dietrich would approach these as representative of the interest of the royalty and prophets, respectively. And we ask, could not the same hand have produced both a spirit of optimism and of pessimism?

SOURCES FOR THE DtrH

Noth's theory of single authorship is dependent on his understanding of the use of sources by the Dtr. The Dtr, in Noth's perspective, did not compose every word of the history; he appropriated blocks of materials from annals and archives; from history writing and hero cycles, and from whole narratives, such as the ark narrative, and the succession narrative. The Dtr took these sources and wove them together according to a precise plan:

> Dtr was the author of a comprehensive traditional work, who scrupulously collected and presented the existing tradition, but who at the same time, organized and outlined the entire work, making it clear and systematic by composing summaries which anticipate and recapitulate.[75]

Noth came to the realization of how the Dtr made use of sources in a study of the book of Joshua. Noth recognized that the book of Joshua consisted of a series of originally independent hero sagas and etiological legends which had been carefully worked into a unified account.[76] Noth

---

[74]Ibid., 287.

[75]Noth, *Ü St.*, 89.

[76]Martin Noth, *Das Buch Josua* (2nd ed.; HAT 1/7; Tübingen: J. C. B. Mohr, 1953). In this Noth followed the lead of Albrecht Alt, "Josua," in

described the traditioning process as he understood it in the following way: the basic material for the DtrH derived from independent legends and traditions that existed in Israel, some of them oral and some written;[77] and the available sources were gathered, selected, arranged and altered as the need arose by the Dtr who worked the originally independent materials into a unified piece.[78] The process was not a gradual evolution into narrative cycles with possible later additions and expansions, as some traditionists would suppose.[79] Noth insisted that the work came into existence in a systematic and consciously determined way by the Dtr who worked with the sources.

Werden und Wesen des Alten Testaments (ed. F. Stummer and J. Hempel; BZAW 66; Berlin: Alfred Töpelmann, 1936) 13-29; reprinted in *Kleine Schriften zur Geschichte des Volkes Israel* (Munich: C. H. Beck, 1953) 1. 176-92. Alt had already proposed an etiological origin for Joshua 1-11 and had also noticed a hero legend in Joshua 10. Both Alt and Noth based their studies on the methodological principles of Gunkel and Gressmann. For a summary of the work of these scholars and a critique of their impact upon subsequent scholarship, see Gene M. Tucker, *Form Criticism of the Old Testament* (Guides to Biblical Scholarship, OT Series; Philadelphia: Fortress, 1971) esp. 4-6, 22-41; and Jay A. Wilcoxen, "Narrative," in *Old Testament Form Criticism* (ed. John H. Hayes; San Antonio, TX: Trinity University, 1974) 57-98.

[77] Of those who agree that the material for the historical books was derived from special sources, the work of Rost is most supportive of Noth. Rost studied the Throne Succession Narrative, the Ark Narrative, the Nathan prophecy and the reports of the Ammonite Wars as independent sources. He introduced the concept of the "Unterquellen" as opposed to the source theory. See Leonard Rost, *Das kleine Credo und andere Studien zum Alten Testament* (Heidelberg: Quelle & Meyer, 1965) 119-253.

[78] Noth, *Ü St.*, 95-100.

[79] Those who understand the traditioning process to take place in narrative cycles account for four steps in the process: 1) individual sagas and traditions, oral and written, existed in Israel; 2) the individual units were taken up into story cycles; 3) the cycles were gradually expanded and reconstructed according to some plan; 4) a redaction by a deuteronomistic hand concluded the whole process. Noth believed that only the first and fourth steps were actually involved in the procedure. For orientation in the relationship of Noth's work to that of the work of other scholars, see Hans-Joachim Kraus, *Geschichte der historisch-kritischen Erforschung des Alten Testaments* (2nd ed. rev.; Neukirchen-Vluyn: Neukirchener, 1969) esp. 455-56.

The introduction of Noth's hypothesis set a course in biblical scholarship markedly contrary to the earlier literary critics.   The popular view
prior to Noth had been that the literary sources J and E, which supplied
the basic material for Genesis to Numbers, continued also into Deuteronomy and Joshua,[80] and according to some scholars, even to Judges,
Samuel, and Kings as well.[81]

The only scholar other than Noth who departed as radically from
the norm of literary criticism was Ivan Engnell.[82]   Like Noth, Engnell

---

[80]The postulate that the literary strata of the earlier books extends
into Joshua is the result of the literary critical studies of J. Wellhausen
(*Prolegomena*, 357; and *Die Composition*, 116-34). Wellhausen considered
Joshua 1-24 in connection with the literary history of the Pentateuch and
spoke of a Hexateuch extending to Judg 2:5.

In essence, this position is maintained by Artur Weiser, *The Old
Testament: Its Formation and Development* (New York: Association
Press, 1961) 144; Sigmund Mowinckel, "Israelite Historiography," in
Annual of the Swedish Theological Institute (ed. Hans Kosmala; Leiden:
E. J. Brill, 1963) 2. 5; and *Tetrateuch-Pentateuch-Hexateuch.   Die
Berichte   über   die   Landnahme   in   den   drei   altisraelitischen
Geschichtswerken* (BZAW 90; Berlin: Alfred Töpelmann, 1964); and,
Georg Fohrer, *Introduction*, 196-205.

For a summary of the situation, see Cuthbert A. Simpson, "The
Growth of the Hexateuch," in *IB* 1. 185-200.

[81]The most trenchant supporter of the hypothesis that J and E are
the main sources for the whole history from Genesis to Kings is Gustav
Hölscher, "Das Buch der Könige, seine Quellen und seine Redaktion," in
Fs. H. Gunkel, *Eucharisterion* (FRLANT 36/1; Göttingen: Vandenhoeck &
Ruprecht, 1923) 158-213; and *Die Anfänge der hebräischen Geschichts-
schreibung* (Sitzungberichte der Akademie, Heidelberg, Philos.-hist.
Klasse, 1942), which works with the J source, in particular. A revised
edition of this work which includes a similar inquiry on the E source is:
*Geschichtsschreibung in Israel: Untersuchungen zum Jahvisten und Elo-
histen* (Lund: Gleerup, 1952).

For a survey of the scholarship that addresses the question of the
documentary sources in the historical books, see Norman Snaith, "The
Historical Books," in *The Old Testament and Modern Study* (ed. H. H.
Rowley; Oxford: Clarendon, 1951) 84-107; Ernst Jenni, "Zwei Jahrzehnte
Forschung an den Büchern Josua bis Könige," *TRu* 27 (1961) 104-14; and
Otto Eissfeldt, *The Old Testament*, 244-48.

[82]"The Pentateuch," in *A Rigid Scrutiny: Critical Essays on the Old
Testament* (ed. and trans. John T. Willis; Nashville: Vanderbilt University,
1969) 50-67. Cf. *Gamla Testamentet. En traditionshistorisk inledning*

supposed that the traditions in the Tetrateuch were quite independent from the traditions in the deuteronomic work. He differed from Noth, however, in that he assigned a far greater role to oral tradition for the process of the transmission and the production of the literature.

Each of the two "masterpieces of world literature,"[83] as Engnell called the Tetrateuch and the Deuteronomic work, originated within a distinct group of traditionists. The Tetrateuch was the product of the P circle, while the Deuteronomic work was the product of the D circle. These circles continued across many generations during which time the traditions of the group were handed down to posterity. Each of these traditions was cumulative of material which was its own contribution, as well as large amounts of other material passed from antiquity in both oral and written forms. Each circle was unique and distinct in its outlook and the material of each circle was stamped by the ideological tendency of the group.[84] The shift to a written form, Engnell believed, occurred in the exilic or post-exilic period. Though the transfer to a static form happened late in the evolution of the tradition, Engnell insisted that the tradition was written as it had been transmitted. Nothing new was added during the final process. The novelty of Engnell's hypothesis rests in his proposal that the creative amalgamation happened within the oral stage.[85]

As forceful as this argument is as a corrective to the extremes of conventional criticism, Engnell must be criticized for giving too much importance to oral tradition. It is true that the fluidity of oral transmission allows for greater creativity in the formulation of traditions. Yet it is questionable whether the complex structure of either of these works, the Tetrateuch and the Deuteronomistic History, could have been fashioned in the course of solely an oral process. It is highly improbable that memory alone would conserve a tradition which had developed to the scope of either the Tetrateuch or the DtrH. It is likewise inconceivable that traditions would not have been written during every stage in the process of transmission, in view of the high regard for the written record evidenced in the multifarious documents that have survived from ancient times from almost every culture in the ancient oriental world. The

---

(Stockholm: Svenska Kyrkans Diakonistyrelses Bokförlag, 1945) 1. 28-30, quoted in Douglas A. Knight, *Rediscovering the Traditions of Israel* (SBLDS 9; Missoula: Scholars, 1975) 264-66.

[83]Ibid., 67.

[84]Ibid., 58-59.

[85]Ibid., 61.

hypothesis of Engnell presents an extreme that, if tempered to permit a more balanced view of the mode of transmission, could be instructive concerning the interplay of sociological factors in the formation of community and tradition.

In his explanation of the composition process, Noth allows for the appropriation of blocks of literary materials and, therefore, correctly accounts for the information which had a long history prior to use within the history. Engnell, on the other hand, offers an explanation for the transmission process that recognizes only oral tradition. While we cannot conceive of a dynamic oral composition for the whole of the history, Engnell's work is suggestive for the work of this paper. The writer believes that the art of oral composition influenced the Dtr and that it was this technique which was followed in the composition of those texts which were composed by the Dtr to weld other sources together in history.

When we say this we do not mean that these Dtr-composed texts existed in an oral stage. They were fashioned literarily. But we suspect, and will test the conjecture in the course of this study, that the Dtr used traditional elements in a way very similar to the use of formulaic langauge in oral composition. Since the content of the Dtr-composed texts consists of traditional language, we call the methodology of the Dtr "traditional composition."

When we speak of "traditional composition," we do not mean tradition criticism.[86] The latter implies the refocusing of theme or of basic tenets of faith in response to critical cultural situations. In "traditional composition," as it is interpreted by those who study the poetry of peoples where oral composition is operative, a speaker builds a completely new poetic piece out of traditional language.[87] The writer is proposing that

---

[86]See the statement by Walter A. Brueggemann, "The Continuing Task of Tradition Criticism," in *The Vitality of Old Testament Traditions,* 115-26; also, Douglas A. Knight, *Rediscovering the Traditions of Israel,* esp. 26-29; Rudolf Smend, "Tradition and History: A Complex Relation," in *Tradition and Theology in the Old Testament* (ed. D. A. Knight; Philadelphia: Fortress, 1977) 49-68; and Walter Harrelson, "Life, Faith and the Emergence of Tradition," in *Tradition and Theology,* 11-30.

[87]For an excellent statement concerning the process of oral composition, see Albert B. Lord, *The Singer of Tales* (New York: Atheneum, 1974) chaps. 1-6.

There is a new interest in oral literature awakened by the work of Lord. Among these we recognize: Walter A. Koch, "Recurrent Units in Written and Oral Texts," *Linguistics* 73 (1971) 62-89; Bennison Gray,

the Dtr methodology of composition or narrative technique can be understood in light of oral composition. The Dtr made use of traditional language in the shape of formularies, technical terms, phrases or words as
the building blocks out of which was articulated a new theological statement. The traditional language, it should be noted, was not chance borrowing, but consciously and deliberately selected elements from tradition
that contribute to the statement being formulated.

We argue in this study that the technique of "traditional composition" was employed by the Dtr in the expression of the speeches and
essays used transitionally within the history. Thus we will demonstrate a
methodology used by the Dtr to be that of "traditional composition." This
is the technique used in the articulation of the dream narrative in 1 Kgs
3:4-15.

"Repetition in Oral Literature," *Journal of American Folklore* 84 (1971)
289-303; Robert Kellogg, "Oral Literature," *New Literary History* 5 (1973)
55-66; Ruth Finnegan, "How Oral is Oral Literature?" *BSO(A)S* 37 (1974)
52-64; and the recent review of the situation by Lord, "Perspectives on
Recent Work on Oral Literature," *Forum for Modern Language Studies* 10
(1974) 187-210.

The interest in the oral phase of composition is extended to biblical
studies. Note that an entire issue of *Semeia* is devoted to a discussion of
the subject: Robert C. Culley, ed., *Oral Tradition and Old Testament
Studies* (Semeia 5; Missoula: SBL, 1976).

The work done on biblical poetry to identify its formulaic nature has
focused solely on the psalms: see William Whallon, "Formulaic Poetry in
the Old Testament," *Comparative Literature* 15 (1963) 1-14; Stanley
Gervitz, *Patterns in the Early Poetry of Israel* (Studies in Ancient
Oriental Civilization 32; Chicago: University of Chicago, 1963); and
Robert C. Culley, *Oral Formulaic Language in the Biblical Psalms* (Near
and Middle Eastern Series 4; Toronto: University of Toronto, 1967).

II

The Dream of Solomon
in 1 Kgs 3:4-15

We turn our attention to the text that has been selected for study. The dream of Solomon will be used as a model for our demonstration of the Dtr-technique of traditional composition. Our purpose in this study is to come to an understanding of the deuteronomistic intention and message by identifying a deuteronomistic methodology of composition.

As we have tried to make clear in the survey of literature in the opening chapter, we are working on the assumption that the DtrH is an integral, coherent, and unified document. What we demonstrate in this study will contribute to the affirmation of that assumption; for, the methodology we will uncover allows for the appropriation of existing literary sources as well as the use of traditional elements which become for the Dtr the building blocks for new literary pieces within the thematic structure of the history.

We enter upon the study of the dream narrative itself at this point. The study will be undertaken according to the following plan. In this chapter, we will review the present scholarly opinion concerning the dream of Solomon; and we will also present our translation of the text. In chapter three, we will demonstrate through the formal structure of the narrative its inner coherence and its integrity. In chapters four to six we will analyze the content of the narrative that we might understand how the traditional elements utilized for the composition of the narrative contribute to a unique definition of kingship.

THE DREAM NARRATIVE IN RESEARCH

Scholarly opinion in regard to 1 Kgs 3:4-15 can be divided into two basic camps. On the one hand, the dream narrative is looked upon as an originally independent piece deriving from the royal ritual tradition of

Judah. On the other, the narrative is viewed as a construct of the Dtr who imposed its content on an ancient dream form.

Arguments for the antiquity of the text 1 Kgs 3:4-15 have been grounded in the comparison of this text with the Egyptian literary genre, the Königsnovelle. The genre itself was first studied by Alfred Hermann.[1] We are indebted, however, to Siegfried Herrmann for the comparison of the Egyptian genre with the text of 1 Kgs 3:4-15 and other biblical texts.[2]

---

[1] *Die ägyptische Königsnovelle* (Leipziger Ägyptologische Studien 10; New York: J. J. Augustin, 1938). Hermann applied the designation Königsnovelle to the body of literature which contained etiological reports of the royal decrees, deeds, and building accomplishments. He noted the fixed style describing a court ceremony during which the king proclaimed his decrees or announced his decisions before the assembled officials. In the description of the events, usually a dream in which the deity made his will known preceded the king's proclamation, thus, the issuance of the king was an expression of the divine will. The speech of the king was the medium through which many aspects of royal ideology were communicated: e.g., the king's divine sonship; his designation from infancy and the deeds of his youth before ascending to the throne; and the bestowal of the kingship and the kingdom to him by divine will.

This genre of literature was found in royal records and on temple inscriptions. Always, the king is presented in these as a representative figure with a specific role in society and never as a personality. The decrees and decisions, the achievements and building accomplishments announced by the king, however, correspond with historical data; what is recorded in the words of the king much be understood as historical fact. This literary genre fixed in a definite pattern the words and events of the king. It adorned and enhanced these with expressions drawn from royal ideology.

[2] "Die Königsnovelle in Ägypten und in Israel," *Wissenschaftliche Zeitschrift der Karl-Marx-Universität*, Leipzig, 3 (1953-54) 51-62. Herrmann discussed the two texts, 1 Kgs 3:4-15 and 2 Samuel 7, and showed that they correspond with the Königsnovelle genre. In the earlier study of A. Hermann (*Die ägyptische Königsnovelle*, 39, n. 64), such a correspondence had already been suggested for 2 Kgs 3:1-28 and 5:1-8:66 (sic!).

Since these earlier works, Klaus Baltzer (*The Covenant Formulary in Old Testament, Jewish, and Early Christian Writing* [Philadelphia: Fortress, 1971] 71-72), suggested that the transfer of office to Joshua in Joshua 1 also is depicted as a court ceremony like that described in the Königsnovelle "albeit with certain changes to adapt it to the situation at hand" (ibid., 71).

Herrmann defined the boundaries of the dream text on the basis of comparison with the activities described of Thut-mose IV on the "Sphinx Stela."[3] In both, the future king received a message from a deity at a sacred place and afterward went from there to the temple in the holy city to offer sacrifice.[4] Herrmann compared also the hymn of praise in vv 6-8 of Solomon's dream with the hymn found in royal records of the day of coronation or on inscriptions in the temple of that king. These royal texts record the king's praise to the god whose son he was and make reference to his designation to kingship from the time of his youth. In such recorded hymns, the Egyptian king was enabled to give proper praise to the gods for the kingship and kingdom that were given by them.[5]

When Herrmann studied the content of the message he found in the biblical dream text, he noted that the terminology of the text corresponds with the terminology in the royal psalms 2, 20, 21, and 89, and also with the messianic texts in Isaiah 9 and 11.[6] On the basis of its correspondence with the Königsnovelle genre and the content common to Judean royal ritual, Herrmann concluded that 1 Kgs 3:4-15 is a royal text that was used as a ceremonial text for the occasion of the king's coronation. Herrmann states:

> On the day of coronation in a divine encounter, the new ruler is given the deed and titles of his kingship. The phrase 'as it is this day' at the end of V. 7 shows that I Kings 3 is a 'ceremonial text,' a type of *hieros logos* which establishes the terms and definitions of the future kingship. The phrase is to be understood as a reference to the coronation day and points finally to the repeated use of expressions which in other Old Testament passages are used again and again in connection with the king.[7]

According to Herrmann, the dream of Solomon was originally a royal text which was used as a ceremonial text for the day when the god, by whom the king was designated, bestowed upon the king the names and titles of his office. Thus, Herrmann asserts that this literary piece was actually a "geschlossene kleine Einheit" (short concise unit) inserted into the context of the Solomon history in 1 Kings 3-11 as an "ursprünglich selbständiges

---

[3]The text of this inscription can be found in *ANET*, 449.
[4]S. Herrmann, "Die Königsnovelle," 53b.
[5]Ibid., 54.
[6]Ibid., 55b-56a.
[7]Ibid., 55b.

älteres Stück" (originally older independent piece).[8] The only exception
to this consideration of unity is v 14. Because v 14 seems obviously to be
from the stock of deuteronomic formulae, Herrmann accounted for its
presence in the ancient ritual text by saying: "V. 14 ist Zusatz des Deu-
teronomisten, der auch in V. 15 eingegriffen hat" (V. 14 is an addition of
the Deuteronomist, who also intervened in V. 15).[9]

Herrmann based his argument for the original function of the text
also on the position it was given within the Solomon history. Herrmann
claimed that the Dtr included this originally independent text into the
history of Solomon in much the same way that a description of the coronation event was often used to introduce significant historical records.
As an illustration, Herrmann referred to the inscription of the enthronement event that introduces the Karnak inscription.[10] We see that even in
the way the dream text was used by the Dtr, Herrmann depends upon
Egyptian examples and precedent for his explanations.

Herrmann is entirely correct in recognizing that the dream of Solomon is patterned after the Königsnovelle genre of Egyptian literature. He
is not correct, however, in his conclusion that, therefore, the text must
have functioned in the life of the Judean kings in the manner that the
Königsnovelle functioned in Egyptian protocol. Such a conclusion is to be
expected, however, of an adherent of traditional form criticism who
would, as a matter of course, associate form and content and *Sitz im
Leben* without question.[11]

---

[8]Ibid., 54a.

[9]Ibid., 54a, n. 1. That v 14 is a deuteronomistic addition is claimed
also by: Georg Fohrer, "Der Vertrag zwischen König und Volk in Israel,"
ZAW 71 (1959) 7-10; Martin Noth, *Ü St.*, 67-68, and *Könige*, 44-46, 50;
C. F. Burney, *Notes on the Hebrew Text of the Books of Kings* (New
York: KTAV, 1970) 29-30; A. Jepsen, *Quellen*, 21-23, 102-4; Otto Eiss-
feldt, *The Old Testament*, 288-89; J. Fichtner, *Das erste Buch*, 73; and
John Gray, *I and II Kings*, 126.

[10]"Die Königsnovelle," 57. Cf. William P. Randolph, "The Development of History Writing in the Scribal Wisdom of Judah," (Diss., Emory
University, 1970) 85. Randolph cites the Solomon throne history as an
example of royal biography structured in the typical biographical pattern
of the ancient oriental writings. These biographies were generally introduced with a description of the establishment of the king's throne. In this
style of biographical writings, the divine election of Solomon which is
conveyed in the dream narrative, is positioned at the head of the Solomon
history.

[11]Under the influence of Hermann Gunkel, form, content and setting
in life are regarded as inseparable. Gunkel's great contribution to biblical

In so doing, Herrmann did not take into consideration the break-
down in genre that occurs gradually as the genre is removed further and
further from its original setting in life. Contemporary critics of traditional form criticism are making us aware that a genre is constituted by a
diversity of typicalities that are not statically fixed.[12]   Knierim, in
particular, has argued that "a genre is no longer to be constituted by its
societal setting."[13] The fact that a narrative is patterned in the structure of a particular genre does not necessarily specify the text as belonging to that genre. Similarly, the meaning of a text is altered by such
variations as its setting, its content, its mood, its concern, its function,
and its intention.[14]

On account of the limitations in form criticism, texts in the Old
Testament that have been approached from that perspective have not
always yielded their true meaning. This limitation has certainly affected
the interpretations that have been given to the dream of Solomon. It
cannot be said that the Königsnovelle genre which was a conventional
literary form for royal sociology and which functioned for Egyptian royal
ideology had been appropriated to the Israelite royal tradition. Neither
the content, the intention, nor the function of the dream of Solomon make
it that genre.

In this study we will demonstrate that the content and intention of
the dream of Solomon had been determined by the Dtr. The Dtr surely
made use of the structural design usually found in the Königsnovelle, as
we will discuss in the next chapter. The borrowing of a formal structure
of a genre, however, does not constitute an appropriation of the genre.

---

interpretation has been the insight that a particular language pattern had
its origin in a specific life situation; the form emerged from and reflected
its *Sitz im Leben*. As significant as this methodology has been for the
recovery of the basic forms of oral tradition that underlie both the poetry
and prose of biblical literature, it is not effective in every application.
On this, see Klaus Koch, *The Growth of the Biblical Tradition: The Form-
Critical Method* (New York: Scribner's, 1969); Gene M. Tucker, *Form
Criticism*, esp. 4-6 and 22-41; John H. Hayes, ed., *Form Criticism* (San
Antonio: Trinity University, 1974), especially the essay by Martin J. Buss,
"The Study of Forms," 1-56.

[12]So, Rolf Knierim, "Old Testament Form Criticism Reconsidered,"
Int 27 (1973) 435-68; and Douglas A. Knight, "The Understanding of 'Sitz
im Leben' in Form Criticism," in *SBLASP* 1974 (ed. George MacRae;
Massachusetts: Society of Biblical Literature, 1974) 1. 105-18.

[13]"Old Testament Form Criticism," 438.

[14]Ibid., 458-67.

For the Dtr, as a matter of fact, the structural design served as the framework, the mold, the pattern;[15] on this structure, adopted as a rhetorical device, the Dtr presented a new content that was his contribution out of Israelite tradition for the purpose of introducing a deuteronomistic design for kingship. The selection of the structure and the imposition of the content were, to be sure, determined by the purpose of the Dtr who was the author of the narrative.

The work of Herrmann, nonetheless, has dominated the interpretation of the dream narrative up to the present time. Differences introduced by scholars along the way alter the conclusions of Herrmann only in minor details. There are some, for example, who while they recognize the antiquity of the basic part of the text, do not agree that the text functioned as a ceremonial text in the royal ritual of Judah. The most radical of these is Otto Eissfeldt.[16] He asserts that the dream content has the character of a legend or tale that probably derived from oral popular tradition. For Eissfeldt, there is no connection between the dream of Solomon and cult. For Fohrer,[17] on the other hand, the text functioned for the legitimation of Solomon's reign. Fohrer argued that Solomon had not attained the throne in the customary way. Since he had not entered into a contract with the people, he had not been legitimately chosen by them. The dream narrative was supposedly written in the time of Solomon for the specific purpose of justifying the irregularity of his succession to the throne. The narrative substituted for the customary contract between king and people and also smoothed over the fact that the contract was lacking.[18]

---

[15]In an insightful work, Dennis McCarthy dealt masterfully with this problem though it was not the major question of his research. In his thesis, *Treaty and Covenant: A Study in Form in the Ancient Oriental Documents and in the Old Testament* (AnBib 21; Rome: Pontificio Instituto Biblico, 1963), McCarthy demonstrated how the covenant form, though it originally belonged in a ritual and legal setting, was employed by the Dtr simply as a rhetorical device and for no other reason. The texts studied by McCarthy are Deuteronomy 4; 29; 30; Joshua 24; 1 Samuel 12 and the book of Deuteronomy as a whole.

[16]*The Old Testament*, 288-89.

[17]"Der Vertrag," 7; and *History of Israelite Religion* (Nashville: Abingdon, 1972) 128.

[18]Fohrer states: ". . . he tried to resolve the defect peculiar to his kingship, coup d'état without election or covenant, by tracing his legitimacy back to Yahweh in the context of a Königsnovelle borrowed from the Egyptian prototype. . . . With Solomon the divine legitimation takes

Gray also understands the narrative to be an adaptation of the Königsnovelle for the purpose of authenticating the royal authority. The narrative was designed, according to Gray, in its specific form as a repetition of the story of the Davidic succession to the throne. At the time of Solomon's succession, however, the claim was made on the basis of Yahweh's covenant with David and his house within the economy of Yahweh's chosen community. In this way, the Davidic covenant was linked with Yahweh's covenant with Israel. In summary, Gray would say that the dream narrative is an extension to Solomon of the promise to David and reinterpretation of that promise to include Yahweh's covenant with Israel.[19]

We also recognize the work of those who do not deny the antiquity of the basic material, but who assign a greater role to the Dtr or a redactor in the reworking of the original source. Among these is Noth himself.[20] Noth claims that vv 5a, 13 and 14a are additions made by the Dtr. He also notes that there are signs of expansions by the Dtr in vv 6-8. Burney,[21] on the other hand, recognizes Dtr expansions in vv 5, 6, and 8. He argues also that vv 10, 12, 14, and 15 are additions made by the Dtr. In this view, the Dtr supposedly retained the older literary unit and without significantly altering its form made additions with words, phrases, or with complete statements and thereby impressed an older written text with his theological viewpoint.

There is a certain truth not to be overlooked in the recognition that the identified texts reflect the deuteronomistic perspective. In these statements are found traditional elements representative of the Dtr interest that have been woven together with traditional elements reflecting the basic tenets of Yahwism and the royal tradition. Those elements that reflect the Torah, in particular, were not added later, but are integral to the dialectic consciously introduced by the Dtr to present the design for kingship. In this study we will show that the Dtr coloration within the narrative is neither additional nor an expansion to an older

---

the place of a temporal royal contract and compensates for the lack of it" ("Der Vertrag," 7). Also, *Israelite Religion*, 128.

[19]John Gray, *I and II Kings*, 120-21; cf. 21-22.

Fohrer also noticed the relationship between the dream narrative and the promise to David in 2 Samuel 7. Fohrer proposed, however, that 2 Samuel 7 follows from the dream narrative and extends to the Davidic dynasty what had concerned Solomon alone in 1 Kgs 3:4-15. So, "Der Vertrag," 10.

[20]*Ü St.*, 67-68; and, *Könige*, 44-46, 50.

[21]*Notes on the Hebrew Text*, 29-30.

source. It is an indication of the skillful combination by the Dtr of elements from tradition, that when combined, create a dialectic between the
Davidic and Mosaic, the conditional and unconditional covenant.

Finally, we recognize the work of Jepsen, whom we discussed
above.[22] Jepsen assigned the dream narrative to the second redactor,
who took the piece from tradition and added it to the existing work of
R^I. The text taken over according to Jepsen, consisted of vv 5-15a.[23] On
account of the content, Jepsen was deterred from assigning vv 4 and 15b
to the basic unit. Jepsen believed that the interest in sacrifice and in
places of worship found in these two texts could only reflect the situation
of the second temple, and therefore, Jepsen decided that vv 4 and 15b be
assigned to the levitical redactor, R^{III}.[24]

As we will demonstrate, every word and every phrase of the dream
narrative is integral to the statement. The dream of Solomon, encom-
passing vv 4-15, was composed at one time with one specific message.
The architecture of the narrative is such that from beginning to end not
one element may be excluded without obliterating the full portrait of
kingship presented there. The source material is ancient, deriving from
the living tradition of the Israelite people. But the source was not appropriated for the historical work as an already existing literary piece to
which later additions were later made. We have in the dream of Solomon
a coherent and integrally-formed composition fashioned upon a conventional structure, and formulated out of traditional elements, but
articulating a new and poignant interpretation of kingship.

Of those who credit the content of the dream of Solomon entirely
to the creative genius of the Dtr, the work of Moshe Weinfeld[25] is most
significant. Weinfeld compared the Solomon dream with other dream
texts found in literature of the ancient orient, and concluded that the
literary form was indeed patterned like the known dream texts, all of
which contain an account of a prophetic vision granting approval for the
construction of a sanctuary.[26] The content of Solomon's dream differs
radically, however, from the content that would be expected in such a
dream. Instead of signalling the construction of the temple, as one might

---

[22]See Chap. I, 12-15.
[23]*Quellen*, 19.
[24]Ibid., 21.
[25]*Deuteronomy and the Deuteronomic School* (Oxford: Clarendon, 1972).
[26]Weinfeld treats the extra-biblical texts of Gudea, Esarhaddon, Nabonidus, and Baal: Ibid., 248-50.

expect, the dream becomes a vehicle through which the deity promises
Solomon judicial wisdom.[27]   Because Weinfeld perceived the tradition of
the dream at Gibeon and Solomon's return to Jerusalem to be "an ancient
and genuine one,"[28] Weinfeld conjectured "that the original dream at
Gibeon also was a prophetic vision whose purpose was to grant divine
approval for the construction of a sanctuary, an undertaking which the
Deity had previously rejected in the Nathan prophecy."[29]   In Weinfeld's
opinion, the Dtr discarded the original content pertaining to the building
of the temple, and "reworked the content material of Solomon's dream at
Gibeon, so as to make it conform with his own conceptions."[30]   The
original dream content was, in Weinfeld's opinion, "objectionable" to the
Dtr, so the Dtr "introduced a new content which was more consistent with
his own views."[31]

    The fact is that Solomon's glory in history, and in particular in the
deuteronomistic presentation of Solomon's history, is founded on his
building accomplishments and the building of the Jerusalem Temple. The
Dtr himself did not ignore this focus of Solomon's life; the writer highlighted the place of the temple in the history of Solomon by making its
construction and dedication the high points of the history. One wonders
on what basis the argument could be made that matter concerning the
building of the temple was "objectionable" to the Deuteronomist. Why
would the Dtr discard content pertaining to the divine approbation for the
building of the sanctuary in view of the importance of the temple in the
history of Solomon, in the life of the nation, and for the DtrH as a
whole?   Why would the Dtr divorce the content of divine approval for
temple building from the particular form appropriate for conveying that
content?   If the Dtr could be held responsible for altering the content of
the dream, surely the reason that the original content was "objectionable"
would not be valid. At one point in his discussion, Weinfeld states that it
was the vision at Gibeon, i.e., the incubation theophany, that conflicted
with the views of the Dtr.[32]   Why then did the Dtr preserve the dream

---

[27]Ibid., 250.
[28]Ibid., 246.
[29]Ibid., 248.
[30]Ibid., 247, 253-54.   The theory proposed by Weinfeld had been
suggested earlier by A. S. Kapelrud ("Temple Building, a Task for Gods
and Kings," Or 32 [1963] 59-60). Kapelrud, too, argued that the author
introduced the wisdom theme in place of the discarded material.
[31]Ibid., 247.
[32]Ibid., 253.

itself while discarding material "more consistent with his own view"?[33]
Weinfeld's arguments are circular with respect to the nature of the dream
of Solomon.

All of this manipulation of form and content was undertaken to
explain the introduction of content which, according to Weinfeld, was the
contribution of the scribal circles of the Hezekian court.[34] The granting
of judicial wisdom to Solomon by Yahweh was matter which was apparently more appealing to the mind of the Dtr whose concern, says Weinfeld, was proper behavior and morality. Weinfeld contends that the
wisdom described in 1 Kgs 2:5-9; 3:16-27; 5:9-14; and 10:1-10, 23-24
actually derived from the pre-deuteronomic wisdom tradition. This early
wisdom concerned the intellectual and pragmatic;[35] whereas the wisdom
expressed by the Dtr concerned behavior and morality.[36] This latter was

---

[33]I have deliberately applied this statement obversely.

[34]Ibid., 9, 161-62, 255. Weinfeld associates the author of Deuteronomy and the Dtr with the scribes of the Hezekian court who were
responsible for the literary activity accomplished in the time prior to the
reign of Josiah until after the fall of Judah.

So also, R. B. Y. Scott, "Solomon and the Beginnings of Wisdom in
Israel," in Wisdom in Israel and in the Ancient Near East (Fs., H. H. Rowley; VTSup 3; Leiden: E. J. Brill, 1969) 262-79. Scott is emphatic in his
view that wisdom as a literary phenomenon originated with the wise men
of the Hezekian court. He contends that the literary efforts and the
attributions of wisdom to Solomon at that time were undertaken in an
effort "to renew the vanished glories of Solomon" in the age of Hezekiah
(278). R. N. Whybray (The Intellectual Tradition in the Old Testament
[BZAW 135; New York: Walter de Gruyter, 1974] 57, 60-61), on the other
hand, cites the Hezekian setting as the locus for the authorship of the
present collection of proverbs prepared for the instruction and entertain-
ment of an adult educated class. Counter to Whybray, Weinfeld assumes
that the scribes of the Hezekian court were responsible for collating the
proverbial sayings and for ascribing the Lebensweisheit to Solomon, but
this wisdom already existed in a literary form (Deuteronomy, 256).

[35]To illustrate the nature of pre-deuteronomic wisdom, Weinfeld
outlines the traditions of Solomon's wisdom which he considers to fall into
the category of pre-deuteronomic wisdom: Solomon is characterized as a
cunning individual (2:5-9; 3:16-29); as possessing extraordinary knowledge
of natural phenomena (5:9-14); as a skilled artisan (10:4); and as a
pragmatically successful ruler (ibid., 254-55).

[36]Ibid., 255. Weinfeld states that "the concept 'wisdom' had taken
on a new meaning which accorded with the new temper of the times," that
is, a time of heightened awareness of moral demands.

"wisdom" interpreted in "an entirely novel manner,"[37] in a judicial sense
and in terms of ability to discern between social good and evil.[38]

It must be realized that the dream text, interpreted as an illustration of a novel concept of wisdom that was introduced by the Dtr, is based
on the assumption that wisdom belonged exclusively to mundane areas of
life prior to the seventh century. This experiential wisdom was supposedly reinterpreted by the deuteronomic circle that it might bring
wisdom into accord with the ethical teachings of Israel under the impetus
of deuteronomic law. Before this time, wisdom and law existed side by
side as two disparate disciplines. This is Weinfeld's point as he states
quite clearly:

> Until the seventh century Law and Wisdom existed as two
> separate and autonomous disciplines. Law belonged to the
> sacral sphere, whereas Wisdom dealt with the secular and the
> mundane. These two disciplines were amalgamated in the
> book of Deuteronomy, and the laws of the Torah were now
> identified with wisdom: '. . . for this is your wisdom and your
> understanding.' (Deut 4:6)[39]

This conclusion based on the assertion that wisdom belonged exclusively to mundane areas of life prior to the seventh century is purely con-
jectural in view of the holistic view of life in the oriental cultures.[40] To
be sure, what does it mean to distinguish between the sacral and secular
in a society founded on the conviction of being the chosen of a God?

We recognize that Weinfeld is correct, nonetheless, in crediting the
Dtr with the integration of law and wisdom. It is an integration, however,
not of law and wisdom understood as representative of the sacral and
mundane. The religious flavor in wisdom teaching does not derive from
assimilation with the Mosaic law. We will discover in this study that an

---

[37]Ibid., 254.

[38]Ibid., 256.

[39]Ibid., 255-56.

[40]See statements concerning this problem in: Ernst Würthwein,
"Egyptian Wisdom and the Old Testament," in *Studies in Ancient Israelite
Wisdom* (New York: KTAV, 1976) 117; and W. Zimmerli, "The Place and
Limit of the Wisdom in the Framework of the Old Testament Theology,"
SJT 17 (1964) 148, now appearing in *Studies in Ancient Israelite Wisdom*,
316.

D. J. McCarthy (review of *Deuteronomy and the Deuteronomic
School* in *Bib* 54 [1973] 450-51) addresses this problem in reference to
another issue.

achievement of the Dtr was the integration of Israelite traditions--Torah
and wisdom, the Mosaic and Davidic--in the articulation of this statement
about kingship. We might add that, in the mind of the writer, wisdom
belongs to the sphere of the royal influence. Therefore, strictly speaking,
the traditions that have been assimilated by the Dtr were principally the
traditions associated with Moses and with David.

At this point in the discussion we will introduce our translation of
the dream of Solomon for the convenience of the reader. Then, in Chapter III we will resume the discussion with an analysis of the structure upon
which the narrative was composed.

THE TEXT OF THE DREAM NARRATIVE

4) And the king went to Gibeon[41]
    to sacrifice there,
    for that was the great high place.
    A thousand burnt offerings
        did Solomon offer
        upon that altar.

וילך המלך גבעֹנה
לזבֹח שם
כי היא הבמה הגדולה
אלף עלות
יעלה שלמה
על המזבח ההוא

5) At Gibeon,
    Yahweh appeared to Solomon
        in a dream by night.
    And God said:[42]
    Ask, what shall I give you?

בגבעון
נראה יהוה אל-שלמה
בחלום הלילה
ויאמר אלהים
שאל מה אתן-לך

6) And Solomon said:
    You have shown your servant
        David my father
        great loyalty,
    when he walked before you
        in faithfulness
        in righteousness,
    and in uprightness of heart
        toward you,
    and you have proven to him
        this great loyalty
    and you have given him a son

ויאמר שלמה
אתה עשית עם-עבדך
דוד אבי
חסד גדול
כאשר הלך לפניך
באמת
ובצדקה
ובישרת לבב
עמך
ותשמר-לו
את-החסד הגדול הזה
ותתן-לו בן

---

[41] Our translation differs from the RSV in favor of a word order that
is closer to the Hebrew text, and in an attempt to provide as literal a
translation as possible without violating clarity.

[42] LXX reads *kyrios* here and in v 11. Because of the consistency in
the text in the use of "Elohim" in the two instances when God speaks, we
prefer to retain the reading of the MT.

to sit[43] upon his throne,
    as it is this day.

ישב על-כסאו
כיום הזה

7)   And now, Yahweh my God,
    you have made your servant king
      in succession to David my father,
   though I am but a little child;
   I do not know going out or coming in.

ועתה יהוה אלהי
אתה המלכת את-עבדך
תחת דוד אבי
ואנכי נער קטן
לא אדע צאת ובא

8)   And your servant is
    in the midst of your people
      whom you have chosen,
    a numerous people,
    that cannot be numbered
      nor counted for multitude.

ועבדך
בתוך עמך
אשר בחרת
עם-רב
אשר לא-ימנה
ולא יספר מרב

9)   And you are able to give[44] your servant
    an attentive heart
      to govern your people,
    to understand (the difference)
      between good and evil;
   for who is able
    to govern your people,
    this burden?

ונתת לעבדך
לב שמע
לשפט את-עמך
להבין
בין-טוב לרע
כי מי יוכל
לשפט את-עמך
הכבד הזה

10) And the request pleased Adonai[45]
    because Solomon asked this word.

וייטב הדבר בעיני אדני
כי שאל שלמה
את-הדבר הזה

11) And God[46] said to him,
   Because you asked this word
    and you did not ask long life
      for yourself
    and you did not ask riches
      for yourself
    and you did not ask for the life
      of your enemies;
   but you asked for yourself
    understanding to discern justice.

ויאמר אלהים אליו
יען אשר שאלת את-הדבר הזה
ולא-שאלת לך ימים רבים
ולא-שאלת לך עשר
ולא שאלת נפש איביך
ושאלת לך
הבין לשמע משפט

---

[43]Against LXX I retain the word ישב in the phrase ישב-על כסאו. This phrase occurs also in 1 Kgs 8:20 and 25.

[44]The text reads a perfect waw-consecutive. Rather than translating this verb as an imperative (RSV), we prefer to translate in such a way as to express a future action which is open to continuing possibility.

[45]LXX reads YHWH here and in v 15. The text was obviously altered to correct a difficult reading.

[46]See n. 42 above.

12)   behold, I now do[47]   הנה עשיתי
          according to your word,[48]   כדבריך
      Behold, I give you   הנה נתתי לך
          a wise and intelligent heart   לב חכם ונבון
      so that no one like you   אשר כמוך לא-
          has been before you   היה לפניך
      and after you will arise   ואחריך לא-
          no one like you.   יקום כמוך

13)   And also what you did not ask   וגם אשר לא-שאלת
          I give to you;   נתתי לך
          both riches and honor   גם-עשר גם-כבוד
      so that there has never been   אשר לא-היה
          any one like you   כמוך איש
      among the kings,   במלכים
          all your days.   כל-ימיך

14)   And if you will walk in my ways   ואם תלך בדרכי
          keeping my statutes and   לשמר חקי
          my commandments,   ומצותי
          as your father David walked,   כאשר הלך דויד אביך
      then I will lengthen your days.   והארכתי את-ימיך

15)   And Solomon awoke, and behold,   ויקץ שלמה והנה
          it was a dream.   חלום
      And he came to Jerusalem,   ויבוא ירושלם
      and he stood before the ark   ויעמד לפני ארון
          of the covenant of Adonai,[49]   ברית-אדני
      and offered burnt offerings and   ויעל עלות
          made peace offerings,   ויעש שלמים
      and prepared a feast   ויעש משתה
          for all his servants.   לכל-עבדיו

---

[47]Here and in v 13 I translate the perfect verb in the present aspect. A divine promise stated in the present carries the assurance of an accomplished fact. See *GKC*, 312, par. 106m. So also, Noth, *Könige*, 42.

[48]With the numerous editions, I prefer the singular reading in view of the repetition of this phrase in vv 10 and 11.

[49]See n. 45 above.

III

Structure and Integrity
of the Dream of Solomon

In Chapter II, we presented one corner in scholarship that draws a comparison between the dream narrative and the Königsnovelle genre of Egyptian literature. We learned from A. Hermann that this genre generally comprised a variety of forms. There could be a dream in which the divine will was communicated to the king; there could be a speech through which the king apprised his servants of the content of the dream; there might be a hymn which enabled the king to praise the god who had bestowed the throne and kingdom. When these elements are present in Egyptian literature, they constitute the Königsnovelle genre. We also noted that the direct comparison of the Königsnovelle genre with the dream narrative by S. Herrmann led to invalid conclusions because of the erroneous assumption that similarity in structure constituted the genre.

In this chapter, we will determine the nature of the dream narrative by analyzing the formal structure upon which the narrative is composed. We will delineate the forms adopted for rhetorical use within the composition, then demonstrate that, not the forms, but the structuring of the content exposes the inner coherence and singular message of the dream.

RHETORICAL FORMS WITHIN THE NARRATIVE

The narrative can be divided into three distinct sections that seem to correspond to units often found in the Königsnovelle. The first division, vv 4-5a and 15, define the outer limits of the text. Within these verses there are actually two separate parts that can be divided into a two-fold chiastic ring about the body of the narrative. That the chiasm and inclusio structure may be obvious, we quote these verses:

a)   The king went to Gibeon to sacrifice there,
               for that was the great high place.
       A thousand burnt offerings did Solomon offer
               upon that altar (v 4).

b)   At Gibeon,
       Yahweh appeared to Solomon in a dream by night (v 5a).

b')   And Solomon awoke, and behold, it was a dream (v 15a).

a')   He came to Jerusalem,
       and stood before the ark of the covenant of Adonai,
       and offered burnt offerings and made peace offerings,
       and prepared a feast for all his servants (v 15b).

The reference to the king's travel to Gibeon and his sacrifice there (a) is balanced by the reference to Solomon's journey to Jerusalem and his worship at the central sanctuary (a'). The parallel design of these verses is precise and forbids the conjecture that one or the other does not belong to this narrative unit.

       With the pattern of events in the dream of Solomon, we compare the sequence of events that surround the divine revelation recorded on the Sphinx Stela. Speaking of Thut-mose IV, the inscription recounts an encounter with a deity at a holy place followed by a journey of the recipient of the communication to the holy city where sacrifice was offered at the sanctuary:

> One of these days it happened that the King's Son Thutmose came on an excursion at noontime. Then he rested in the shadow of this great god. Sleep took hold of him, slumbering at the time when the sun was at (its) peak. He found the majesty of this august god speaking with his own mouth, as a father speaks to his son, saying. . . .

> When he had finished these words, then this king's son awoke, because he had heard these [words]. . . and he understood the speech of this god. (But) he set silence in his heart, (for) [he] said: ". . . Come, let us go to our house in the city. They shall protect the offerings to this god which ye will bring to him: cattle, . . . , and all green things. We shall give praise to . . . the image made for Atum-Harmakhis. . . ."[1]

The events recorded in this inscription are remarkably similar to those in the dream of Solomon. It is not unthinkable that the Dtr had a text such

---

[1] *ANET*, 449.

as this in mind when he composed the dream narrative. We can expect that the Dtr, who was fond of emulating forms for rhetorical purposes,[2] would select a model from royal literature for his own construct. The Dtr borrowed a framework pattern, but he enfleshed that framework with selective content to set the stage for Solomon's reign, and thus to designate the dream narrative as programmatic for the history of Solomon.[3]

The medium for divine communication indicated on the Sphinx Stela is apparently a dream. We surmise this from the references to falling asleep and awaking. In the biblical text, the medium of communication is also a dream, but here that is explicitly stated. The dream is named at the beginning and again at the end of the dream. Moreover, the Dtr conveyed the event of the dream by the use of clearly recognizable forms to announce the beginning and the ending of the dream. The verification of the dream form will be accomplished when we undertake the content study.[4] At this point we call attention only to the obvious, that the function of the dream form is to provide a frame for the content of the dialogue and supplies the vehicle for the communication of the dialogue.

In the outer framework of the narrative, there are two distinct elements: 1) the setting at the sanctuaries, and 2) the event of the dream. Each is an independent rhetorical feature and each possesses its own function in the narrative. But with delicate artistry the Dtr appropriated these familiar patterns of expression and skillfully utilized them to introduce and close the body of the narrative. Later in this study we will demonstrate that these rhetorical patterns, while being structured typically, cloak a substance that differs radically from that presented in the extra-biblical models.

In the plan of the narrative, the setting of the dream provides the frame for the dialogue between Yahweh and Solomon. The dialogue itself is introduced with the question: Ask, what shall I give you? (v 5b). The direct answer to the question and the continuing discourse are structured upon the verbs introduced in the initial question, the verbs "ask" and "give." A skeletal base consisting of these verbs forms the backbone for the introduction of traditional content. The structure looks like this:

---

[2]This is a presumptuous statement. But we are confident that this Dtr technique of composition will become evident in the course of this study and future studies in the deuteronomistic methodology for using forms and traditions.

[3]This will be elaborated in Chap. VI.

[4]See the analysis of the dream in Chap. VI.

God:	Ask, what shall I give you?
Solomon:	You are able to give . . .
Transition:	The request pleased Adonai because Solomon asked this
God:	Because you asked this

and you did not ask
and you did not ask
and you did not ask

but you asked for yourself . . .

behold, I now do . . .
behold, I give you . . .

and also what you did not ask

I give you . . .

The structure is self-evident. The king is always the one who "asks" while God "gives" both what is asked and what is not asked.

The remarkable fact is that the burden of the content is borne upon the interplay between the two verbs "ask" and "give." A consideration of the object of these verbs allows us to lay out the significant content of the dream. Solomon asks very specific ability for himself. He states that God is able to give him

an attentive heart to judge (v. 9b), and
understanding (to distinguish) between good and evil (v 9c)

In response to Solomon's request, it is reiterated that Solomon had asked for

understanding to discern what is right (v 11f)

In response, God gives him

a wise and intelligent heart (v 12b).

Four times the content of what Solomon requests is repeated in a different way. In each of the four instances the verb upon which the content is contingent is either "ask" or "give." From the consistency in the structure it is apparent that, though the content of the request is phrased variously, each of the expressions is a rhetorically equivalent statement. Each manifests a tonal variation of the one precise responsibility of kingship, that of governing the people with justice. The gift for which Solomon asks and that which is given to him enables him to carry out his responsibility as leader. Upon the structure of these verbs, the Dtr has presented one characteristic of a king who is loyal to covenant.

The narrative is so expressed that we are able to notice one other characteristic of kingship within the dialogue. This particular description of kingship is vehicled on the negative aspect of the verb "ask":

> Solomon <u>did not ask</u> for long life
> riches
> the life of (his) enemies (v 11).
> But also what (he) <u>did not ask</u>
> God <u>gave</u> him both riches and honor (v 13).

The content contingent upon the verb "did not ask" differs noticeably from the content contingent upon the verbs "ask" and "give." In each, the content reflects a quite different tradition of kingship. What we observe in the case of the verb "did not ask" is a naming of gifts that identify the king as being in harmonious relationship with the God upon whom his reign is dependent.[5]

The structure of the dialogue sets up a contrast between two quite different traditions about kingship and two g ups of distinguishing factors. Careful attention to the structure will yield rich insight into the kinds of elements that have been brought together into a coherent literary piece for the purpose of setting into relief the deuteronomistic interpretation of kingship.

Within the lines of the dialogue, a second structure can be outlined. This is the dialogic pattern of I-You which is appropriate in an exchange between two parties. The I-You interchange is consistent throughout:

> God: What shall <u>I</u> give <u>you</u>?
> Solomon: <u>You</u> are able to give (<u>me</u>) . . .
> God: Because <u>you</u> asked
> and <u>you</u> did not ask
> and <u>you</u> did not ask
> and <u>you</u> did not ask
> but <u>you</u> asked
> behold, <u>I</u> now do . . .
> behold, <u>I</u> give <u>you</u> . . .
> what <u>you</u> did not ask <u>I</u> give

There is a boldness in this presentation. It is also unique as the manner in which the deity usually communicated to a king.

----

[5]The meaning of these gifts will be discussed in detail in Chap. V.

In the extra-biblical texts available to us, whenever the deity makes his will known through the medium of the dream, the divine message is simply communicated.[6] Other gods speak in monologue.[7] Yahweh communicates in dialogue.

The Dtr deviated radically from the usual mode for the communication of the divine will to a king. The uniqueness of the pattern for the delivery of the message is a convincing indication of the Dtr's creativity in the use of conventional forms of royal literature. It is also an indication that the Dtr depends upon Israelite tradition as the controlling factor in his presentation. For it is the case that communication in dialogue quite specifically roots the king in the covenantal tradition. The Israelite king, in the perception of the Dtr, is not like the kings of the ancient orient. He is associated with his God by covenant. It is this covenant relationship between the king and Yahweh that the Dtr intends to dramatize through the dialogical discourse.[8]

The third section of the dream narrative is expressed in the form of a hymn. This is vv 6-8. In this prayer of praise Solomon acknowledges that the throne of Israel had been given to him by Yahweh.

A hymn of praise on the lips of the king acknowledging his dependence upon a particular deity is an important component of the Königsnovelle genre. The hymn was the conventional device used in the royal literature to indicate the association of the king with his patron-god. As the substance of the hymn, the king attributed his kingship to the will of the god by proclaiming his relationship with the deity and the special protection granted him from the time of his youth.

---

[6]For a discussion of the dream, its form and the message, see A. Leo Oppenheim, *The Interpretation of Dreams in the Ancient Near East* (Transactions of the American Philosophical Society, n. s. vol. 46, part 3; Philadelphia: The American Philosophical Society, 1956) 186-87.

[7]A single text from Mari records an account of a dream in which a dialogue occurs between the god Dagan and his worshipper. (This text appears in translation in Oppenheim, *Dreams*, 195.) Because the account departs in every respect from the conventional dream-form, Oppenheim suggests that the incident was based "on an actual visionary experience which the person who was so privileged saw fit to report to the officials as a dream" (195b). Its type more closely models the "full report," a report presented in the form of a letter addressed by the king to his god immediately following a successful military campaign.

[8]We will present examples of the use of dialogue in Israelite tradition in Chap. V.

We find in the dream narrative that the Dtr utilized the form of a hymn to introduce the historical circumstances of the inauguration of Solomon's reign. In the rhetorical pattern appropriate for the king's response to the god for his kingship and his kingdom, the Dtr expressed the specific phenomena of the king's governance of the chosen people of Yahweh and of the transition of the leadership from David to Solomon.

There is division within the hymn itself based on a logic of the content. In three movements, the circumstances of the setting have been established. The first movement in v 6a sets the stage of the relationship between Yahweh and David:

> You have shown great loyalty to your servant David, my
>   father
> when he walked before you in faithfulness, in righteousness,
>   and in uprightness of heart . . .

The second movement in vv 6b - 7 presents the reality of Solomon's accession to the throne within the context of his succession to David:

> and you have proven to him this great loyalty
> and you have given him a son to sit upon his throne,
>   as it is this day.

> And now, Yahweh my God, you have made your servant king
>   in succession to David my father,
> although I am but a little child;
> I do not know how to go out or come in.

The final movement in v 8 refers to the special significance of that throne: the kingdom in which Solomon reigns is the community of the chosen people of Yahweh.

> And your servant is in the midst of your people whom you
>   have chosen, a numerous people that cannot be numbered
>   nor counted for multitude.

In this dramatic trilogy, Solomon's reign is disclosed as being legitimately in succession to David and as being in the kingdom of a covenant community. The rulership of the Israelite king is presented here as being quite different from other forms of kingship, for the kingdom is quite a unique sort of kingdom. In the hymn, as in the other forms within the narrative, the Dtr structured the form so that even there the intention becomes evident.[9]

---

[9]The content of the hymn and the implications of the content will be discussed in Chap. IV.

Solomon spoke words, in the form of a hymn, which reveal his historical circumstance as the successor to David and as king of the special people of Yahweh. The hymn does not provide the answer to the question posed by God in the narrative, though the hymn follows directly after the question. The hymn expresses the motivation for Solomon's request. Because Yahweh has willed that he legitimately reign over Israel in place of his father David, Solomon asks for the ability to govern the people who have been charged to him. The hymn form is simply and plainly a rhetorical device that enabled the Dtr to set forth the circumstances that make the request understandable. Except for the knowledge gained through the hymn, the reader would be unaware of the actual posture of Solomon before Yahweh and of his position in relation to the Israelite people. In the hymn, the scene is set for Solomon to ask for the ability to govern, that justice may prevail among the people.

As we considered each of the sections of the narrative, we recognized that the narrative is built out of what we have called typical royal forms. Each of these forms has been adopted by the Dtr from the royal literature and adapted by him with deliberate intention for the dream of Solomon. The fact that these precise forms could, in the Egyptian royal scene, constitute a literary genre has, up to the present, blinded scholars to the fact that the Dtr has utilized the forms with freedom and originality. As a component of the dream narrative, each of the forms has been appropriated as a suitable vehicle to set forth the Dtr's own perception of kingship. This is to say that the Dtr used these forms to articulate content made up of a dialectic between the traditions of Yahwism and the traditions of royal ideology. In the interface between these two streams of tradition,[10] the Dtr definition of kingship is expressed.

While each form is distinguishable and has a clearly defined structural plan, these forms cannot be misconstrued for independent units. In the following section we will demonstrate that the forms are woven together by the content in continuous flowing expression out of formulaic language.

---

[10]The expression "streams of tradition" was introduced by O. H. Steck as a rubric for the pre-given elements from the intellectual world that influence Old Testament writing. See "Theological Streams of Tradition," in *Tradition and Theology in the Old Testament*, 183-214.

THE INTEGRITY OF THE NARRATIVE

The inner coherence of the narrative is such that not one single element may be removed without adumbrating the message in the text. Each form is indispensable, as is every expression that was selected as a building block toward the statement about kingship.

The cohesion between the forms has been effected by the fact that the content runs in continuous discourse. The narrative was written in continuous prose, one idea or motif leading to the next in a progressive build-up to a central point, then descending with statements that balance or contrast to effect the dialectic of traditions that speak the definition of kingship. Within the inclusio structure, it is possible to account for the conjoining of each element. The use of catch words and ideas is observable; so is repetition by parallel expression.

In this discussion we will show how each consecutive phrase and key idea carries the account forward as one after the other is picked up and developed.

Beginning at v 6, each successive motif is built upon a previous word or phrase. Solomon speaks with reference to the relationship between Yahweh and David in the words:

you have shown to your servant great loyalty (v 6a)

In his next point, Solomon speaks of his own involvement in that relationship:

you have proven to him this great loyalty (v 6b)
and now, you have made your servant king (v 7a)

One part of the statement repeats the phrase "great loyalty"; the other repeats the phrase "your servant."

Solomon continues to speak about his own relationship with the people of the kingdom:

your servant is in the midst of your people (v 8a)

and you are able to give your servant
an attentive heart to govern your people (v 9ab)

The phrase "your servant" is taken over from the previous statement in v 7a. To this is added the key concept "your people." V 9ab is then formulated upon the repetition of these two key motifs: "your servant" is the focus of 9a and "your people" is the focus of 9b. This latter use of "your people" is part of the extended expression "to govern your people." This precise phrase is repeated in the next line:

who is able to govern your people

In the composition of vv 6-9, it is observable that the statements are composed on key motifs that successively unfold in the articulation of a smooth and flowing discourse. The key phrases we have underlined govern the composition; but within the confines of those limits, the Dtr employed formulae from tradition for variation but also for precision in the articulation of his message.[11]

To illustrate, the key motif "great loyalty" is really part of a formulaic expression "to show loyalty" (עשה חסד). A variation of this and also formulaic is the phrase, "to prove loyalty" (שמר חסד). The two times the Dtr used the motif "loyalty," he expressed it in a different formulary known to him from tradition.

An illustration of coherence within the speech that is closely akin to accretion on the basis of meter is observable in lines 7cd:

> I am but a little child
> I do not know going out or coming in

These two lines אנכי נער קטן, and לא אדע צאת ובא are attracted to each other by their poetic form.[12] Both seem to be poetic fragments, but since each contains a formulary from tradition, the Dtr obviously is demonstrating his skill by the way he adopted two traditional phrases-- נער קטן and צאת ובא --into poetic form. These lines are not fragments from poetry; the poetic form is an indication of the creativity with which the Dtr introduced the two significant phrases pertinent to kingship into the narrative. It is noteworthy that the two poetic lines are elaborations upon the motif "your servant."

In v 8, the motif "your people" designates the particular community in which Solomon is king. This point is made by grouping together a series of expressions from tradition that identify Yahweh's people. The narrator builds upon the phrase "your people" with the expressions, a "chosen" people, "a numerous people" and a people "that cannot be numbered nor counted for multitude." Each of these formulae is drawn from tradition and each contributes a relevant dimension to the portrait being painted of the people in Solomon's kingdom.

In vv 9-12, the Dtr defined the task of king also by the technique of accumulating traditional formulae. The king's obligation is "to govern"

---

[11]At this point in our discussion we will not attempt to verify the formulaic nature of the expressions we use for illustration. That is the task in Chaps. IV-V.

[12]Notice that the question in v 5b also falls into the category of being expressed as a poetic fragment: שאל מה אתן-לך.

(vv 9b and d). The series of expressions: "an attentive heart" לב שמע
(v 9b); "understanding to distinguish between good and evil" להבין בין
טוב לרע (v 9c); "understanding to discern what is right" הבין לשמע
משפט (v 11e); and "a wise and intelligent heart" לב חכם ונבון (v 12b)
are borrowed from royal ideology and function to elucidate the task of the
Israelite king. We noted above that these formulae are bound into the
narrative upon the structure of the interplay between the verbs "ask" and
"give." We call attention also to the fact that the formularies themselves
are structured chiastically. The concept "an attentive heart" (לב שמע)
corresponds with "a wise and intelligent heart" (לב חכם ונבון), and the
function "understanding to distinguish between good and evil" (להבין
בין-טוב לרע) corresponds with "understanding to discern what is right"
(הבין לשמע משפט).

The verbs "ask" and "give" govern the narrative in vv 9-14, in the
manner that the key motifs "great loyalty," "your servant," and "your
people" limit the narrative in vv 6-8. The verbs "ask" and "give" vehicle
another set of motifs that set forth a different perspective about kingship. On the negative aspect of "ask," the Dtr hinged the series "long
life," "riches," "the life of your enemies," and "riches and honor." Each is
a traditional element relevant to kingship and each names a blessing
which the king might expect for faithful execution of his rulership.

Another element belonging in the category of blessings is the
expression "length of days" used in v 14b. This component hinges not on
the verb "ask" but is integral to an if-then statement. It supplies the
substance for the consequence of the condition. The conditional statement, that is often considered to be an interpolation,[13] is securely linked
into the narrative by the phrase "length of days." The crucialness of the
condition for the interpretation of the narrative will become more obvious
in our delineation of the overall structuring of the narrative in the last
section of this chapter.

In vv 12 and 13, we have already referred to the content expressed
in traditional formulae and contingent upon the verb "give." At this time,
we call attention to the fact that the two verses follow the same inner
logic, as if the pattern of one determined the pattern for the second. The
content of these verses is formulaic throughout, but the differing content

---

[13]Noth (Könige, p. 44) states that v 14b could have belonged to
v 13. He says this because he takes v 14a to be an addition to the text,
and because he considers that "length of days" may be the third element
in the series "riches and honor and life." Cf. Prov 22:4; 8:18.

has been patterned on the principle of repetition. Because of the complexity of these verses, we set them side by side that the structural logic may become apparent:

I do according to your word	also what you did not ask
I give you	I give to you
a wise and intelligent heart	both riches and honor
(v 12a)	(v 13a)

The introductory line in each case reiterates what has been expressed several times before. V 12a, "I do according to your word," repeats v 10b, ". . . Solomon asked this word," and v 11a, "Because you asked this word." V 13a, "What you did not ask," repeats what has been expressed three times in v 11bcd. This illustrates that the narrator employed the technique of repetition within the narrative itself to carry along the flow of the discourse and to provide the way into new content.

The second half of vv 12 and 13 correspond in both content and structure:

so that no one like you	so that there has never been
has been before you	any one like you
and after you will arise	among the kings
no one like you (v 12b).	all your days (v 13b).

The statement in v 12 functions in a significant way in the deuteronomistic presentation of kings. We suspect that the analogous statement in v 13b is present in the narrative by attraction, i.e., to fill out the pattern in v 13 to make it correspond to v 12.

We have shown that there is a logic to the way the narrative has been composed. We have also seen that it would be difficult indeed to exclude any particular element since the components of the narrative are either contingent upon a clearly defined structure, are expressed in a pattern identical to another, or contribute significantly to a definition or description. We claim, therefore, that this narrative, built up of traditional elements that are conjoined upon a carefully conceived plan, is indeed an example of traditional composition. By this we mean that traditional materials have been apropriated to a new end.

In our consideration of the narrative technique, we have thus far identified two principles of Dtr's methodology. 1) The Dtr employed conventional literary forms of royal literature as a rhetorical device to convey novel content. 2) The Dtr filled out these forms with logically presented content expressed in traditional language. That the components of the content are traditional formulae will be demonstrated in subsequent chapters.

At this point we have still to identify the overall structure that governed the Dtr's use of the forms and content.

THE INCLUSIO DESIGN AS STRUCTURE

In the formal construction of the narrative, the adopted literary forms lose their force. An over-arching structure that governed the mind of the narrator in the presentation of the content gives the narrative its shap . It is out of the imposed structural design that the intention of the narrative becomes clear.

An outer structural frame in vv 4 and 15b sets the limits of the narrative:

And the king went to Gibeon to sacrifice there,
    for that was the great high place.
A thousand burnt offerings did Solomon offer
    upon that altar (v 4).

And (Solomon) came to Jerusalem,
and stood before the ark of the covenant of Adonai,
and offered burnt offerings and made peace offerings,
and prepared a feast for all his servants (v 15b).

This framework for the narrative also creates the effect of transition that is significant in the position the Dtr has given the dream narrative within the DtrH.

The inner structural frame in vv 5a and 15a announces the onset and the termination of the dream:

At Gibeon,
Yahweh appeared to Solomon in a dream by night (v 5a).

And Solomon awoke, and behold, it was a dream (v 15a).

The dream setting creates the context for theophany that the deity might communicate his divine will in a mode appropriate for kings. Thus the dream acts as the vehicle for the content of the dream. Moreover, the dream setting in the sanctuary serves to hinge the dream itself with the outer framework which is situated in a sanctuary.

The narrative itself unfolds in the symmetry of two inclusio rings around a central focus. The outer inclusio circle balances the circumstance of the Davidic covenant with the conditions of Torah:

You have shown to your servant
  David my father great loyalty
<u>when</u> he walked before you   <u>if</u> you will walk in my ways
       in faithfulness,   keeping my statutes and
       in righteousness,   my commandments,
and in uprightness of heart   as your father David walked
      toward you (v. 6a).   <u>then</u> I will lengthen your days
                                    (v. 14).

Two apparently contradictory traditions are set in balance. The "when he walked . . ." stands in a creative tension with "if you will walk. . . ." Out of this tension, the Dtr's purpose to bring the Davidic covenant into harmony with Torah is effected. That purpose is most clearly dramatized in the contraposition of the two opposing traditions: the Davidic and the Mosaic.

The two statements "you have shown loyalty" and "then I will lengthen your days" also stand in opposition. Two different traditions are represented. The one states the unconditional divine promise, the other names a blessing of creation that was adopted as a cliche in the DtrH to name a consequence for covenant loyalty.

Out of their chiastic structure these two texts speak their meaning. The "when . . ." and "if . . ." clauses are enclosed by the "you have shown loyalty" and "I will lengthen your days." The force of these statements declares the position of Solomon with Yahweh. The king comes under promise but he is also subject to Torah; the king shares in the promise of covenant and in the blessings of creation.

While the outer inclusio delineates the relationship of the king with Yahweh, an inner inclusio circle focuses upon the king himself. The first half of this inclusio sets into perspective the legitimacy of Solomon's kingship:

      and you have proven to him this great loyalty,
      and you have given him a son to sit upon this throne as it is
         this day (v 6b).

      And now, Yahweh my God, you have made your servant king
         in succession to David my father,
      though I am but a little child;
      I do not know going out or coming in (v 7).

The opposing portion of the inclusio pattern names qualifications, but primarily it enumerates the benefits that come to a faithful king:

      Because you asked this word
      and you did not ask long life for yourself
      and you did not ask riches for yourself
      and you did not ask for the life of your enemies;
      but you asked for yourself
         understanding to discern what is right (v 11),

behold, I now do according to your word.
Behold, I give you a wise and intelligent heart
so that no one like you has been before you
and after you will arise no one like you (v 12).

And also what you did not ask I give you;
    both riches and honor,
so that there has never been any one like you
among the kings, all your days (v 13).

Both sections of this description function in the narrative to reverse notions about kingship. The king does not attain the throne by power or by inheritance as do kings in the ancient oriental cultures. Kingship is given to Solomon as the result of the divine promise (v 6b); it is Yahweh who has made Solomon king (v 7a). The point is made that "riches, honor, and life," the "life of the enemy" and "a wise and intelligent heart," all of which express the properties of a royal potentate, do not rightfully belong to Solomon on account of his kingship. These are gifts which are given to the king; and they are, moreover, given as the gratuitous blessings to either the covenant partner or the creature by the Lord of creation.

    The central issue for the narrative is named in the center of the inclusio circle:

And your servant is in the midst of your people
    whom you have chosen, a numerous people,
        that cannot be numbered, nor counted for multitude (v 8).

And you are able to give your servant
    an attentive heart to govern your people,
    to understand (the difference) between good and evil;
for who is able to govern your people,
    this so great (people) (v 9)?

The people among whom Solomon is king are a special people; they are the people of election and those who live under promise. The focus is upon the people in the series of descriptions in v 8 as well as by the question at the end of v 9. At the core of this mini-inclusio, the focus is upon the king. Solomon is given kingship, not for his own prestige and security; his is the obligation "to govern this people" (v 9a and d). His rulership imposes obligations upon him, since in this position the king is responsible before Yahweh.

    Even before we have investigated the express meaning of the narrative, the structure in itself unfolds for us vibrant and dynamic content. Moving out from the focus of the narrative, wherein the essence of Israelite kingship is expressed, the definition of kingship deepens with the content of the widening circles. Encompassing the kernel text, the tension between faith and power dimensions in kingship is heightened in the declaration that kingship and authority are divinely given. The responsibilities of kingship are further elaborated in the contraposition of two distinct theological perspectives: the promise to David because of his loyalty and service is set in contrast with the stipulations of covenant obedience. The force of the contrast makes the affirmation that while the king is secure under the Davidic promise, he is yet bound by the stipulations of Torah.

IV

Content of the Dream Narrative
in Verses 6-8

In the previous chapters we noted that the dream of Solomon was composed out of forms common in royal literature so that the dream appears to be modelled after the Königsnovelle. We have also exposed a clearly defined overall structure that blurs the divisions between forms and unites the content composed of traditional elements into a unified and coherent narrative.

Our purpose is to demonstrate that the interlocking of the varied forms and unique content could not have been achieved in a sequence of reworkings over a period of time. Nor could the text have consisted simply of a nucleus to which additions were made in the course of its literary history. We are demonstrating that the rich and vibrant statement made in the dream narrative is a coherent literary unity created by the Deuteronomist to articulate a specific theological position regarding kingship. Every individual component of this carefully composed narrative is fraught with meaning toward the definition of kingship which the author intended for his readers.

We have considered the integrity of the unity in its structural design. In the following chapters we will investigate each element from tradition that was used for the expression of this particular interpretation of kingship. We will demonstrate the profound sophistication with which traditions, in the shape of technical terms, formularies, or motifs, combined in the articulation of the deuteronomistic design for kingship.

For the purpose of order, we will approach the dream narrative in three parts according to the forms we have already defined: the hymnic, response, vv 6-8; the question and answer, vv 5b, 9-14; and the framework, vv 4-5a, 15. Our study of the traditional elements used in the development of each section will be handled in three separate chapters corresponding with these three sections.

In each section, we will approach the text according to the following method:

1) identify the traditional elements used in the composition,
2) locate the traditional elements in tradition and consider the meaning of each component in tradition,
3) consider the meaning of the traditional elements as they are used by the Dtr to contribute to a design for kingship.

We will begin our study with an analysis of the traditional elements used in the composition of vv 6-8.

COVENANT BETWEEN YAHWEH AND THE KING

Yahweh's Fidelity to Covenant

A keynote idea in the dream narrative is expressed in the first words of Solomon's response to God. Solomon begins speaking by making reference to the relationship between Yahweh and his father David:

You have shown great loyalty (גדול) חסד עשה
to your servant David my father (v 6a).

The phrase חסד עשה[1] constitutes the nature of the relationship between Yahweh and David.

Biblical evidence which we will consider for the use of עשה חסד sets its context indubitably as that of entering into a solemn treaty under oath. The implication of the treaty, according to the evidence, establishes that the agreement applies to the contractual partners as well as to future generations of each of the families involved, and affects the land in the possession of each party.[2] To demonstrate that the formula עשה

---

[1]The descriptive modification to the phrase, גדול, is not generally present in tradition. It occurs elsewhere only in Num 14:19; Ps 108:5; and Gen 19:19.

[2]A treaty applying to the descendants of the parties who swear the oath of treaty and affecting the land in possession of each is not new with the treaties represented in the biblical texts. A treaty made between the Hittites and Egypt reads: "Behold, I, as the Great Prince of Hatti, am with (Ramses Meri-Amon), in good peace and in good brotherhood. The children of the children (of) the Great Prince of Hatti are in brotherhood and peace with the children of (Ra)mses Meri-(Amon), the great ruler of Egypt, for they are in our situation of Brotherhood and our situation (of peace. *The land of Egypt*), with the land of Hatti (*shall be*) at peace and in brotherhood like us forever. Hostilities shall not occur between Them

חסד in the biblical tradition is a technical term for loyalty to a sworn agreement, we will look to texts considered to be tenth century writings before considering the use by the Deuteronomist.[3]

The covenant between Jonathan and David is significant to demonstrate our purpose.[4] In the course of the Accession Narrative, Jonathan is

---

forever." (*ANET*, 200a Cf. the treaty between Hattusilis and Ramses II, *ANET*, 202ab.)

[3]The tenth century writings include: the Yahwist narrative--see G. von Rad, *Old Testament Theology*, 1.39-56; 136ff; H. W. Wolff, "The Kerygma of the Yahwist," *Int* 20 (1966) 131-58, now appearing in *The Vitality of the Old Testament Traditions*, 41-66; and Peter F. Ellis, *The Yahwist: The Bible's First Theologian* (Collegeville, MN: Liturgical, 1968). A late date for the Yahwist has been proposed by Norman E. Wagner, "Abraham and David?" in *Studies on the Ancient Palestinian World* (Fs. F. V. Winnett; eds. J. W. Wevers and D. B. Redford; Toronto: University of Toronto, 1972) 117-40; and John Van Seters, *Abraham in History and Tradition* (New Haven: Yale University, 1975).

On the Accession Narrative, see G. von Rad, *Old Testament Theology*, 1.308-9.

On the Succession Narrative, see L. Rost, "Die Überlieferung von der Thronnachfolge Davids," in *Das kleine Credo und andere Studien zum Alten Testament* (Heidelberg: Quelle & Meyer, 1965) 119-283; G. von Rad, *Old Testament Theology*, 1.310-18; and "The Beginnings of Historical Writing in Ancient Israel," in *The Problem of the Hexateuch*, 176-204; W. Brueggemann, "David and His Theologian," *CBQ* 30 (1968) 156-81; "On Trust and Freedom: A Study of Faith in the Succession Narrative," *Int* 26 (1972) 3-19; *In Man We Trust: The Neglected Side of Biblical Faith* (Richmond: John Knox, 1972) 52-63; R. N. Whybray, *The Succession Narrative: A Study of II Samuel 9-20; I Kings 1 and 2* (SBT, 2nd series 9; Naperville, IL: Alec R. Allenson, 1968); David M. Gunn, "David and the Gift of the Kingdom (2 Sam 2-4, 9-20, 1 Kgs 1-2)," *Semeia* 3 (1975) 14-45. That the history of David is the work of the Dtr is held by R. A. Carlson, *David, the Chosen King: A Traditio-Historical Approach to the Second Book of Samuel* (Uppsala: Almqvist & Wiksell, 1964).

On the Joseph Story, see n. 23 above, p. 67.

[4]The covenant itself is detailed in 1 Sam 18:1, 3-4. V 3 reads: "Jonathan made a covenant with David," with the phrase כרת ברית, a technical term for covenant making. Cf. 1 Sam 23:18 and 20:17. On this phrase, see: Ludwig Koehler, "Problems in the Study of the Language of the Old Testament," *JSS* 1 (1956) 4-7; James Barr, "Covenant," in *Dictionary of the Bible* (2d ed.; rev. by F. C. Grant and H. H. Rowley; New York: Scribner's, 1963) 183b-185; Gottfried Quell, "The OT Term בְּרִית," *TDNT* 2.106-24; Frank M. Cross, "A Brief Excursus on *berît*, 'Covenant,'"

asked to show his fidelity to the covenant he had made with David.[5]
Because David's life is endangered by Saul, and Jonathan is in a position to
help David, David says:

> Therefore deal kindly (עשה חסד) with your servant, for you
> have brought your servant into a sacred covenant[6] with you
> (1 Sam 20:8).[7]

There is a second incident when a covenant is sworn between Jonathan and David. On this occasion it is David who is asked to show loyalty
to the covenant. Jonathan requests that David keep covenant not only
with him but also with his house:

> If I am still alive, shall you not show me the loyal love (עשה
> חסד) of the Lord, that I may not die?[8] You shall not cut off
> your loyalty from my house forever. When the Lord cuts off

---

in *Canaanite Myth,* 265-73; Dennis J. McCarthy, "*berît* in Old Testament
History and Theology," *Bib* 53 (1972) 110-21; and *Treaty and Covenant: A
Study in Form in the Ancient Oriental Documents and in the Old Testa-
ment* (new edition and completely rewritten; AnOr 21A; Rome: Biblical
Institute Press, 1977) 17-21, 91-96; cf. 254-56.

For a different viewpoint, see: E. Kutsch, "Gesetz und Gnade:
Probleme des alttestamentlichen Bundesbegriffs," *ZAW* 79 (1967) 18-35;
and "Der Begriff ברית in vordeuteronomischer Zeit," in *Das ferne und
nahe Wort* (Fs. L. Rost; ed. Fritz Maass; Berlin: Alfred Töpelmann, 1967)
133-43; Lothar Perlitt, *Bundestheologie im Alten Testament* (WMANT 36;
Neukirchen-Vluyn: Neukirchener, 1969).

[5]For an analysis of the treaty between Jonathan and David, see D. J.
McCarthy, "*Berît* and Covenant in the Deuteronomistic History," in
Studies in the Religion of Ancient Israel (VTSup 23; Leiden: E. J. Brill,
1972) 68-71.

[6]RSV. The Hebrew reads: "a covenant of YHWH."

[7]We point out the phrase "your servant" in this context of covenant. Apparently Jonathan as son of the king assumes the position of
suzerain. David, on the other hand, refers to himself as "servant," the
vassal partner in the covenant relationship.

[8]This is the translation of the writer. RSV reads: "If I am still
alive, show me the loyal love of the Lord, that I may not die," with the
LXX. If the Hebrew text is retained, the only problem is with the initial
לא. This could easily be taken to be an example of dittography because
of the repetition of לא introductory to five consecutive phrases. We
drop לא and treat the second phrase as a question. Thus, we have solved
the textual problem and have a clearer insight into what Jonathan is
demanding.

everyone of the enemies of David from the face of the earth, Jonathan and his house shall not be cut off from David (1 Sam 20:14-16).[9]

The position of Jonathan and David is reversed from that in the first covenant in 1 Sam 18:3-4. Instead of Jonathan being the suzerain, this account presents him envisioning David as future king. In this light, he begs David not to annihilate him and his descendants as kings usually did with the previous royal family.[10]

From these two reports of the covenant between David and Jonathan, it is clear that the covenant between them was mutually contracted and therefore understood to place the demand of loyalty upon both of them and their descendants. A summarization text confirms this:

> . . . we have sworn both of us in the name of the Lord saying, "The Lord shall be between me and you, and between my descendants and your descendants, for ever" (1 Sam 20:42).

When David began his reign, a major responsibility for him was to remain faithful to the covenant with Jonathan. He addressed this concern by asking:

> Is there still anyone left of the house of Saul, that I may show him kindness (עשה חסד) for Jonathan's sake (2 Sam 9:1)?

To a servant of the house of Saul, David repeats his inquiry:

> Is there not still some one of the house of Saul, that I may show the kindness of God (עשה חסד אלהים) to him (2 Sam 9:3)?

When David was informed that the crippled son of Jonathan survived the fall of the Saulides (2 Sam 4:4), David requested that Mephibosheth be brought to him. Thereupon to Mephibosheth, Jonathan's son, David said:

> Do not fear, for I will surely show you kindness (עשה אעשה- חסד) for the sake of your father Jonathan, and I will restore to you all the land of Saul your father; and you shall eat at my table always (2 Sam 9:7).

---

[9]RSV also reads v 16 with LXX: "Let not the name of Jonathan be cut off from the house of David." By retaining the Hebrew rendering, there is emphasis upon the house of Jonathan and not the house of David. This translation makes more sense in the light of the context. Cf. D. J. McCarthy, "Bᵉrît and Covenant in the DtrH," 71-73.

[10]Though the covenant was made between Jonathan and David, Saul also makes this request of David. See 1 Sam 24:21.

David showed himself loyal to the agreement he had made with Jonathan by restoring the land of Saul to Mephibosheth. Implicit in the treaty negotiation is consideration for the posterity of the original treaty partners and for their possessions, particularly the land. The technical expression עשה חסד is consistently used in these texts to connote the one idea of fidelity to covenant.

The relationship between David and Jonathan may have been simply one of friendship. However, that does not correspond to the evidence of the text. The implications of the relationship, as it is presented in the biblical accounts, extends to the family and the land, thus indicating that there was a formal agreement sworn between the parties that had political ramifications. The evidence of the context, especially the reference to the effect of the relationship upon the family of Saul, speaks to a covenant agreement that is more than an informal relationship. The phrase עשה חסד is used precisely in those statements where the continuation of the relationship is discussed. Thus, we conclude that עשה חסד is a technical term for loyalty to covenant.

A second instance of David's concern to remain loyal to a treaty relationship is found in reference to the treaty with the King of Ammon.[11] At the death of Nahash, the King of Ammon, David attempted to renew the covenant by swearing loyalty to Nanum, the son of Nahash:

> I will deal loyally (עשה חסד) with Nanum the son of Nahash,
> as his father dealt loyally (עשה חסד) with me (2 Sam 10:2).

The expressed desire to renew the agreement is phrased in the technical term עשה חסד, the phrase meaning to be loyal to a treaty. In the course of events, however, David's effort to renew the agreement was spurned by Nanum, thus violating the bond between the nations.[12] The consequence of this rejection was war between the peoples and the subsequent subjugation of the land and people of Ammon under the rulership of David.[13]

---

[11] The biblical text does not preserve an explicit account of a covenant agreement having been made, though evidence suggests that the treaty may have been sworn between Saul and the King of Ammon (1 Sam 11:1-11). In any case, the implication of the renewal effort by David with the son of Nahash at the death of his father is that a covenant had been established.

[12] 2 Sam 10:1-14.

[13] See 2 Sam 10:6-14; 11:1; 12:26-31. Usually the renewal of the treaty implies the restoration of land. Here the reverse is effected since the treaty renewal was rejected.

The relationship described in this narrative could have been none other than a treaty between nations which had to be renewed when one or other partner died. Thus David seeks for a covenant renewal with the son of Nahash at his father's death. The words used in that negotiation are precisely עשה חסד, the technical phrase for remaining loyal to covenant. That a treaty is the context is quite clear in the fact that the consequence of the termination of the relationship was war between the nations and the subsequent subjugation of one to the other.

There is one significant illustration of a treaty negotiation presented in the 'J' narrative which we will consider. This is the sworn agreement between Abraham and Abimelech in Gen 21:22-24.[14] In this situation, Abraham is invited to swear to a relationship with Abimelech, with Abimelech's offspring and posterity (v 23a). The oath which is called forth from Abraham is based on the fact that just as Abimelech had been loyal (עשה חסד) to Abraham, so Abraham must do (עשה-) to Abimelech and to the land on which he sojourns (v 23b). This treaty is concluded with Abraham's oath: "I will swear" (v 24).

We have here another instance to demonstrate the solemn nature of the treaty, its demand that each party show loyalty (עשה חסד) to the other and to the descendants of the other. The treaty also states explicitly that Abraham is bound to loyalty to the land under the jurisdiction of Abimelech. From these examples it is clear that a treaty sworn between two individuals and their descendants includes and pertains to the territory under the jurisdiction of the parties involved.

The example of the negotiation between Abraham and Abimelech explicitly states that the agreement was made under oath, indicating the solemn nature of the covenant. Here, too, the negotiation is expressed in the words עשה חסד. It is beyond doubt that עשה חסד is a formulary from early Israel used to indicate loyalty to a sworn agreement. Thus, we have a technical term for being faithful to covenant.

In every instance in which עשה חסד is used in a negotiation between human partners, the context is one of covenant. Thus, we have established עשה חסד to be technical language for covenant loyalty. That עשה חסד is technical language for covenant loyalty must be kept

---

[14]See Dennis J. McCarthy, "Three Covenants in Genesis," *CBQ* 26 (1964) 179-89; and "Covenant Relationships," in *Bibliotheca Ephemeridum theologicarum lovaniensium XXXIII. Questions disputées d'Ancien Testament: Méthode et Theologie* (ed. C. Brekelmans; XXII session des *Journées Bibliques de Louvain* [Louvain University Press] Editions J. Duculot, Gembloux, Belgium, 1974) 91-103.

in mind as we continue our examination of texts in which Yahweh is one of the covenant partners.

Each of the accounts we have considered to this point deals with treaties negotiated between human partners. It was the Yahwist, the author of the oldest narrative tradition, who applied the phrase עשה חסד to the relationship between Yahweh and the Fathers. As we will see, the Yahwist tied together Abraham and his descendants as bearers of Yahweh's promise of land and progeny under the umbrella of Yahweh's fidelity by using the phrase עשה חסד.

The content of the promise, as it is understood by the Yahwist, is summarized in Gen 12:1-4a.[15] In the composition of the narrative, the Yahwist presented stories and incidents about each of the descendants of Abraham which are built upon the promise of land and progeny and which acknowledge Yahweh's fidelity in keeping his promise.

The story of Rebekah, daughter of Abraham's kinsmen, who will become the wife of Isaac, illustrates our point very well.[16] In order that the promise made to Abraham be fulfilled in Isaac, it is necessary that Isaac seek a wife from his own family and not from among the daughters of the Canaanites.[17] Yahweh's fidelity to his promise will be demonstrated in the successful mission of Abraham's servant who was sent to bring back a wife from among Abraham's kin in Haran.[18] It is for the success of this mission that the servant intercedes by calling upon the god of Abraham:

> O Lord, God of my master Abraham, grant me success today,
> I pray thee, and show steadfast love (עשה חסד) to my master
> Abraham. . . .
> By this I shall know that thou hast shown steadfast love (עשה
> חסד) to my master (Gen 24:12, 14b).

---

[15]See Hans W. Wolff, "The Kerygma of the Yahwist," *Int* 20 (1966) 131-58; now appearing in *The Vitality of Old Testament Traditions,* by Walter Brueggemann and Hans W. Wolff (Atlanta: John Knox, 1975) 41-66.

[16]On the composition of Genesis 24, see Wolfgang M. Roth, "The Wooing of Rebekah," *CBQ* 34 (1972) 177-87. Cf. J. Van Seters, *Abraham in Tradition,* 240-48.

[17]Gen 24:3-4. A woman from Abraham's own would insure the perpetuation of the progeny out of a single family from which the nation would arise.

[18]A servant is sent to procure a wife, lest Isaac return to the land of his origin and dwell there with a wife (Gen 24:5-7). Under the promise, Isaac's place of dwelling is properly the land given to Abraham.

The prayer continues with the acknowledgment that Yahweh has indeed shown loyalty (עשה חסד) to Abraham, and that Yahweh has not forsaken his promise because he has led the servant to the kin of Abraham and the maiden who will be the wife of Isaac:[19]

> Blessed be the Lord, the God of my master Abraham, who has
> not forsaken his steadfast love and his faithfulness toward my
>   master,
> as for me, the Lord has led me in the way to the house of my
> master's kinsmen (Gen 24:27).[20]

The Yahwist narrator developed this account to show how the promise with Abraham, i.e. Yahweh's relationship, continued in Isaac, the descendant of Abraham. Yahweh showed his fidelity to the promise by sending a wife, through whom the promised nation would be perpetuated to guarantee the continuation of the promise. Also, because Rebekah consented to leave her home and come to Isaac, Isaac is enabled to continue to live upon the land given in promise.

On account of the meaning of the formulary עשה חסד which we have shown to be technical language for loyalty to the covenant, the presence of this expression in this narrative indicates that the relationship between Yahweh and the Patriarchs must have been understood to be one of covenant. The promise depends upon the covenant relationship; it is the sign of that relationship. The promise being fulfilled, as it is in the narrative about Isaac, demonstrates the loyalty of Yahweh to the covenant between himself and the Fathers: he showed loyalty, עשה חסד: and he did not forsake covenant, לא-עזב חסד. Covenant and promise are thus synonymous terms, for the one obtains its meaning from the other.

Neither the word "covenant" (ברית), nor a word for "promise" (דבר) occurs in any of these texts.[21] Covenant is expressed by the formulaic

---

[19]Gen 24:14b, 27.

[20]The verb "forsake" generally means "violation" of covenant. This is another way of saying that Yahweh "showed loyalty" to his chosen. See Deut 29:24 (Eng 25); 1 Kgs 19:10, 14; and passim in the DtrH.

[21]The promise and covenant are directly linked in the covenant account of Abraham. As the tradition is recounted in Genesis 15, a covenant was made with Abraham which ratified the promise of the possession of the land by the descendants of Abraham. Genesis 15 remains problematic, however. There is great controversy over the antiquity of the tradition presented there. See the arguments introduced by John Van Seters for the exilic dating of Genesis 15, and the bibliography cited

עֲשֹׂה חֶסֶד which is used to indicate the divine fidelity to the descendants and their maintenance on the land given to them in promise. Promise is expressed in the content of the promise: the descendants and land that are given as the sign of Yahweh's fidelity to covenant relationship. The words for "covenant" and "promise" and a distinction in their connotation appear in the narrative literature only much later. In the Yahwist narrative, we may alternate and interchange the referents, covenant and promise, for the concepts are not delineated as they will be in later literature. In the Yahwist tradition, the technical expression for covenant loyalty, עֲשֹׂה חֶסֶד, indicates explicitly Yahweh's loyalty to promise which is the content of his covenant with the Patriarchs.

The promise continues through Jacob, the son of Isaac and Rebekah. In the struggle between Jacob and his brother Esau, the Yahwist dramatizes for the readers the struggle for the survival of the people of the promise. Jacob had gone to another country to save his life after he had cunningly secured the birthright for himself. When Jacob prepared to return to his homeland, the place where Esau continued to dwell, Jacob feared that Esau might "come and slay us all, the mothers with the children" (Gen 32:12). The slaughter of the women and children would indeed mean the death of all for it would mark the death of the nation. Using human ingenuity, so characteristic to the Yahwist's presentation, Jacob divided his company into two parties so that should one be destroyed at least one group of his family would survive (Gen 32:7-8). The prayer of Jacob at the conclusion of the mission reveals that the safe passage across the Jordan is understood to be a direct expression of Yahweh's fidelity to his promise:

> God of my father Abraham and God of my father Isaac, . . . I am not worthy of the least of all *the steadfast love* and all the faithfulness *which thou hast shown* to thy servant,[22] for with only my staff I have crossed this Jordan; and now I have become two companies (Gen 32:10a-11).

In this story of Jacob Yahweh showed his loyalty to covenant by preserving the descendants of Jacob and by bringing them safely back to the place given to them for their homeland. The promise continues because Yahweh has remained loyal in covenant and has given safety to Jacob the bearer of the promise.

---

there: "The Covenant of Abraham: Genesis 15," in *Abraham in History and Tradition*, 249-78.

[22]The technical term is adjusted to fit into the flowing style of the narrative: הֶחֱסָדִים . . . אֲשֶׁר עָשִׂיתָ.

The story of Joseph has also been woven into the Yahwistic pattern of the Patriarchs.[23]   Yahweh showed his fidelity to Joseph by bringing him into the favor of the prison keeper from whence he was established in Pharaoh's household and made overseer of the land of Egypt.   The tradition declares that Yahweh was present with Joseph and gave him success:

> But the Lord was with Joseph and showed him steadfast love
> (עשה חסד), and gave him favor in the sight of the keeper of
> the prison (Gen 39:21).

The events in the prison and Joseph's position there brought him eventually into the house of Pharaoh from where he provided food for the survival of his father and brothers and from where his family was given land upon which to live and multiply until they should return to Canaan, the land of the promise.   The tradition carries the message that because of the position of Joseph, his father and brothers survived during the famine upon the provisions and in the land of Egypt.   The survival of Joseph's family ultimately meant the survival of the whole people who would one day return to the land of promise.   Through Joseph as through each of the descendants of Abraham, Yahweh acted for his people; he showed his

---

[23]The relationship between the Yahwist Narrative and the Joseph Story has been understood variously.   Gerhard von Rad ("The Joseph Narrative and Ancient Wisdom," in *The Problem of the Hexateuch*, 292-300) suggests that the story was produced in the Solomonic or post-Solomonic era, under the influence of wisdom circles, perhaps in the context of the royal court, as was the 'J' narrative. Cf. Claus Westermann, "Die Joseph-Erzählung," in *Calwer Predigthilfen V* (Stuttgart: Calwer, 1970) 11-118; and G. W. Coats, "The Joseph Story and Ancient Wisdom: A Reappraisal," *CBQ* 35 (1973) 285-97.

W. A. Brueggemann ("Life and Death in Tenth Century Israel," *JAAR* 40 [1972] 96-109) relates the Joseph story with other tenth century literature on the basis of similarity of theme.   In a recent study, George W. Coats (*From Canaan to Egypt: Structural and Theological Context for the Joseph Story* [CBQMS 4; Washington, DC: The Catholic Biblical Association of America, 1976] esp. 55-79) convincingly argues for a structural and theological consistency between the Joseph story and the work of the Yahwist.   The point of this study is to demonstrate that the Joseph story was created to serve the function of transition between the patriarchs and exodus.

For other viewpoints, see L. Ruppert, *Die Josepherzählung: Ein Beitrag zur Theologie der Pentateuchquellen* (Munich: Kösel, 1965); and D. B. Redford, *A Study of the Biblical Story of Joseph: Gen 37-50* (VTSup 20; Leiden: E. J. Brill, 1970).

fidelity to them and thus kept them alive to live upon the land of promise.   Yahweh showed loyalty עשה חסד; he remained true to his covenant relationship with his people.

In our consideration of the formulary עשה חסד, we have discovered that we have a technical term for keeping covenant.   Every instance of the use of the phrase is in the context of a covenant negotiation.   In settings with human partners, the question is always the continuation of the relationship that exists between the parties.   It was a matter of "being loyal" in the case of David and Jonathan, a covenant between the family of David and of Saul, in which Jonathan was the sovereign at one time, then David.   This covenant, as was the nature of covenants, continued between David and Mephibosheth, the survivor of the family of Saul.   The technical term עשה חסד was used in that negotiation for being faithful to an established covenant.

In another instance, David sought to renew the covenant to show fidelity to the Ammonites by entering into a covenant with the new king who assumed authority in that kingdom.   The formulaic עשה חסד was used to make that request for remaining loyal to the covenant.   This attempt, as we have indicated, was futile thereby leading to war between the nations.

The meaning of the technical term is clear from the contexts in which we find it.   We have a clear example of language deriving from the world of kings which was used in negotiations for the continuation of covenant between respective nations.   The formulary does not mean "entering into covenant."   It is language, rather, for the renewal of covenant or to convey the idea of "being loyal" to an established covenant.

We have observed that the Yahwist adopted this language to express his understanding of the relationship between Yahweh and the Patriarchs.   In a consistent manner, in the case of each of the descendants of Abraham, the Yahwist related the narrative in such a way that the relationship that had been established between Yahweh and Abraham is reaffirmed independently by Isaac, by Jacob, and by Joseph.   The setting in each instance is threat to the descendants and the loss of the land, the content of Yahweh's promise to Abraham.   Thus, we discover that for the Yahwist, the promise is founded upon covenant.   Isaac declares that Yahweh is loyal (עשה חסד), in giving him a wife and providing that he remain in the land.   Jacob confesses that Yahweh is loyal to covenant (עשה חסד), in keeping the women and children safe on their return to the land.   Joseph affirms Yahweh's faithfulness to covenant (עשה חסד), in providing for the chosen people in Egypt through the position of Joseph, thereby keeping them alive to return to their own land.

The Yahwist clearly and consistently applied the technical term in instances of Yahweh's fidelity to his promise, the content of which are the descendants and the land. Thus, the Yahwist employed language from the political/royal setting to the relationship between Yahweh and the Patriarchs. Appropriately, that language implied a covenant extending beyond the parties involved to the family and land under the jurisdiction of that family. These elements are crucial in the narration of the story about Yahweh's relationship with his people.

It is this tradition of Yahweh's fidelity to his promise that is translated to David and his kingdom in the royal psalm:[24]

> Great triumphs he gives to his king and shows steadfast love (עשׂה חסד) to his anointed, to David, and his descendants for ever (2 Sam 22:51 = Ps 18:15).[25]

The psalm declares that the fidelity of Yahweh extends not only to David but includes the descendants of David as well. In regard to the land of promise, it could be said that the victory given by Yahweh guaranteed that the king retain the limits of the kingdom. These ideas were expressed in the promise made to David through the prophet Nathan.[26]

---

[24] The connection between the Abraham and Davidic traditions continues to be problematic. Earlier scholarship explained that there was a mutual reflection of one tradition upon the other: the Abraham tradition reflects the Davidic period, and at the same time, the Abraham covenant influences the Davidic covenant. This is the stance of the writer along with: G. E. Mendenhall, "Covenant Forms in Israelite Tradition," *BA* 17 (1954) 71-72; and "Covenant," *IDB* 1. 717-18; D. N. Freedman, "Divine Commitment and Human Obligation," *Int* 18 (1964) 419-31; R. E. Clements, *Abraham and David: Genesis 15 and its Meaning for Israelite Tradition* (SBT 2nd series 5; London: SCM, 1967).

More recent studies argue that there was no early connection between the Abraham and Davidic traditions. So, Norman E. Wagner, "Abraham and David?" in *Studies on the Ancient Palestinian World,* 117-40; John Van Seters, *Abraham in History and Tradition*; and Thomas L. Thompson, *The Historicity of the Patriarchal Narratives: The Quest for the Historical Abraham* (BZAW 133; New York: de Gruyter, 1974).

[25] On the antiquity of this poem, see F. M. Cross and D. N. Freedman, "A Royal Song of Thanksgiving: II Samuel 22=Psalm 18," *JBL* 72 (1953) 15-34; now appearing in *Studies in Ancient Yahwistic Poetry* (SBLDS 21; Missoula: Scholars, 1975) 125-58. In their reconstruction, the authors question the originality of the final colon. See n. 116, p. 158 of the latter publication.

[26] 2 Sam 7:11b-12, 15-16.

Early tradition, as we have seen, had expressed the notion of
Yahweh's fidelity to his promise by the technical term עשה חסד in
application to both the patriarchs and to David. The Dtr used the language that was known to him from tradition to speak of Yahweh's fidelity
to David. Thus Solomon addresses Yahweh with the declaration:

> you have shown great loyalty (עשה חסד גדול) to your
> servant David, my father (1 Kgs 3:6a).

Solomon appeals to Yahweh's fidelity to the covenant with David to
legitimate his own participation in that covenant. He appeals as the
descendant of David to whom jurisdiction in the kingdom, the land of the
promise, is being transferred. Since the phrase עשה חסד indicates
fidelity to covenant with the implication that the covenant continues for
future generations of the covenanting families, the phrase was deliberately chosen and strategically placed in the composition of the dream
narrative to mark the transition from David to Solomon. While Solomon
referred to Yahweh's faithful relationship with David, the implication is
that the same relationship is open to himself. Indeed, Solomon affirms
that this is so since he, the son of David, is given the throne as a sign of
Yahweh's promise.

The extension of the promise to Solomon, to be sure, is made explicit in the repetition of the idea in the phrase שמר חסד:

> And you have kept for him this great loving kindness (1 Kgs
> 3:6c).[27]

In contrast with the terminus technicus, עשה חסד, this latter expression
for fidelity to covenant, שמר חסד, generally occurs in contexts of a
relatively younger origin where it has become a confessional formulary.[28]

The exception to this is the use of Ps 89:29 (Eng 28):

> My steadfast love I will keep for him forever,[29] and my cove-
> nant will stand firm for him.

---

[27] We note that here as in v 6a, the word חסד is modified by גדול.
See n. 1, p. 58, above. This repetition supports our theory of the literary
unity of the narrative. The use of גדול חסד in the context of עשה
would attract the same phrase with שמר though elsewhere the phrases
without the modifier would be expected.

[28] Deut 7:9, 12; 1 Kgs 8:23 = 2 Chr 6:14; Dan 9:4; Neh 1:5; 9:32. In
all of these examples the phrase is שמר הברית והחסד, a traditional
formulary used in the confession of Yahweh's fidelity.

[29] The text reads אשמר-לו חסדי.

Here the allusion is precisely the promise to David. We presume the antiquity of Psalm 89 and its correspondence with 2 Samuel 7, though the details of this correspondence will not concern us.[30] In any case, the Deuteronomist drew upon Psalm 89 for his expression of the continuation of the Davidic promise to Solomon. Solomon declares that Yahweh has kept covenant, he has proven his loyalty because Solomon, the descendant of David, is upon the throne of the kingdom.

The language used by the Dtr is formulaic and borrowed from Israel's own tradition. It is the tradition of Yahweh's covenant with his chosen-- be it the Patriarchs or David. The Dtr fitted the formulae into the narrative to emphasize, first of all, the nature of the relationship between Yahweh and David and subsequently with Solomon; and secondly, to designate Solomon the son of David upon the throne as the sign of the fulfillment of the promise.

Summary

In this discussion, we have shown that the Deuteronomist chose two formulae from tradition which convey the idea of Yahweh's fidelity in covenant. The first, עשה חסד, was borrowed from the royal/political sphere. It was appropriated early to the biblical tradition to express the relationship between Yahweh and the patriarchs as well as between Yahweh and the king.

The second phrase, שמר חסד, became formulaic at the hand of the Deuteronomist. This does not mean that the Deuteronomist created the formula. This theologian simply adopted an expression which Psalm 89, celebrating Nathan's oracle, shows to have been familiar to Temple worshippers. Something which the cultic sphere thus illustrates has been added to the material of the royal/political tradition.

Both formulae adequately interpreted for the purpose of the Deuteronomist the relationship of Yahweh toward the king. In both expressions the focus is upon Yahweh's fidelity; the loyalty of the God of Israel is shown to be unquestionable. Yahweh had demonstrated his loyalty to Abraham and to the descendants of Abraham in giving them progeny and in preserving them upon the land given to them. The Royal Psalms show an understanding that Yahweh had promised to show his loyalty to David

---

[30]On this question, see J. L. McKenzie, "The Dynastic Oracle: II Sam 7," *TS* 8 (1947) 187-218; and Artur Weiser, *The Psalms. A Commentary* (Philadelphia: Westminster, 1962) 591.

in the same way. In this, David is presented as one of the descendants of Abraham.

In the composition of the dream narrative, the Dtr employed precisely these expressions to affirm that, in fact, Yahweh has been faithful to his promise to David. The use of this particular language indicates that the dream narrative follows upon the promise recorded in 2 Samuel 7 as the fulfillment of that promise. The Dtr, by using these formulae, declares that Yahweh's fidelity is seen in the elevation of a son of David to the throne of the kingdom as Yahweh had promised. Yahweh has shown his loyalty (עשה חסד) to David; he has proven his loyalty (שמר חסד) to David by giving him a son to reign after him.

The King's Obedient Service

In his response to Yahweh, Solomon continues with the affirmation that Yahweh's fidelity was the reciprocal, the other side of the coin of David's loyal service:

he walked before (הלך לפניך) you . . . (1 Kgs 3:6a).

In such an assertion there is the intimation that relationship with Yahweh involves faithful service; that is, covenant and obedience are interrelated. The phrase הלך לפני expresses loyal service or obedience to the suzerain. We will consider evidence for the meaning of the phrase in biblical texts and also in extra-biblical texts.

In the Yahwist narrative, the idiom הלך לפני is used in close connection with the promise of progeny. Abraham, when he sent his servant to secure a wife for Isaac, assured him that his mission would be successful because he (Abraham) had been faithful in his service of Yahweh:[31]

The Lord, before whom I walk (הלך לפני) will send his angel with you and prosper your way; and you shall take a wife for my son from my kindred and from my father's house (Gen 24:40).

Abraham is confessing that he had been a loyal servant of Yahweh, that the relationship with Yahweh on his part was in order and therefore, he could rely upon Yahweh's fidelity to him in sending a wife for his son to

---

[31] The connection between Yahweh's fidelity to the promise and the obedience of Abraham is stressed in the early narrative tradition. See Gen 18:19; 22:16-18; 26:3-5, 24.

insure the perpetuation of his family. Yahweh's loyalty in acting is directly related to Abraham's fidelity before Yahweh in this text. In this early tradition, there is a direct connection between Yahweh's loyalty to his covenant promise and the fidelity of the covenant partner. There is responsibility on both parties in the covenant. The phrase הלך לפני in this context indicates the faithfulness of Abraham in living rightly, i.e., in a godly direction.

The formulary הלך לפני occurs in the prayer of Jacob/Israel upon Ephraim and Manasseh, the sons of Joseph, that through them the promise may endure unto future generations:

> The God before whom my father Abraham and Isaac walked
> (התהלכו לפניך)
> the God who has led me[32] all my life long to this day
> the angel who has redeemed me from all evil, bless the lads;
> and in them let my name be perpetuated,
> and the name of my fathers Abraham and Isaac
> and let them grow into a multitude in the midst of the earth
> (Gen 48:15-16).

The words of the hymn allude, in the first place, to the loyal service before Yahweh on the part of Jacob's ancestors. Jacob appeals to this fidelity to covenant in praying for the fulfillment of the promise in his sons. Precisely because of the fidelity before Yahweh on the part of the Fathers, Jacob is able to trust in the promise. This is to say that the promise endures on the basis of the continuance of the relationship upon which the promise was founded.

Moshe Weinfeld,[33] in his attempt to identify Yahweh's covenant

---

[32]The Hebrew reads הרעה, literally, the God who shepherds me (v 15b). This is significant in that shepherd belongs to ancient Near Eastern terminology for kingship. This designation for God as shepherd implies the rulership or kingship of Yahweh before whom the servant does courtly service.

[33]*Deuteronomy and the Deuteronomic School*, 74-81; and "The Covenant of Grant in the Old Testament and in the Ancient Near East," *JAOS* 90 (1970) 184-203.

Weinfeld distinguishes between the "grant" and the "vassal" treaty, associating the Abraham/David promissory covenant with the treaty of grant. He argues that the promise of land and progeny is the counterpart of the reward granted to the servant for loyal service. The comparison is made principally to verify that the biblical literature in question is the product of the seventh century Hezekian court. He claims that his dating

with Abraham and David with the "royal grant," points specifically to the phrase לפני הלך as an example of language which occurs in Assyrian grant texts. An example is the grant of Assurbanipal to his servant Baltaya:

> Baltaya--whose heart is devoted to his master, served me with truthfulness and acted perfectly in my palace, grew up with a good name, kept the charge of my kingship.[34]

Another grant text will illustrate the formulaic diction repeated in this type:

> Nabû-šar-uṣṣur, the general of Aššurbanipal the king of Assyria, a friend and companion . . . who served me faithfully and who loyally performed his duties in my palace . . .[35]

The phrase for serving faithfully,[36] and for acting perfectly or performing loyally,[37] is found in both texts. Weinfeld understands these Akkadian expressions to be the correlative of the Hebrew הלך לפני, though the Akkadian equivalent would be *ina pāni alāku/attaluku*.[38] The idea of loyal service is surely expressed in these Assyrian texts, but the literary equivalence for the purpose of arguing a date of writing is just not present. Moreover, in regard to the promise of land and progeny as the content of the grant treaty, Weinfeld's argument is not tenable. In the Assyrian grants, the reward for loyalty to the king is generally freedom from taxation for the use of land,[39] or the gift of land for the purpose of supplying

---

is accurate because an equivalent for the phrase הלך לפני and for other biblical terms occurs in Assyrian texts of that era.

[34] Quoted from Weinfeld, *Deuteronomy*, 75.

[35] Translated from: J. Kohler and A. Ungnad, *Assyrische Rechtsurkunden in Umschrift und Übersetzung nebst einem Index der Personen-Namen und Rechtserläuterungen* (Leipzig: 1913), by Y. Muffs (*Studies in the Aramaic Legal Papyri from Elephantine* [Studia et Documenta 8; Leiden: E. J. Brill, 1969] 134-35). See pp. 203-4 for notes on the text.

[36] In Akkadian: *ina maḫ-ri-ya ina ki-na-a-ti i-zi-zu-ma*. So, Weinfeld, *Deuteronomy*, 75, n. 1; and Muffs, *Aramaic Legal Papyri*, 134, 1. 14.

[37] In Akkadian: *it-tal-la-ku šal-me-iš qi-rib ekalli-ya*. So, Weinfeld, *Deuteronomy*, 75; and Muffs, *Aramaic Legal Papyri*, 134, ll. 15-16.

[38] See Weinfeld, *Deuteronomy*, 77, n. 4; and Muffs, *Aramaic Legal Papyri*, 203.

[39] The text of Aššurpanipal to Nabû-šar-uṣṣar reads: "I lifted my eyes and considered . . . the fields and gardens which, under my aegis, he had acquired . . . (all of these) I acknowledged in a written document as free from taxation." So, Muffs, *Aramaic Legal Papyri*, 135, ll. 19-20.

offerings to the temple.[40]

A more pertinent illustration of this formulary is found in a Hittite text of Hattusilis III. There the situation is quite similar to what we find in the biblical reference. The Hittite king describes himself as being obedient before the gods, precisely by "walking before" them according to the divine ordinances:

> My Lady Ishtar always rescued me . . .
> The goddess, My Lady, always held me by the hand.
> Because I, for my part, was an obedient man, (and)
> because I *walked before* the gods in obedience . . .
> Thou, goddess, My Lady, dost always rescue me.[41]

The Hittite reads: *A-NA PA-NI DINGIR*^{MEŠ} . . . *iyahhat*. This statement may validly be taken in the sense of "I walked before the gods," with "walk" (*iya-*) corresponding to the Hebrew הלך, with the parallel meaning of "live one's life."   The modifying phrase, *para handandanni*, may be translated "in obedience,"[42] but a more accurate interpretation is "in accord with right direction,"[43] with "right" meaning "god-given."[44]

In context, the Hittite king is understood to live in accord with divine direction, and because of this stance, the king can expect the divine help of Ishtar. Though the king is designated by Ishtar and thus there is an established relationship between the king and the goddess, yet the king must conform to the will of the deity. The king is receptive to divine help only when he has proven himself faithful to the goddess by living in accord with the god-given direction.

The formulaic הלך לפני derives from the royal sphere where it indicates the loyal service of the king to the god by whom the throne was given.

---

[40]See J. N. Postgate, *Neo-Assyrian Royal Grants and Decrees* (Studia Pohl: Series Maior I, Pontifical Biblical Institute, 1969), passim.

[41]"The Apology of Hattusilis," 4.43-50, in *A Hittite Chrestomathy*, by Edgar H. Sturtevant and George Bechtel (William Dwight Whitney Linguistic Series; Philadelphia: Linguistic Society of America, University of Pennsylvania, 1935). Cf. Albrecht Goetze, "Ḫattušiliš: Der Bericht über seine Thronbesteigung nebst den Paralleltexten," in *Hethitische Texte in Umschrift, mit Übersetzung und Erläuterungen* (ed. Ferdinand Sommer; Leipzig: J. C. Hinrichs'sche Buchhandlung, 1925) 10-11.

[42]So, Sturtevant in "The Apology of Hattusilis."

[43]So, Goetze, "Ḫattušiliš," 1. 48.

[44]I am grateful to Dennis J. McCarthy for confirming the accuracy of my interpretation of the Hittite phrase and for providing me with assistance in expressing the correlation between the texts.

In the Yahwist narrative tradition, the formulaic expression from royal tradition was employed to explain the obligation of the Patriarchs to Yahweh who had bound himself by covenant promise. Theirs was not a relationship with Yahweh without obligation. The Yahwist theologian reflects that the promise was fulfilled when Abraham and the fathers "walked before Yahweh," that is, they live their lives in accord with Him.

In the dream narrative Solomon speaks of David as one who "walks before" Yahweh. This means that David has remained faithful in his relationship with Yahweh who gave David the throne. This means that David's fidelity has been demonstrated specifically in his being in accord with Yahweh's will, or, what the Dtr intends to be understood, with Torah.

In the formulary הלך לפני, we have a concept of royal decorum as in the Hittite text. The formula is a technical term for the loyalty of the king to contrast with the expression that designates the loyalty of Yahweh. The phrase has been used by the Yahwist narrator in presenting the Patriarchs as figures who live in accord with Yahweh, God of the promise;[45] it was used by the Dtr in designating David as a king who lives in accord with Yahweh, by whose promise throne and dynasty are guaranteed.

In the structural outline of the narrative in Chapter III, we identified a correspondence between vv 6 and 14.[46] We noted that, though the content of each reflects a different tradition, the Dtr intended that the parallel design should indicate a congruity between these traditions. V 14 contains the "if" statement of Torah; whereas v 6 expresses the "when" David "walked before." Having learned the precise meaning of the formulaic הלך לפני, it is obvious that the king is imaged, as a royal figure who lives in accord with his God; and, that the God-given directives by which the king lives are precisely the Torah.

Other examples for the use of the idiom for obedience come from the hand of the Deuteronomist. All the uses, as a matter of fact, occur within the History of Solomon.[47] In our consideration of these texts, we will gain some insight into the way the Deuteronomist made use of such skillfully composed texts to weave together the components of the history.

---

[45]The attribution to Abraham of the idiom הלך לפני had become fixed in tradition, for we find the 'P' author using precisely this expression in the covenant text: "I am El Shaddai, walk before me, and be blameless, and I will make my covenant . . ." (Gen 17:1-2).

[46]Cf. pp. 53-54.

[47]1 Kgs 2:4; 8:23, 25; 9:4. The one exception is 2 Kgs 20:3 which occurs in the account of Hezekiah.

In the dream text, as we have seen, Solomon in speech form makes reference to David's obedience to Yahweh by using the idiom הלך לפני (1 Kgs 3:6b[a]). Solomon uses the idiom again in his prayer at the dedication of the Temple:

> O Lord, God of Israel,
> there is no God like thee,
> in heaven above or on earth beneath,
> keeping covenant and showing steadfast love
>   to the servants who walk before thee (ההלכים לפניך)
>   with all their hearts (1 Kgs 8:23).

At this precise point, Solomon makes reference to himself along with David as "servants" who "walk before" Yahweh. The clues to the meaning of the plural servants are found in the two subsequent verses. In v 24, Solomon refers to Yahweh's faithfulness in his dealing with David; then, in v 25, requests the same for himself. For our purpose in discussing the phrase הלך לפני, we notice that an obedient Solomon expects an affirmative answer. The promise to David had already been fulfilled because of his obedience; now Solomon unites himself with David as an obedient servant and asks that Yahweh show his fidelity in fulfilling the promise on his behalf also.

The use of הלך לפני in 1 Kgs 8:23 is not without design. Nor is the position of this verse accidental. The formula הלך לפני is consciously chosen as is the verse strategically placed to unite Solomon with David as an obedient heir to the promise.[48] The selection of this idiomatic expression and its use within the compositional design of the Temple prayer demonstrates the deliberate use of formulae by the Deuteronomist.

The technical term הלך לפני is found in three other texts of the Deuteronomist, focusing in upon an entirely different situation for Solomon. These are the conditional statements of the Davidic promise:

> If your sons take heed to their way, to walk before me (הלך
>   לפני) in faithfulness, with all their heart and with all
>   their soul,

---

[48]The context of the temple prayer demands that Solomon present himself as one who is obedient before Yahweh. All of his prayer is made in supplication for himself and for the people. Did he not "walk before" Yahweh, he would not be receptive to the divine help from God who acts benevolently for those who live in his covenant love.

The theology presented here corresponds with that in the dream text as well as with the earlier portrayal of Abraham and his descendants.

there shall not fail you a man on the throne of Israel (1 Kgs
    2:4).

There shall never fail you a man before me to sit upon the
    throne of Israel,
if only your sons take heed to their way, to walk before me
(הלך לפני) as you have walked before me (1 Kgs 8:25).

If you will walk before me (הלך לפני), as David your father
walked, with integrity of heart and uprightness . . .
then I will establish your royal throne over Israel for ever,
as I promised David your father, saying,
"There shall not fail you a man upon the throne of Israel"
    (1 Kgs 9:4-5).

Each of these texts is characterized by the conditional particle אם. They
are repetitive in that each is constructed upon two formularies. The one
is the idiom for obedience, הלך לפני; and the other is the promise:
"There shall not fail you a man upon the throne of Israel." Each text is
formulated as a speech: the first is spoken to Solomon by David; in the
second, Solomon himself quotes the words of David spoken to him; in the
third, Solomon is addressed by Yahweh in a second dream. The texts are
strategically placed within the Solomon history: one bridges the reign of
David and Solomon, the second is spoken when Solomon is at the height of
his power, and the third is spoken just prior to the downfall of Solomon.
With these texts, the Deuteronomist has woven the material of the Solomon History into a narrative whole.

    The content of these texts applies exclusively to Solomon. This has
been noted by Richard Nelson in his recent dissertation.[49] He points out
that the reference to "sons" in the first two texts is made explicit in the
third text with its direct address to Solomon. A transition has been
recorded by the Deuteronomist from the sons who tried for succession to
the throne to the one who was finally seated upon the throne.[50] By this
precision in narration, the Deuteronomist "indicates that the crisis of the
fulfillment or non-fulfillment of this promise must be worked out within
the confines of I Kings 2-11, the reign of Solomon."[51] Nelson also points
out that the promise of dynasty, expressed as "throne of Israel" in each of
the three texts, refers to the state of Israel. The oracle is therefore

---

    [49]"The Redactional Duality of the Deuteronomistic History," Diss.,
Union Theological Seminary in Virginia, 1974.
    [50]Ibid., 204-9.
    [51]Ibid., 209.

directed to Solomon following his reign and the loss of the Northern tribes to the kingdom of the Davidids.[52] Nelson has contributed significantly to our understanding of the methodology of the Deuteronomist by showing how, by the use of these conditional statements, the Deuteronomist made a theological comment upon the loss of the throne of Israel to the Davidic dynasty because of the disobedience of Solomon.[53]

Nelson has shown how these particular texts function in the structure of the history. We have noted the particular formulaic components of these speeches especially the idiom for obedience הלך לפני. In the tradition to which we have referred, the phrase הלך לפני carried the implication of obedience as the sine qua non for receiving the divine promise. In these texts which apply specifically to Solomon and the loss of the Northern Kingdom to the Davidic dynasty, the condition for participating in the promise is explicitly stated as a matter of obedience. It is probable that the condition itself, the אם, is theologically significant. Knowing that the Northern Kingdom had been separated from Judah, the Deuteronomist prepared the readers in the structural development for the loss by stating the promise in explicit conditional terms. The same could be said for the conditional statements in 1 Kgs 6:12 and 11:38. In both cases, the historian prepared for the reverse of the promise through the use of the conditional statements. The hand of the Dtr is visible in the formulation of each of the speeches, for we find that they are skillfully formulated to carry the theological impact intended by the author and they are deliberately placed to weave together the other sources used for the composition of the history.

The use of הלך לפני in the history of Hezekiah remains to be considered. The words of Hezekiah are spoken when he is at the point of death. He prays:

> Remember now, O Lord, I beseech thee,
> how I have walked before thee (התהלך לפני)
> in faithfulness and with a whole heart, and
> have done what is good in thy sight (2 Kgs 20:3 = Isa 38:3).

The expression put upon the lips of Hezekiah is similar to the deuteronomistic statements made by David, Solomon, and Yahweh. The technical term הלך לפני used here means obedience to the divine will in a sense very close to that in the Hittite text of Hattusilis. Hezekiah, by his

---

[52]Ibid., 209-11.

[53]R. D. Nelson, "Dynastic Oracle in DTR. A Workshop in Recent Trends," in *SBLASP* 10 (ed. George MacRae; Missoula: Scholars, 1976) 5.

assertion of loyalty to Yahweh, presumes upon the fidelity of Yahweh toward him. As the Davidic king upon the throne of Judah, he can expect physical help and, to be sure, receives it as the sign that Yahweh is faithful to his promise. The integrity of the covenant between Yahweh and Hezekiah is thus expressed in their mutual fidelity.

The Dtr presents Hezekiah referring to himself as obedient in the same mode that Solomon spoke of David. Clearly this is intentional, for, according to the Dtr, both David and Hezekiah are cast in a favorable light.[54] Had the situation been otherwise, the Dtr might have formulated the prayer of Hezekiah conditionally, and so also the promise to David.

In this survey of texts, we have shown that the formulary הלך לפני was equivalently expressed in the Hittite court documents to indicate the obedience of the reigning king to his patronal deity. In the biblical tradition, הלך לפני clearly implies the loyal service on the part of the patriarch or king toward Yahweh with whom he is related in covenant. We have here a formula from ancient Near Eastern royal language used for theological purposes in the Old Testament.

The early narrative history recounts how, because of the obedience of the ancestral fathers, Yahweh kept his promise to give them descendants and prosperity in the land. In the case of the Dtr, הלך לפני expresses two different aspects of relationship. The meaning of the formulary as such is not altered. As we would expect, the Dtr works with skill in his appropriation of formulae from tradition to make a theological point. This theologian speaks without reservation of the obedient service of David and Hezekiah. In application to both, the formulary is used to express this loyalty in positive statements: David walked before (הלך לפני) Yahweh in trustworthiness, in righteousness and in uprightness; Hezekiah walked before (הלך לפני) Yahweh in trustworthiness and with integrity.

The Dtr presents Solomon, on the one hand, speaking of himself as a loyal servant through the use of the phrase הלך לפני only in conjunction with his father David in reference to the promise. Solomon unites himself with his faithful father as being also an obedient follower of Yahweh in his prayer asking that Yahweh show loyalty to himself as he had to David in giving him a son to reign after him. The other uses in connection with Solomon all occur within conditional statements: "if you walk before me, then. . . ." We have suggested that this condition of

---

[54] 1 Kgs 13:3-8 for Hezekiah; and 1 Kgs 11:34, 36; 15:4-5; and 2 Kgs 8:19 for David.

obedience is a literary device used by the Dtr to foreshadow the deterio-
ration of Solomon's relationship with Yahweh. In the deuteronomistic
presentation of the history, Solomon did, in fact, turn away from loyalty
to Yahweh. Whereas Solomon was set upon the throne by Yahweh, the Dtr
portrayed him as an obedient servant in the one instance when he was
obviously in covenant--at the dedication of the temple. This situation was
to change in the progress of history. The author prepared for Solomon's
change of heart by foreshadowing with conditional statements the possibility of Solomon's subsequent disloyalty to Yahweh.

In the dream narrative, the declaration of obedience is without
condition and in reference to David. The formulary הלך לפני is juxtaposed with עשׂה חסד to indicate the mutual loyalty between Yahweh and
his chosen king. Because David remained steadfastly loyal to his God,
Yahweh acted reciprocally to his servant. Yahweh gave to David a son to
be on the throne in fulfillment of the promise that his house and kingdom
would endure.

The relationship between Yahweh and David as it is presented by the
Deuteronomist does not differ from that between Yahweh and the patriarchs presented in the Yahwist narrative account of history. In both
cases, the covenant partner presumes upon the fidelity of Yahweh in view
of loyal service. This is not the same as the conditional statement introduced by אם. The covenant relationship implies mutual loyalty; the bond
exists only so long as both parties remain loyal. By stating explicitly that
Yahweh was faithful (through the use of the formulary עשׂה חסד) and
that David was also faithful (through the use of the formulary הלך
לפני), the Deuteronomist is simply stating that Yahweh and David were
intimately related in covenant. Moreover, where the covenant exists, the
promise is effected. This is to say that out of the covenant between
Yahweh and Abraham, the people Israel became a reality in the land of
Canaan; and out of the covenant between Yahweh and David, a son was
given to reign in the kingdom of his father.

We turn our attention to the qualifiers of the formula הלך לפני.
We observe that the texts found within the Yahwist narrative in which
this expression is used are without qualification. Abraham says simply:
"Yahweh before whom I walked . . ." (Gen 20:40); and Jacob says "Yahweh
before whom Abraham and Isaac walked . . ." (Gen 48:15).

All the other texts which come from the hand of the Deuteronomist
use the formula הלך לפני together with characteristic modification.
In the dream narrative, Solomon says of David that he

walked before (Yahweh) in faithfulness[55]
in righteousness, and
in uprightness of heart.[56]

These expressions are applied to David, as we will see, because in the royal and sapiential traditions, they are characteristics of the ideal royal leader. The same is true for the accumulation of qualifiers in the other deuteronomistic texts.[57]

The meaning of these formulae is closely tied with the interpretation of the idiom הלך לפני. We showed that the basic meaning was to live one's life in accord with divinely-given directives. Just how that royal decorum was carried out by David before his God is expressed in the three phrases בישרת לבב, בצדקה, באמת.

The first of these expressions, faithfulness (אמת), occurs frequently in contexts in close conjunction with חסד.[58] The combined use of חסד and אמת was noted by Nelson Glueck in his study of the word חסד. He argues that חסד includes the concept of אמת. In so saying, he is referring to the use of the two terms in a phrase joined by a conjunction, in which case, חסד ואמת would be regarded as a hendiadys, the term אמת having the value of an explanatory adjective.[59]

---

[55]The phrase באמת follows the formula הלך לפני and introduces other descriptive qualifiers also in 1 Kgs 2:4 and 2 Kgs 20:3.

[56]The phrase בישרת לבב follows the formula הלך לפני also in 1 Kgs 9:4. Cf. Ps 101:2c.

[57]Phrases following הלך לפני elsewhere in the DtrH are: "with all your heart and soul" (1 Kgs 8:23); "with integrity of heart" (1 Kgs 8:4; Ps 101:2c); "with a whole heart" (2 Kgs 20:3 = Isa 38:3; 1 Kgs 15:3). It is beyond the scope of this paper to root each of these in the royal and sapiential traditions. We will pursue only those formulae found in the dream narrative.

[58]The combination of חסד and אמת expresses an indissoluble bond of loyalty (Gen 47:29; Josh 2:14; Ps 85:11); it indicates in particular God's faithful relationship with his people (Gen 24:27; Exod 34:6; 2 Sam 15:20// 2:6).

[59]*Hesed in the Bible* (Cincinnati: Hebrew Union College, 1967) 35-102, esp. 55 and 71-73.

Regarding the combination of these two terms, H. W. Wolff comments that "אמת emphasizes the enduring quality of responsible relationships" and "חסד underlines its intensity." So, *Hosea. A Commentary on the Book of the Prophet Hosea* (trans. by Gary Stansell; Hermeneia; Philadelphia: Fortress, 1974) 67.

In the dream narrative, the two terms are not joined together as they generally are in the biblical tradition; each term forms part of a fuller phrase which is balanced against the other. The one phrase, עשׂה חסד, describes the loyalty of Yahweh to covenant; the other, הלך לפני באמת, indicates fidelity to covenant on the part of the king. When the terms חסד and אמת are used together in this way, they convey an attitude of mutual loyalty which constitutes covenant.

In the royal and sapiential tradition, the terms occur in the phrase חסד ואמת with a meaning very similar to that of covenant as it is conveyed in the dream. The psalmist prays for the king thus:

> Prolong the life of the king;
> may his years endure to all generations!
> May he be enthroned for ever before God;
> bid love and faithfulness (חסד ואמת) watch over him
>   (Ps 61:7-8)![60]

In this phrase, we understand the mutual loyalty between God and king. In this sense, חסד ואמת could be understood to be synonymous with covenant. By the covenant relationship between God and the king, the king is preserved upon the throne given to him by Yahweh. This is to say that the life of the king upon the throne and his relationship with God in covenant are understood in tradition as being integral.

This understanding that the throne of the king is given by God and endures upon the mutual loyalty between God and king is testified in Proverbs:

> Loyalty and faithfulness (חסד ואמת) preserve the king
> and his throne is upheld by loyalty (חסד) (Prov 20:28).[61]

and in Psalm 89:

> Righteousness and justice are the foundation of thy throne;
> loyalty and faithfulness (חסד ואמת) go before thee (v 15).

----

[60] With this text we compare Prov 9:10-11:
The beginning of wisdom is reverence for Yahweh,
and knowledge of the Holy One is understanding,
because through him your days will be multiplied
and he will increase for you the years of your life.
This translation is taken from M. Dahood (*Psalms* II), 87. RSV takes בי in line c as first person as if the reference were to Wisdom. The third person is a better reading in light of its parallelism with line d.

[61] Cf. Prov 3:3; 14:22; 16:6. In each case the phrase carries a meaning similar to that of covenant itself.

Without his relationship with Yahweh, the king does not reign. On the other hand, the king can trust that Yahweh will preserve him upon the throne as long as he remains faithful before Yahweh.

We can be certain that the term אֱמֶת pertains to the attitude on the part of the king, for in Proverbs an instruction is given for one specific way that the king might demonstrate his fidelity:

> the king who judges the poor with equity (בֶּאֱמֶת)
> his throne will be established forever (Prov 29:14).

The king's principle obligation was that of governing the people. When the king carried out this function in accordance with Torah,[62] he acted loyally before his God and witnessed that he was indeed living in accord with his God.

The king likewise showed himself to live in accord with Torah when he acted in righteousness (בִּצְדָקָה). In the royal and sapiential traditions, this term expresses relationship with Yahweh as well as relationship in the human community. Of צְדָקָה, von Rad says:

> It is the standard not only for man's relationship to God, but also for his relationship to his fellows, reaching right down to the most petty wranglings--indeed, it is even the standard for man's relationship to the animals and to his natural environment. צְדָקָה can be described without much ado as the highest value in life, that upon which all life rests when it is properly ordered.[63]

The king is secure upon his throne when he acts in righteousness, so say Proverbs:

> It is an abomination to kings to do evil,
> for the throne is established by righteousness (בִּצְדָקָה)
>   (Prov 16:12).

The messianic hymn in Isaiah reflects this understanding. The life of the king upon the throne and his practice of righteousness are interconnected:

> Of the increase of his government and of peace
>   there will be no end,
> upon the throne of David, and over his kingdom

---

[62]Exod 23:1-3, 6-8; Deut 19:15-21.

[63]*Old Testament Theology,* 1.370; see 370-83; and " 'Righteousness' and 'Life' in the Cultic Language of the Psalms," in *The Problem of the Hexateuch,* 243-66.

> to establish it, and to uphold it
>> with justice and with righteousness (בצדקה)
> from this time forth and for evermore (Isa 9:6 [Eng 9:7]).

The royal tradition seems to say that Yahweh keeps covenant with the king by preserving him upon the throne; and the king keeps covenant with Yahweh by dealing with those in his charge in accord with God's direction.

In a royal hymn of victory, the king acknowledges that Yahweh has been faithful to him:

> The Lord rewarded me according to my righteousness
>> (Ps 18:20, 24 = 2 Sam 22:21, 25).

This statement begins and ends a recounting of specific ways in which the king has acted "in righteousness." This listing is expressed in the form of a "confession of innocence,"[64] the content of which concerns relationships on the human level.

In Psalm 72 special blessing is requested for the king that he might carry out his particular task with righteousness:

> May he govern your people with righteousness (Ps 72:2).
> . . . .
> may he defend the cause of the poor of the people
>> give deliverance to the needy,
>> and crush the oppressor (Ps 72:4)!

The king acts בצדקה when he lives by Torah in caring for the poor and removing evil from the realm. Proverbs are consistent with the idea that a ruler demonstrates his fidelity in the way he executes his authority toward the people in the kingdom:

> When the one in authority is righteous,
>> the people rejoice;
> but when the wicked rule,
>> the people groan (Prov 29:2).

> The righteous knows the rights of the poor;
> the wicked do not understand such knowledge (Prov 29:7).

We get some idea of just how integral kingship and righteousness was to the ancient mind when we consider the most primitive of royal poems. It declares:

---

[64] The content and probable setting of this form in the life of the king was presented by the writer elsewhere: see H. A. Kenik, "Code of Conduct for a King: Psalm 101," *JBL* 95 (1976) 391-403.

The one ruling over man, he is righteous (2 Sam 23:3)!

The third way that David showed loyalty to Yahweh is expressed by the phrase "in uprightness of heart" (בישרת לבב).

In regard to the meaning of this phrase, we notice, first of all, the synonymity of ישר לבב (uprightness of heart) and צדקה (righteousness); these terms occur in parallelism in Psalms,[65] as well as in Proverbs.[66] Very little is said about the specific mode of action of the "upright." Proverbs states:

> The highway of the upright turns aside from evil
>   (Prov 16:17a).

This is a very vague statement to be sure. A more complete image is given to us, however, in Job, a model of an "upright" person. Tradition says of him that he "turns away from evil" and also that he is "one who fears God."[67] The description is that of a person who lives in proper relationship with God. But Proverbs contributes to the meaning by making the point that the actions of the "upright" have an impact within the human community:

> The mouth of the upright delivers men (Prov 12:6b).

We might interpret this statement as implying the one whose authority is to pass judgment and thus has power for weal or woe.

While examples are not so explicit as to the duties of the "upright of heart," we learn from Proverbs that this person is truly a recipient of blessing. To the "upright" the Lord has shown his faithfulness:

> (The Lord) stores up sound wisdom for the upright (Prov 2:7a).
> The upright will inhabit the land (Prov 2:21a).
> The tent of the upright will flourish (Prov 14:11b).

The "upright" have enjoyed the special favor of God:

> The upright are in (the Lord's) confidence (Prov 3:32b).
> The upright enjoy (God's favor) (Prov 14:9).
> The prayer of the upright is (the Lord's) delight (Prov 15:8b).

---

[65]Pss 32:11; 64:11; 97:11; and 94:15.

[66]Prov 8:8-9 and 21:18.

[67]Job 1:1, 8; 2:3. With the description of Job, compare Prov 3:7:
Be not wise in your own eyes;
fear the Lord, and turn away from evil.

These proverbs recount ways in which the "upright" person enjoys the special blessing of Yahweh. In this blessing is evident a vital relationship between God and his chosen. Divine blessing, the sign of covenant with God, is not without influence in society:

By the blessing of the upright a city is exalted (Prov 11:11a).

This is to say that the actions on the part of the faithful ruler possess efficacy for his kingdom.

We have considered the three terms which describe the manner of David's "walking before" Yahweh--באמת, בצדקה, and בישרת לבב. Each term, we have shown, is rooted in the royal and sapiential traditions and derives the substance of its meaning out of the relationship upon which the king's reign is founded. In each there is the element of covenant, the import of relationship with Yahweh for the existence and the maintenance of the throne, and the impact of the royal activity upon the constituency, the special people of Yahweh.

The Dtr presents David as Yahweh's faithful one who serves his God in the manner most appropriate for a king. The ways of David's actions all hold implications for the life of the kingdom. Each of the phrases about "how" David lives in accord with his God is rooted in the royal and/or sapiential tradition; they are specifications of the way a king exercises his authority, and they are the requirements for his continuation upon the throne. For, to be king, it is necessary to be in accord with the order that resides in the Sovereign Deity. For the Israelite king, this order is specified in Torah.

David, cast in the light of the wisdom teachings is modelled like the royal son who listens to and acts according to the instructions of authority. He is heir to the directives for life that are collected in the sapiential tradition. The image is deliberately presented to display the king in a stance of obedience.

At this time, we will not discuss in full the impact of the term "servant" (v 6a), but will only mention that "servant" is predicated of David in this context of the royal son. He is servant, i.e., vassal to Yahweh. Being vassal casts a different hue to the image of the royal son. In the mind of the Dtr, David is indeed heir to the royal sapiential tradition. He acts in accord with those directives that experience has proven to be life-giving for society. But, for the servant/vassal, covenant depends upon living in accord with the stipulations of the covenant. As king, David is heir to Torah, the stipulation for covenant. His relationship with Yahweh and his actions on behalf of the Israelite community, which is his kingdom, are defined by Torah.

The Dtr has consciously and intentionally set two traditions side by side. One images the king in the tradition of royal wisdom. Out of that tradition the king is presented as royal son, heir to the teachings, instructions, and directives that have derived from experience as the guidelines for the successful ruler. The other images the king in the tradition of vassalship. According to this tradition, the king is obliged to the observance of the stipulations for covenant. In either case, the king's obligatory observance of authoritative directives is highlighted. The transformation of the king's role to that of a partner with Yahweh in a conditional covenant is accomplished in the dialectic of vv 6 and 14:

when he <u>walked before you</u>	<u>if</u> you <u>will walk in my ways</u>
in faithfulness	keeping my statutes and
in righteousness	my commandments
and in uprightness of heart	
toward you	

On the one hand, the king's observance is identified with sapiential teachings. On the other, the observance is clearly that of Torah. A more complete image of the king is contained in the combination of these structurally balanced verses. The Dtr collected together from traditions all possible ways of designating the king as obedient steward. The king הלך לפני (walks before), lives in accord with God. He does this by acting באמת (in faithfulness), בצדקה (in righteousness), בישרת לבב (in uprightness of heart), ideals specified in the wisdom tradition for the king who maintains harmony with the divine order by his just dealings in society. In the biblical wisdom tradition, these ideals had already been transformed under Yahwism. The king is designated as "servant" in the same context. Parallel to the image of the king presented in v 6 is the statement of condition specified by Torah. Whatever are the observances of the ancient Near Eastern king, these are transformed by Torah for the king among the Israelite people.[68]

THE DISTINCTIVE PEOPLE
OF THE SOLOMONIC KINGDOM

The previous sections have dealt with formulae from tradition which were used by the Deuteronomist to define the mutual relationship between Yahweh and the king. These next pages will focus upon the termin-

---

[68]See Deut 17:18-20.

ology selected by the Deuteronomist to identify the people who comprise the kingdom of Solomon.

The People of Election

The people over whom Solomon reigns are a distinctive group. They are distinguished by the Deuteronomist as "your people" (עמך) in v 8a and again in vv 9b and d.

The people specified as עמך (your people) are the ones whom Yahweh freed from the bondage of Egypt. Yahweh's word: "Let my people go"[69] fills out the conflict between Yahweh and Pharoah which led to the liberation of the Israelites from Egypt. These are the people for whom Moses intercedes:

O Lord, . . . your people (עמך) whom you brought forth out of the land of Egypt with great power and with a mighty hand (Exod 32:11).[70]

This people is the nation whom Yahweh chose to make his own. They are significantly called in tradition: a "holy people" (עם קדש);[71] "the people of the Lord" (עם יהוה);[72] "a people of his possession" (עם סגלה);[73] "a people, a heritage" (עם נחלה).[74] In familiar expression, these are intimately termed "my people"[75] by Yahweh; or, in prayer before Yahweh, they are called "your people,"[76] indicating that they belong to Yahweh alone.

In the Exodus tradition, the phrase "my/your people" occurs only in the imperative, "Let my people go" and in words spoken directly to Yahweh by Moses.[77] The familiar address for Yahweh's people, adopted from the Exodus tradition, was especially suited to the oratorical style of the

---

[69]Exod 5:1; 7:16, 26 (Eng 8:1); 8:16 (Eng 8:20), 17 (Eng 21); 9:1, 13, cf. 9:17; 10:3, 4.

[70]Cf. Exod 5:23; 32:12; 33:16.

[71]Deut 7:6; 14:2; 26:19; 28:9; cf. Exod 19:6.

[72]Deut 27:9; 2 Sam 1:12; 6:21.

[73]Deut 7:6; 14:2; 26:18; Ps 135:4; Mal 3:17; cf. Exod 19:5.

[74]Deut 4:20; 9:26, 29; 1 Kgs 8:36;, 51, cf. 8:53.

[75]2 Sam 7:7, 8, 10, 11; 1 Kgs 8:16; 1 Sam 2:29; 9:16, 17; 2 Sam 3:18; 5:2; 1 Kgs 6:13; 16:2; 2 Kgs 20:5.

[76]2 Sam 7:23, 24; 1 Kgs 8:30, 33, 34, 36[2], 38, 41, 43, 50, 51, 52; Deut 9:26, 29; 21:8[2], 26:15.

[77]See the texts in notes 69 and 70 above.

Dtr and was frequently used by this author. It is noteworthy that this
familiar address is most prevalent in texts created by the Dtr.[78]

The dream narrative, 1 Kings 3, as we are demonstrating in this
study, corresponds in style with the texts created by the Dtr. Here also,
the people addressed as "your people" are those delivered from the slavery
of Egypt because of Yahweh's special love. The Dtr makes quite clear
that the people in the midst of whom Solomon is king are Yahweh's own,
those saved by him in exodus from the slavery of Egypt:

> Your servant is in the midst of your people,
> whom you have chosen (1 Kgs 3:8a).

The special people of Yahweh are designated more precisely as those
"chosen" (בחר) by Yahweh. The verb בחר was introduced in the deuteronomic tradition with the specific meaning "choose" to indicate the idea
of election.[79]

The verb בחר is linked with those designations for the special
people of Yahweh we have already noted:

> For you are a people holy to the Lord your God;
> the Lord has chosen (בחר) you to be a people for his own
>   possession
> out of all the people that are on the face of the earth (Deut
>   7:6 and 14:2).

The term בחר is the Dtr's own specification for the people of election.
It is noteworthy that, in the use of this term for the people of election,
the Dtr combined the term with designations for the people out of the
Exodus tradition, specifically the "holy people" and "a people for his own
possession" from Exod 19:5-6.

---

[78]See the texts in notes 75 and 76 above.

[79]The election motif derives from two distinct traditions--the
patriarchal and the exodus-conquest complex.   So, K. Galling, *Die
Erwählungstraditionen Israels* (BZAW 48; Giessen: Alfred Töpelmann,
1928); H. H. Rowley, *The Biblical Doctrine of Election* (London: Lutterworth, 1953); Th. C. Vriezen, *Die Erwählung Israels nach dem Alten
Testament* (ATANT 24; Zurich: Zwingli, 1953); K. Koch, "Zur Geschichte
der Erwählungsvorstellung in Israel," *ZAW* 67 (1965) 205-26; and G. Mendenhall, "Election," in *IDB* (Nashville: Abingdon, 1962) 2. 76-82. Cf.
Byron Shafer, "The Root *bḥr* and Pre-Exilic Concepts of Chosenness in the
Hebrew Bible," *ZAW* 89 (1977) 20-42.

The term does not designate the people of the Exodus exclusively, for the Dtr applied בחר also to the Patriarchs and their descendants, who are likewise the chosen of Yahweh:

> the Lord set his love upon your fathers and chose (בחר) their
>   descendants after them,
> you above all peoples . . . (Deut 10:15).

The attribution of the term to the patriarchal tradition is significant, for throughout the DtrH, the Dtr reflects the integration of the Mosaic and patriarchal traditions. In fact, the Dtr uses the verb בחר in connection with the combined election traditions. Both the patriarchs and their descendants and the people brought out of Egypt are the "elected" of Yahweh:

> the Lord set his love upon you and chose (בחר) you . . . it was
> because the Lord loves you, and is keeping the oath which he
> swore to your fathers, that the Lord has brought you out with
> a mighty hand, and redeemed you from the house of bondage,
> from the hand of Pharaoh of Egypt (Deut 7:7-8).

> because he loved your fathers and chose (בחר) their descen-
> dants after them, and brought you out of Egypt with his own
> presence, by his great power (Deut 4:37).

The combination of traditions, such as we observe in these two texts, is the hallmark of the Dtr. Both these statements are taken from speeches of Moses. In them the Dtr combined those formulae and expressions from tradition that together present a full image of what it means to be called Yahweh's chosen. These texts reflect the Dtr narrative technique; they are speeches which are composed out of traditional formulae which, when precisely combined, present a wholly new image of the people of Yahweh.

The verb בחר, as we have indicated, does not appear in biblical texts earlier than the deuteronomistic in application to the people of election, though the concept of election belongs to the earliest streams of tradition. In the earlier traditions, both the patriarchs and their descendants and the people of the exodus are the elected people. It was left to the Dtr, however, to specifically so designate them.

The choice of this term for use in the dream narrative presents a rich image of the people. בחר (chosen) carries the theological content, according to the Dtr, of both the exodus and patriarchal traditions. The term combines in itself the variegated experiences of election which the Dtr intended the readers to understand. This term, pregnant in theological meaning as it is, together with the possessive reference to the people

(עָמַד) give a skillfully articulated and theologically precise picture of the people about whom the Dtr is speaking when he describes the membership in the Solomonic kingdom.

The People of Promise

The Deuteronomist was not content with the description of the people as simply "your people" and the one "you have chosen." To these the author added two other definitions of the people in the midst of whom Solomon is king. These are:

a numerous people (עַם רָב),
that cannot be numbered nor counted for multitude (1 Kgs 3:8b).

The designation עַם רָב occurs most often in conjunction with the descendants of Joseph.[80] Near the end of the Joseph Story, Joseph explains to his brothers that what had happened to him was in the plan of God "that many people (עַם-רָב) should be kept alive, as they are today.[81] The idea of Joseph's descendants being of great magnitude was not the creation of some story teller, but is in accord with early tradition about the Joseph tribes. In Josh 17:14-18, the tribe of Joseph complains[82] to Joshua about the fact that they have been given "but one territory and one portion as an inheritance, although (it is) a numerous people (עַם-רָב) since the Lord has blessed (them).[83] This report tells us that the multitude of people is the sign of the Lord's blessing.

The tradition of Joseph's family being blessed with a multitude of descendants is found in some of the oldest poetry in the biblical tradition. In the blessing of Jacob upon the sons of Joseph, Jacob prays:

---

[80]Other than application to Joseph's descendants, the phrase is used in a general reference to a vast crowd in 2 Sam 13:34, and to a great army in Josh 11:4.

[81]Gen 50:20. See G. Coats (*From Canaan to Egypt*, 45-46), for a discussion of this text in the context of the story line.

[82]This too is an element of tradition. Several times the family of Joseph is presented as discontents: they mutter against Gideon, Judg 8:1-3; against Jephthah, Judg 12:1-7; and against David, 2 Sam 20:1-3.

[83]The expression עַם-רָב is repeated three times in this particular context, in vv 14, 15, and 17. The emphasis is clearly upon the numerousness of the tribe.

let them grow into a multitude (לרב)
in the midst of the earth (Gen 48:15-16, esp. v 16).

Here Ephraim the younger is favored over Manasseh the first born. Yet tradition extends also to Manasseh the blessing of magnitude:

> . . . he also shall become a people, and he also
> shall be great; nonetheless his younger brother
> shall be greater than he, and his descendants
> shall become a multitude of nations (Gen 48:19; cf. v 20).

In the last blessing of Jacob upon his twelve sons, the themes of fruitfulness and blessing are characteristic of Joseph:

> From . . . El-Shaddai, who blesses thee:
> Blessings of heaven above,
> Blessings of the Deep, beneath,
> Blessings of breasts and womb,
> Blessings of father and mother, man and child
> Blessings of the mountains of old,
> Blessings of the eternal hills;
> Let them be on the head of Joseph
> On the brow of the leader of his brethren.[84]

With this is to be compared the image of the tribes of Joseph projected in the last blessing of Moses upon the tribes of Israel. We quote only the last lines of the blessing because they tell of the multitude of the family of Joseph:

> Behold the myriads of Ephraim!
> Behold the thousands of Manasseh (Deut 33:17c).[85]

As a result of our study, we learn that the tribe of Joseph is traditionally designated as "a numerous people" (עם-רב). Every application of this formulary, apart from the uses in the History of Solomon, is made in reference to the family of Joseph which metaphorically could be the Northern Kingdom.[86]

---

[84]Translation by F. M. Cross and D. N. Freedman (*Studies in Ancient Yahwistic Poetry,* 75-76, and notes 79-85, pp. 91-93).

[85]Translation by Cross and Freedman, ibid., 101; and notes 62-63, p. 117.

[86]The tribe of Joseph makes up the greater portion of the Northern Kingdom. Because of its greatness and size, the name Ephraim has traditionally been substituted for the kingdom of the North. Especially is this true of the pre-exilic prophetic references to the North: so, Hos 4:17; 5:3, 5, 9, 11, 12, 13 and passim; Isa 7:2, 5, 8, 9, 17. The name Joseph likewise indicates Israel: so, Amos 5:6, 15; 6:6; Pss 80:2; 78:67; 77:16.

It is curious that this particular designation has been selected by the Dtr to draw a profile of the people in the Solomonic kingdom. We are aware that formularies are not used without reason; they are employed by the Dtr with great precision. This is not a matter of simply conveying an idea of greatness. Before we address this question, it must be pointed out that the attribution of עם רב to the people in the kingdom of Solomon is not limited to the dream narrative. Hiram king of Tyre speaks to Solomon in this way:

Blessed be the Lord this day
who has given to David a wise son to be over
this great people (עָם-רָב) (1 Kgs 5:21 [Eng 5:7])[87]

In a summary statement, the Dtr says of the kingdom:

Judah and Israel were as many (רבים)
as the sand by the sea (1 Kgs 4:20).[88]

The attribution of a numerous people (עם רב) to the people of the Solomonic kingdom is intentional for it occurs in reference to no other kingdom, not to the United Kingdom of David nor to the individual kingdoms of Israel or Judah. Could it be that the association of the kingdom of Solomon with the designation for the tribe of Joseph known for its magnitude is both politically and theologically significant? We mentioned above that the tribe of Joseph, especially the name Ephraim, has traditionally substituted for the Northern Kingdom. The North by comparison with the Southern Kingdom encompassed a much vaster territory and contained a greater number of people. This was the עַם-רָב as distinct from Judah.

The question surely to be asked is why would the Dtr distinguish the kingdoms in this manner in the dream narrative? What was the Dtr attempting to say about the people? I believe that the Dtr's purpose is obvious. - The Dtr wished to represent the historical reality as it was during the reign of Solomon. The Solomonic kingdom encompassed the North as well as the South. On account of the proportions of the kingdom

---

[87] Without analyzing this exclamation of praise in detail, we call attention to its composition. This statement consists of a series of components that are found in the dream narrative and also elsewhere in the History of Solomon: e.g., "give David a son," 1 Kgs 3:6d; "a wise (son)," 1 Kgs 2:9; 3:12b; cf. 2:6; 5:9 (Eng 4:29); 10:4, 6, 7, 8; "great people," 1 Kgs 3:8b, cf. 4:20.

[88] In this text, Judah and Israel replace the word עם. The grouping is, with the plural form of רב in agreement with the dual subject.

and the numerousness of the inhabitants, the Dtr would accentuate the
fact that the kingdom includes the עָם-רָב. Because the North was subsequently lost to the Davidic monarchy, the point is well made. During
Solomon's reign, however, the king did indeed reign over the עָם-רָב.

To put greater emphasis upon the multitude of the עָם-רָב, the
Deuteronomist added the phrase

"that cannot be numbered nor counted for multitude לֹא-
ימנה ולא יספר מרב" (1 Kgs 3:8c).

For all purposes, this phrase seems to be general in its meaning and applicable to anything which is of great size.[89] This is true to some extent,
though a look at contexts in which the expression most often occurs
suggests a more specific connotation.

The patriarchal promise as it is recounted in the earliest traditions
puts great emphasis upon the vast number of promised descendants.
These are compared with the "dust of the earth,"[90] "the stars of heaven,"[91] and the "sand of the sea."[92] In each case the comparison is made
to emphasize the inability of the descendants to be counted or numbered. Let us look at the statements of promise:

I will make your descendants as the dust of the earth; so that
if one *can count* the dust of the earth, your descendants also
can be counted (Gen 13:16, with the verb מנה)

Look toward heaven, and *number* the stars, if you are able *to
number* them . . . so shall your descendants be (Gen 15:5, with
the verb ספר).

I will do you good, and make your descendants as the sands of
the sea, which *cannot be numbered for multitude* (Gen
32:13).[93]

---

[89] The Deuteronomist himself has done this in applying the precise
expression to illustrate the magnitude of the offerings which were being
sacrificed upon the altar on the day of the Temple dedication. See 1 Kgs
8:5; 2 Chr 5:6.

[90] Gen 13:16; 28:14.

[91] Gen 15:5; 26:4; 27:17; Exod 32:13; Deut 1:10; 10:22; 28:62.

[92] Gen 32:13 (Eng 12); 22:17; Isa 10:22; 48:19; Hos 2:1 (Eng 1:10); Jer
33:22.

[93] With this text is to be compared the promise spoken to Hagar concerning Ishmael: "I will so greatly multiply your descendants that they
cannot be numbered for multitude" (Gen 16:10). Both texts conclude with
the formulary לֹא-יספר מרב .

In the first two illustrations, the idea of inability to count is expressed in a phrase that uses the verb מנה (count) in the first example, and ספר (number) in the second. It should be noted that the Dtr preferred not to select from one or other of these, but appropriated both into the formulary לא-ימנה ולא-יספר.

In view of such artistry and exactitude in the use of traditional language, can it ever be said that the technique of the Dtr is other than a systematic articulation of a theological perspective out of elements drawn from tradition?

The formulary, as it appears in the dream, contains one more element, the phrase "for multitude" (מרב) so that the entire phrase reads לא-ימנה ולא-יספר מרב (cannot be numbered nor counted for multitude). This additional element as an integral component of the formulary is observable in the third illustration above. The formulary לא-יספר מרב occurs in the cited example and also in Gen 16:10, a statement about the descendants of Ishmael. It occurs, of course, in the dream narrative with the additional verb לא-ימנה.

The expression as it is articulated by the Dtr echoes the precise formulation from the earlier narrative tradition. In that tradition, the context is always that of the promise of descendants. There can be no doubt, therefore, about the precise content that is intended by the Dtr in the inclusion of the formulary in the dream narrative.

The content is that of the promise of descendants. But what is the force of this tradition within the dream narrative? When the Dtr describes the people as too numerous to be counted, his intention is obviously to pinpoint the people of Solomon's kingdom as the descendants that had been promised to Abraham. The nation under the rulership of Solomon is thus related in the scheme of promise-fulfillment to the great nation that had been promised to Abraham. The great glory of Solomon, at the moment of history being told, is his rulership in a nation which traces its ancestry to the Father to whom Yahweh had spoken the promise of these many descendants.

THE IDENTITY OF THE COVENANT GOD AND THE KING

The Identity of God

The dream narrative incorporates several designations for God, namely, *Elohim, Adonai* and *Yahweh*. The impulse, and indeed, the critical response to this phenomenon has been to recognize in the different designations evidence for the continuation of the tetrateuchal sources into Kings.[94] For others, the names verify redactional work upon an originally ancient and coherent royal ceremonial text.[95]

We submit and will argue that the distinctive designations for God function in the narrative in the same manner as the traditional formulae. Each title is pertinent to a specific tradition. Each represents a dimension of the deity that illuminates the nature of the relationship between the king and God, and the king and the people of God. Hence each title contributes significantly to the design for kingship which is the task of the Dtr. This is to say that the divine designations are skillfully and intentionally located in the narrative in relation to the traditions that are generally associated with that title. Rather than being a haphazard accumulation of titles, we have instead, the multifaceted dimensions of relationships that give meaning to the design for kingship.

The designations *Elohim* and *Adonai* will be discussed in Chap. V in conjunction with the traditions that are associated with the particular dimensions of God reflected in those titles. At this point, we will consider only the reference of the special name of YHWH in tradition and the implications in the use of the name in the dream narrative. Because the traditional application of the name YHWH is self-evident, our discussion will be cursory with the limited intention to make explicit the obvious.

The name YHWH is the special name by which God revealed himself to the chosen people:

God said to Moses, "I am who I am."[96]

This revelation does not introduce a God who had not been known by the people. Rather, tradition stresses that YHWH is the God of the Fathers:

God said to Moses, "YHWH, the God of your father, the God of Abraham, the God of Isaac, and the God of Jacob, has sent me to you": this is my name for ever, and thus I am to be remembered throughout all generations (Exod 3:15).[97]

---

[94]See Chap. I, n. 80 and n. 81, p. 23, for a review of scholarship on this issue.

[95]This matter has been discussed in Chap. II. See p. 33.

[96]Exod 3:14; cf. 6:2-3. See the discussion on "The Name Yahweh" by Frank M. Cross ("Yahweh and ꜗĒl," in *Canaanite Myth and Hebrew Epic*, 60-75).

[97]See F. M. Cross, "Yahweh and the God of the Patriarchs," *HTR 55* (1962) 255-59; and more recently, "The Religion of Canaan and the God of Israel," in *Canaanite Myth and Hebrew Epic*, 1-75.

According to tradition, it is YHWH who observed the plight of his people in the slavery of Egypt, who brought them out of bondage,[98] and who gave them passage through the sea,[99] to make them a people of his own.[100] Through the saving events of the delivery from Egypt, YHWH revealed himself to the people and chose them for his own possession. In the experience of the exodus, the nature of YHWH was revealed to the people; and the people understood themselves to be the chosen of YHWH. In the experience of salvation, the ground was prepared for the special relationship of covenant.

The name YHWH is thus associated in particular with the election of Israel to be Yahweh's people (עמך), his "own possession" and "holy nation"[101] whom the Dtr designates as the "chosen" (בחר). Both עמך and בחר are attributions by which the Dtr has described the people in the kingdom of Solomon (1 Kgs 3:8a).

As tradition recounts the revelation of the name YHWH, the God so identified is revealed to be the God of Abraham and Isaac and Jacob, the ancestors of the people of the exodus. YHWH is the God who had called Abraham out of his country and from his family to a new land.[102] YHWH chose Abraham to be father of the nation;[103] to him was issued the promise of a great land for himself and for his descendants,[104] who would be numerous beyond counting.[105]

YHWH is thus traditionally the God of the promise. YHWH is associated, in particular, with the promise of a great number of people, in the formulaic עם-רב; and of numerous descendants, those not able to be counted (לא יספר מרב).

The use of the divine name YHWH by the Dtr in the hymnic portion of the narrative in v 7 is quite precisely by design. As the Dtr attempts to portray the relationship between God and the king, he does this specifically by establishing the relationship between God and the people in the realm of the king. These people are a people because YHWH is their God. Their God is YHWH who revealed himself in the promise of the land and in the saving events of the exodus. The people are the descendants of

---

[98]Exodus 3-13.

[99]Exodus 14-15.

[100]Exodus 19, 24.

[101]Exod 19:5-6; cf. Deut 7:6; 14:2.

[102]Gen 12:1; 15:7.

[103]Gen 12:2.

[104]Gen 12:7; 13:14-15, 17.

[105]Gen 13:16.

the Fathers to whom YHWH promised the land, and they are the people who had been delivered from bondage that they might live upon the promised land that is the kingdom of Solomon.

Significantly and in continuity with the earlier election traditions, it is by the name YHWH that God promises David the throne and the kingdom.[106] In the dream, YHWH comes to Solomon (v 5); and Solomon addresses the divine visitor with the special name, "Yahweh, my God" (v 7). Solomon, in so doing, identifies himself as the successor to David to whom was promised a son upon the throne; and Solomon acknowledges that the people and kingdom are the descendants and land that had been promised.

The Identity of the King

Three times in the course of the dialogue, Solomon speaks of himself as "your servant" (עבדך) in direct address to YHWH (1 Kgs 3:7a, 8a. 9a). Implicit in the reference "servant" is the implication that the one so designated is the vassal in a covenant relationship. Such a relationship implies obedience on the part of the vassal, and loyalty on the part of the sovereign in protecting his servant.[107] In tradition, whether it be the Yahwist narrative tradition or the DtrH, the designation "servant" always implies a relationship between parties of unequal status. The greater guarantees protection on the condition that the subordinate party demonstrates loyal service.

We have noted earlier in our discussion that David is called "servant" in the context that emphasizes the king's living in accord with God. With the introduction of the motif "servant" into this context, the Dtr had boldly slanted a tradition that in royal ideology expressed harmony between the king and the patron-god to indicate a relationship that was conditioned upon the obedience of the vassal.

There is hint of this transformation of the tradition from royal ideology to a conditioned relationship already in the Yahwist narrative. There, in the patriarchal narratives, the designation "servant" recurs in contexts that speak of the promise of descendants. Abraham refers to himself as "servant" before the strangers who visit him at Mamre to announce the birth of a son.[108] That which seemed humanly impossible is

---

[106]2 Sam 7:1, 4, 5, 11[2].

[107]For comparative extra-biblical material on "servant," see C. Lindhagen, *The Servant Motif in the Old Testament* (Uppsala: Lundequistska Bokhandeln, 1950) 6-39.

[108]Gen 18:3, 5.

given to Abraham as a proof that Yahweh shows loyalty to a covenant partner who has shown loyal service. Jacob refers to himself as "servant" when he acknowledges that Yahweh has shown loyalty in keeping the family of Jacob safe in their journey to the land of promise.[109] Lot, too, who belonged to Abraham's family, experiences the protection of the Sovereign. He and his family are kept safe from the destruction of Sodom.[110] Isaac is called "servant" by the servant of Abraham who had been sent to obtain a wife for Isaac.[111]

In all of these texts, with the exception of the narrative of the divine visitation to Abraham to announce the birth of a son, the technical term for Yahweh's fidelity, עשׂה חסד, occurs in the same context with "servant."[112] In every case, it is the question of Yahweh's fidelity in keeping his promise. In all of these texts, there is no question about the faithfulness of Yahweh; in fact, the patriarchal narratives throw the emphasis upon the loyalty of Yahweh, and away from the "servanthood" of the recipients of the promise. The latter element is present, nonetheless. There remains the implication that the recipients are "servants," and therefore, because the promise is fulfilled, the fidelity of the servants is self-evident.

In contrast with the patriarchal narratives, to be sure, the narratives about Moses and Caleb as "servants" cast the focus straightforwardly upon the loyalty of the one designated as "servant." Moses, "servant" of Yahweh, acts as the spokesman for Yahweh;[113] he faithfully communicates Yahweh's will to the people,[114] and he mediates before Yahweh on

---

[109]Gen 32:11 (Eng 32:10).

[110]Gen 19:2, 19. This text was not mentioned in our study of the formulary עשׂה חסד. It is to be noted, therefore, that the formulary occurs in v 19 together with the designation "servant" just as these expressions occur together in each of the texts we are summarizing here.

[111]Gen 24:14.

[112]Since the text is plainly and explicitly about the fulfillment of the promise and therefore the loyalty of Yahweh to his promise, there is no need for the formulaic reference. In all the other cases, it is not so clear that the issue is the fulfillment of the promise. The technical term עשׂה חסד focuses the reader to the issue of the covenant promise.

[113]Exod 4:10.

[114]Num 12:7, 8. For a poetic reconstruction of this text, see F. M. Cross, "Priestly Houses of Early Israel," in *Canaanite Myth and Hebrew Epic*, 203-4.

behalf of the people.[115] Caleb identified as "servant" is described by Yahweh himself as one who "has followed me faithfully."[116] Though the emphasis is upon the service of the subordinate partner in the case of Moses and Caleb, nonetheless, Yahweh is implied to be loyal in his protection and concern for his covenant partner.

The same covenant tradition underlies both narrative accounts. The Abraham accounts stress the fidelity of Yahweh;[117] whereas the Mosaic/Caleb accounts stress the responsibility of the vassal/servant. The relationship, in each account, is founded on the assumption that the covenant partners are of unequal status. Israel grew in the understanding that Yahweh's loyalty to his promise could be trusted. There remained the experience of human frailty that taught Israel about its potential for obstructing its participation in the benefits of the promise.

In the DtrH, two figures in particular carry the designation "servant." Moses is "servant" *par excellence* in agreement with the image of Moses in the earlier Mosaic tradition.[118] The Dtr presents Moses living his life faithfully before Yahweh and acting in his leadership role for the good of the people. David also is "servant" in the mind of the Dtr.[119] Whatever the nature of the Davidic covenant, it is certain that the Dtr

---

[115]Num 11:11, cf. Exod 14:31.

[116]Num 14:24; cf. Deut 1:36; Josh 14:8, 9.

[117]Because of the stress upon the activity of Yahweh in the Abraham tradition, it has been assumed that Yahweh's covenant promise was without condition. Indeed that is the case because of the nature of Yahweh. But the human partner with Yahweh is still "servant" and capable of disloyalty. The response of the "servant" does not interfere with the nature of Yahweh; it simply means that the "servant" obstructs his/her participation in the promise.

[118]The title "servant of YHWH" is a favorite for Moses within the DtrH. Josh 1:1, 13, 15; 8:31, 33; 11:12; 12:6; 13:8; 14:7; 18:7; 22:2, 4, 5; 2 Kgs 18:12; and Deut 34:5 with which is to be compared Josh 24:29 and Judg 2:8.

[119]David identifies himself as "servant": 2 Sam 7:19, 20, 21, 26, 27, 28, 29; 24:10; and Solomon calls David "servant": 1 Kgs 3:6; 8:24, 26.

David is called "servant" in an oracle of Yahweh: 1 Kgs 11:13; by an agent: 2 Sam 3:18; by prophets: 2 Sam 7:5, 8 (Nathan); 1 Kgs 11:32, 34, 36, 38; 1 Kgs 14:8 (Ahijah); 2 Kgs 19:34; 20:6 (Isaiah); and by the psalmist: Ps 89:4, 21. Also in summary statements, David is designated as "servant": 1 Kgs 8:66 and 2 Kgs 8:19.

On the king as the servant of Yahweh, see C. Lindhagen, *The Servant Motif*, 280-84.

transformed the Davidic role to that of a vassal.[120] The Dtr presents David, like Moses, in an ideal light who has lived faithfully before Yahweh and who exercised his authority to maintain the life of the community.

Psalm 89 must be addressed in this discussion because its content corresponds so closely with the promise to David in 2 Samuel 7,[121] and because the tradition of the Davidic promise is blurred in the psalm. The psalm holds in tension two royal traditions: the tradition of the decree of an eternal dynasty, and the tradition of the vassalship of the king. The two traditions are spoken together within a single oracle:

I have made a covenant with *my chosen one,*
I have sworn to David *my servant;*
"I will establish your descendants for ever
and build your throne for all generations" (Ps 89:4-5
    [Eng 89:3-4]).

The designation "my servant" is placed in parallelism with "my chosen." The servant is charged with the obligation of loyal service to Yahweh

---

[120]That the Davidic covenant was conditional in the pattern of a vassal treaty has been proposed by a number of scholars who have approached the question from different perspectives. Roland de Vaux ("La roi d'Israël, vassal de Yahvé," in *Mélanges Eugène Tisserant* [Studi e Testi 231; Vatican City, 1964] 199-33; now appearing as "The King of Israel, Vassal of Yahweh," in *The Bible and the Ancient Near East* [trans. D. McHugh; New York: Doubleday, 1971] 152-66), argues that the Davidic king was vassal of Yahweh in virtue of a covenant in strict vassal treaty form, and the anointing of the king was the rite which signified his vassalship. Philip Calderone (*Dynastic Oracle and Suzerainty Treaty* Logos I; Manila: Ateneo de Manila University, 1966), proposed that the Nathan oracle was similar to the vassal treaty in concept and ideology, but not in form. He states that the promise of a long dynastic rule was fitted into the covenant structure to fulfill the need of theological legitimation, and thus satisfy the demands of conservative elements who feared this secular institution, and to forestall opposition from former adherents of Saul and other Northerners (p. 69). Frank M. Cross ("The Ideologies of Kingship in the Era of the Empire: Conditional Covenant and Eternal Decree," in *Canaanite Myth,* 219-73), theorizes that David, a charismatic leader, was linked more closely with Saul, the covenant being limited by the traditional law of the league and by prophecy. Cross argues that the Judean royal ideology began with Solomon and his dynastic temple and not with David.

[121]On the correspondence between 2 Samuel 7 and Psalm 89, see John L. McKenzie, "The Dynastic Oracle: II Sam 7," *TS* 8 (1947) 187-218.

through the faithful execution of his kingship; the chosen is put upon the throne by a sovereign king to whom the designated king owes service.[122] In these verses, the decree of an eternal dynasty stands in opposition to the image of the king whose reign is conditioned and dependent. Because these two foci are continually stressed in carefully structured opposition,[123] we suspect that the eternal promise to David, in the DtrH and in Psalm 89, functioned to emphasize the eternal fidelity of the Sovereign King, and not the eternal dynasty of the vassal king.

Another strophe within Psalm 89 bears out this conjecture:

I have found David, *my servant*;
with my holy oil I have anointed him;
so that my hand shall ever abide with him,
my arm also shall strengthen him (Ps 89:21-22 [Eng
    89:20-21]).

The king is confirmed in vassalship with the designation "my servant"; and the king is anointed with oil, the anointing being an effective sign that the king reigns as a vassal king.[124] Though the king as vassal may be jeopardized, the promise of Yahweh is secure. The king may rely upon the presence and the support of his sovereign Lord. This verse reflects the reality of which Israel grew in understanding: Yahweh can be expected to be faithful to his king; but the vassal king may depart from loyalty in his service to Yahweh.

---

[122]In the tradition of the monarchy, David is the chosen of Yahweh and was for this reason anointed by Samuel (1 Sam 16:8-13, cf. Ps 78:70). On one occasion David speaks of himself as "chosen" and claims that he was chosen above Saul and his house. So, 2 Sam 6:21.

The way a man was legitimated upon the throne was the claim that he was chosen. Hushai acknowledges Absalom as king because "the Lord and this people and all the men of Israel have chosen (him)." See 2 Sam 16:18. On the human and divine choice of the king, see G. W. Ahlström, "Solomon, the Chosen One," *HR* 8 (1968) 93-110.

[123]An example would be the tendencies we identified in the Abrahamic and Mosaic traditions as these were presented by the Yahwist narrator. See above n. 117.

[124]So, R. de Vaux, "The King of Israel," 162ff; cf. Z. Weisman, "Anointing as a Motif in the Making of the Charismatic King," *Bib* 57 (1976) 378-98. On the two anointings of the king, see E. Kutsch, *Salbung als Rechtsakt im Alten Testament und im Alten Orient* (BZAW 87; Berlin: Alfred Töpelmann, 1963).

Like David, the Dtr presents Solomon as "servant." Solomon so speaks of himself in the dream narrative (1 Kgs 3:7a, 8a, 9a), and again in his prayer at the temple dedication (1 Kgs 8:28, 30, 36, 52, 59). The designation identifies Solomon as vassal in a covenant relationship with his God, Yahweh. Being "servant" implies, however, that the king exercises his tasks of leadership for the good of the people. He is "servant" in the midst of Yahweh's people (v 8a), and he is "servant" who exercises his duties in accord with God-given direction, with Torah (v 9a).

The single motif "servant" casts kingship in quite a different light from the kingship that derives from the ideologies of the ancient orient, or from the kingship that basks in the light of the promise of an eternal dynasty. "Servant," juxtaposed as it is with different traditions within the dream narrative, transforms each of those traditions into a *novum* of royal theology.

Little Child

Solomon identifies himself as "servant" and he also indicates that he is a "little child." He says in a cryptic statement:

I am a little child אנכי נער קטן (1 Kgs 3:7b).

The expression נער קטן (little child) seems to reflect the tradition in Egyptian royal ideology that the king was chosen from time of infancy to take the throne. One text tells of the nomination of Thut-mose III while he was yet an infant:

(The god Amon)--he is my father, and I am his son.
He commanded to me that I should be upon his throne
while I was (still) a nestling. . . .[125]

In another Egyptian text, Sesostris III states that even while he was still a child, he was designated to govern the land; and even before he was born, he was set apart to live in the palace.[126]

In biblical contexts, this concept of being "a little child" takes on an important theological function, for it suggests that the king so designated is completely dependent and without the natural capacity to succeed on

---

[125] *ANET*, 446a, ll. 1-2.

[126] Quoted from S. Herrmann, "Die Königsnovelle," 54; and A. Hermann, "Die ägyptische Königsnovelle," 49.

his own power.[127]   The motif of being "little child" (נער קטן) functions
with precisely this meaning in the narrative presentation of the choice of
David.   When David was set aside to be king, he was the youngest of the
sons of Jesse:

> Samuel said to Jesse:
> "Are all your sons (נערים) here?"
> He said:
> "There remains yet the youngest (הקטן)" (1 Sam 16:11).

The account of David's victory over the Philistine giant makes the point
well.   David was "but a youth" (1 Sam 17:33, 42), whereas the one against
whom he fought had been "a man of war from his youth" (1 Sam 17:33).
The point of this narrative is that the victory belonged to Yahweh.   David
was figuratively, yet literally, the נער קטן, through whom Yahweh
could act.   Thus David, the ideal king in the mind of the Dtr, is presented
as one without natural capacity for success and utterly dependent for
victory upon the God by whom he had been designated to be king.

The motif of being "a little child" functions significantly in the
prophetic tradition.[128]   This is a crucial application for the motif to
illustrate the precise implication of being "a little child."   For the prophet
to be an effective spokesman for Yahweh, he must be utterly dependent
and trusting; he must speak the word that is given to him and not his own
thoughts.

Two prophets in particular carry the distinction of being "little
child."   Both accounts come under the influence of the Dtr.[129]   The Dtr
stresses that when Samuel was called to be prophet, he was only a youth

---

[127]Walter A. Brueggemann makes some significant suggestions
about the theological meaning of "little" in a study on Amos 7.   See
"Amos' Intercessory Formula," *VT* 19 (1969) 386-88.

[128]On the association between the prophet and the royal court, and
therefore a fluidity between the prophetic and royal traditions, see Claus
Westermann, *Basic Forms of Prophetic Speech* (Philadelphia: Westminster, 1967) 98-128.   Westermann compellingly argues for the correlation
between the prophetic messenger formula and the messenger speech with
which the court envoy introduced the words of the king.   See the other
studies synthesized by Westermann in the same work, 14-89; and J. F.
Ross, "The Prophet as Yahweh's Messenger," in *Israel's Prophetic Heritage*
(New York: Harper & Brothers, 1962) 98-107.

[129]On the question of the relationship between Jeremiah and the
DtrH, see especially, E. W. Nicholson, *Preaching to the Exiles. A Study of
the Prose Tradition in the Book of Jeremiah* (New York: Schocken, 1971).

(נער).[130]   Samuel holds a distinctive position as the spokesman for Yahweh within the DtrH, particularly in the inauguration of the monarchy.[131]   In the case of Jeremiah, Jeremiah protested the call to be prophet because of his youth or "littleness":

> . . . Behold, I do not know how to speak, for I am only a youth
> (נער)
> . . . Do not say, 'I am only a youth (נער); for to all to whom I
> send you you shall go, and whatever I command you you shall
> speak . . . (Jer 1:6-7).[132]

Precisely in the admission of being "a child," Jeremiah is directed to speak the words which Yahweh will give him. The prophet thereby also shows himself to be 'servant' to Yahweh.[133]   The two motifs-- נער קטן (little child) and עבד (servant)--are very near in meaning, but it must be recognized that each derives from a separate tradition. The former has its source in the Egyptian royal ideology about the choice of the king from infancy; the latter from the legal sphere and the suzerainty treaty. The Dtr effectively makes the theological point about the subordination and necessary dependence of the king by setting these motifs side by side.

The use of the motif נער קטן in messianic texts of Isaiah are especially instructive for our purpose in trying to understand the connotation of this expression. There נער קטן is used to describe the ruler for the new age who will be an ideal king, dependent upon Yahweh and obedient to his will. In the messianic prophecy of Isa 11:1-9, we read:

> The wolf shall dwell with the lamb,
> and the leopard shall lie down with the kid,
> and the calf and the lion and the fatling together,
> and a little child (נער קטן) shall lead them (v 6).[134]

In light of our study on the meaning of the motif, the model of the ideal king who will reign in that new age is quite unique. The king will be one utterly incapable of ruling by his own power; he will lead Israel by the power of Yahweh. He will be only a child, that is to say, dependent and obedient.

---

[130]1 Sam 3:1, 8; cf. vv 7, 20-21.

[131]Cf. 1 Samuel 8-12.

[132]See Norman C. Habel, "The Form and Significance of the Call Narratives," *ZAW* 77 (1965) 305-9.

[133]On the prophet as servant, see C. Lindhagen, *The Servant Motif*, 277-80.

[134]See J. L. McKenzie, "Royal Messianism," *CBQ* 19 (1957) 25-52.

The sapiential teachings in Proverbs have something to say about the littleness of the king. True, the Proverbs say nothing explicitly about being נער קטן, but the teachings do convey that idea under the term "humility," and the idea of "servant" by the expression "fear of the Lord." Proverbs suggest that the king be dependent and submissive before Yahweh as a necessary requisite for success in ruling:

> The reward for humility and fear of the Lord is
> riches and honor and life (Prov 22:4).[135]

> The fear of the Lord is instruction in wisdom,
> and humility goes before honor (Prov 15:33).

> A man's pride will bring him low,
> but he who is lowly in spirit will obtain honor (Prov 29:23).

> Before destruction a man's heart is haughty,
> but humility goes before honor (Prov 18:12).

These teachings are addressed forthrightly to the king. The blessings promised to the king--honor, riches, and life--demand the prior condition of humility, of lowliness in spirit and fear of the Lord. The sapiential tradition which is closely linked with royal thought says in its own language what the technical expression נער קטן (little child) in the narrative tradition conveys about the ideal king.

There is deep significance in Solomon's declaration "I am a little child." The king admits of his dependence upon and submission to Yahweh. The image of the "little child" together with the various images of kingship so far discussed present a leader who owes allegiance to Yahweh (הלך לפני); who is related to Yahweh as vassal (עבד), and who is without power of his own (נער קטן) to function as king.

These images are drawn together by the Dtr out of very different traditions of kingship. The Israelite king, in the mind of the Dtr, does not model any particular one of these images. It is from the integration of all of these models for kingship that the design for kingship in Israel emerges.

The design for kingship so far presented by the Dtr, complex in its simple view of an ideal king before Yahweh, remains unfinished. Thus far, the design includes only one focus: it images the ideal king in relationship with Yahweh. The Dtr has yet to define the specific functions of the king

---

[135]The terms--riches and honor and life--are the blessings given to Solomon in the course of the dream dialogue. These will be discussed in Chap. V, pp. 152-63.

108   Design for Kingship

in relationship to the people in his charge.[136] The Dtr will draw that
aspect of kingship also from a diversity of royal traditions.

In contrast with the attitude before Yahweh conveyed in the formula
"little child" (נער קטן), the king functions in the specific capacity as
leader of the armies which defend the people and land of Yahweh. The
role of the king as leader in warfare is expressed in the statement:

I do not know going out and coming in (1 Kgs 3:7c).

The phrase צאת ובא (going out and coming in) appears to be a common
expression for passage through the gates of the city.[137] Because the
leader of the army and his troops set out for battle and returned through

---

[136]On account of the way we have chosen to structure our study,
the design for kingship with respect to the king's roles in society will be
discussed here as well as in Chap. V. At this time, we consider only
those functions of the king that are named in the formulae used within the
hymn section. Others are named with the dialogue between Solomon and
Yahweh.

[137]The phrase in question occurs with the general meaning in the
portion of the blessings and curses in Deuteronomy 28 which are sym-
metrically arranged and balanced:
Blessed shall you be when you come in (בבאך)
and blessed shall you be when you go out (בצאתך) (Deut 28:6)
Cursed shall you be when you come in (בבאך)
and cursed shall you be when you go out (בצאתך) (Deut 28:19)
The contexts, Deut 28:3-6 and 16-19, from which these lines are taken,
are recognizable as a kind of recitation, possibly used in ritual. There is a
formal symmetry between the sections of blessings and curses. See G.
von Rad, *Deuteronomy: A Commentary* (Philadelphia: Westminster,
1966) 173-75.
The liturgical use of the poetic formulary may account for its occur-
rence in psalms, e.g. Ps 121:8 and 2 Kgs 19:27 = Isa 37:28. The ritual
connotation of the terms has been argued by G. W. Ahlström, "Solomon,
the Chosen One," 105-8.
Elsewhere the formula indicates freedom of movement. Such is the
case in Jeremiah: "Now Jeremiah was still going in and out (בא ויצא)
among the people, for he had not yet been put in prison" (Jer 37:4). The
formula also indicates lack of freedom of movement as in situations of
siege: "Now Jericho was shut up from within and from without--none
went out and none came in (אין יוצא ואין בא)" (Josh 6:1). "Baasha
king of Israel went up against Judah, and built Ramah that he might
permit no one to go out or come in (יצא ובא) to Asa king of Judah"
(1 Kgs 15:17; cf. 2 Chr 16:1).

the main gates of the city with much fanfare, the formula appropriately became a technical expression for warfare. This can be verified by consideration of several texts.

> Achish, leader of the Philistine forces spoke to David:
> As the Lord lives you have been honest, and to me it seems right that you should march out and in (צאתך ובאך) with me in the campaign; for I have found nothing wrong in you from the day of your coming to me to this day (1 Sam 29:6).

This dialogue between Achish and David took place just prior to the Philistine attack upon Israel. The leaders of the Philistines feared that David and his men might prove troublesome in battle against the land of their own people. The expression צאת ובא (going out and coming in) in this context connotes military activity.

The expression צאת ובא (going out and coming in) is used also in the report of Saul's commissioning David to go into battle against the Philistines:

> So Saul removed him from his presence, and made him a commander of a thousand; and he went out and came in (ויצא ויבא) before the people (1 Sam 18:13, 16).[138]

The formulary follows immediately after the charge given to David which is to lead the thousand. The phrase צאת ובא could only mean military leadership in this context.

The two texts we have just quoted are significant because they have been structured into the narrative account to frame the report of the transition from Saul to David. In the context of each text, there is the refrain of victory:

> Saul has slain his thousands
> and David his ten thousands (1 Sam 18:7b and 29:5b).

The full attention is given to David the victor. In the first case, David is successful against the Philistines against whom he was sent by Saul because "Saul was afraid of David."[139] In the second case, David is dismissed from the ranks of the Philistines with whom he had sought refuge

---

[138]The formulary expressed in the *hifil* form reads "lead/led out and bring/brought in." Saul's charge to David to lead the Philistine wars is recalled in the deuteronomistic report of the designation of David to be king: ". . . when Saul was king over us, it was you that led out and brought in (מוציא והמבי) Israel" (2 Sam 5:2).

[139]1 Sam 18:12; cf. vv 14-16 and 27-30.

in his escape from Saul. This latter event immediately precedes the death of Saul and the rise of David to power. It appears that the formula צאת ובא (going out and coming in) has been deliberately utilized in the narrative at these junctures to mark the transition in leadership from Saul to David.

The phrase צאת ובא occurs within the DtrH only with the specific meaning of participation in battle. The Dtr has used it in the accounts of neither the Judges nor Saul. It is significantly applied only to Moses and Caleb and to David.

The well-known speech of Moses at his farewell to the people and in anticipation of the leadership of Joshua is expressed within an installation form.[140] At the point in the context with which we are interested, Moses states his present age, then announces that he is no longer able to lead the people:

> I am a hundred and twenty years old this day;
> I am no longer able *to go out and come in* (לצאת ולבוא)
> (Deut 31:2).[141]

The announcement pertains to Moses' leadership of the people as they proceed toward the land and there must fight for its acquisition. As Moses continues to speak, we know that our interpretation is accurate, for Moses says:

> The Lord your God himself will go before you; he will destroy these nations before you. . . . And the Lord will do to them as he did to Sihon and Og, the kings of the Amorites, and to their land, when he destroyed them. And the Lord will give them over to you . . . (Deut 31:3-5a).

A similar speech pattern is put upon the lips of Caleb when he lays claim to the land promised him because of his loyalty:

---

[140]Regarding this genre, see Norbert Lohfink, "Die deuteronomistische Darstellung des Übergangs der Führung Israels von Moses auf Josue," *Scholastik* 37 (1962) 32-44; and Dennis J. McCarthy, "An Installation Genre?" *JBL* 90 (1971) 31-41.

[141]Cf. Num 27:17 and 21, the 'P' account of the installation of Joshua. The 'P' writer relied upon the same tradition to express one important charge of Moses and Joshua, their leadership in battle; and this specifically at that point marking the transition from the one to the other.

> I am this day eighty-five years old. I am still as strong to this
> day as I was in the day that Moses sent me;[142] my strength
> now is as my strength was then, for war, and for going and
> coming (ולצאת ולבוא) (Josh 14:10b-11).

That the meaning of צאת ובא is leadership in battle is stated with
unquestionable clarity in this text.

The situation being presented differs from that of Moses, however.
Moses was not to accompany the people beyond the Jordan and there lead
them in battle, whereas Caleb is laying claim to the land of Hebron which
he asserts he is well able to take from the Anakim who presently dwell
there (Josh 14:12). Caleb states that his strength at present is as it was
forty years previously when Moses sent him ahead to spy upon the land.
Furthermore, his fidelity in keeping the ways of Yahweh assure him
success as he goes forth to drive the inhabitants from the land.[143]

The settings for these texts are each speeches put upon the lips of
Moses and of Caleb by the Dtr. Both Moses and Caleb have been presented in tradition as faithful followers of Yahweh who can expect success from the hand of Yahweh. Moses' claim of inability in warfare
prepared for the inauguration of Joshua's leadership. Caleb's claim to
strength, on the other hand, prepared for his assumption of leadership in
battle that he might lay claim to the land of Hebron for his family.

One specific function charged to each leader in Israel, according to
tradition, was that he should be leader in battle.[144] In this capacity, he
acted on behalf of Yahweh, the presupposition in every case being that
the leader "followed in the way of Yahweh" and therefore was reliant
upon Yahweh to give victory. The figures with whom the expression צאת
ובא has been linked fit the image described here.

---

[142]The accounts of Moses' sending Caleb to spy out the land are
found in Num 13:17b-14:25; Deut 1:19-40, esp. v 36; and Josh 14:6-14.

[143]Deut 1:36 and Josh 14:8, 9.

[144]See 1 Sam 8:19-20. The text reads: "No! but we will have a king
over us, that we also may be like all the nations, and that our king may
govern us and go out (ויצא) before us and fight our battles." This description of kingship has its roots in the tradition of the Judges: ". . . he
judged Israel; he went out to war" (Judg 3:10). The purpose of warfare
was to deliver the nation by saving it from the hand of the enemy. See
Judg 2:16, 18; 3:9, 15; 6:14, 36; 7:7; 8:22; 10:1. Saul, whose kingship was
modelled after the charismatic Judges, was also called to deliver the
nation. See 1 Sam 10:1, 27; 11:13.

The phrase in question, צאת ובא, functions primarily in those texts which mark a transition in military leadership. We have noted the transition from Moses to Joshua in Deuteronomy 31; and the transition from Saul to David in 1 Samuel 18 and 29. In the dream narrative, the statement "I do not know going out or coming in" marks the transition in kingship from David to Solomon. The phrase צאת ובא as we have shown, states that function which is considered most important for the one in the leadership role. He is charged with the authority to lead the people of Yahweh in battle.

Solomon, as the legitimate ruler, assumes that responsibility for the people. However, the power to succeed in battle is not his own; it is Yahweh who is the Lord of Hosts. There is purpose in the juxtaposition of the formulae נער קטן and צאת ובא by the Dtr in the dream narrative. In the first expression, the king declares that he is dependent upon Yahweh with the submission of a child. Immediately afterward, in a similarly formulated statement, he affirms that as leader in battle he is dependent.[145] He is asserting that it is Yahweh who gives victory to the king.[146] The juxtaposition of these formulae draws a portrait of the king acknowledging his inability to accomplish victory by his own forces and skill; and he is confessing his absolute dependence upon the God who alone will give victory and success.

Besides being leader in battle and there exercising authority in place of the Lord of Hosts, the king acts for Yahweh in another way. The king is said to be "in the midst of" (בתוך) Yahweh's people (1 Kgs 3:8a).

To be בתוך (in the midst of) indicates a form of presence upon which a relationship is established. This is most evident from the frequent use of "in the midst of" to express the divine presence.

A great comfort to Israel was the assurance that Yahweh "will go forth in the midst of Israel."[147] It was upon this knowledge that the intimate relationship between Yahweh and his people was founded. The Dtr likewise placed special emphasis upon the reality of the divine

---

[145]The Dtr intended that these two formulae be read in conjunction with each other. He has clearly indicated this fact by the way he deliberately formulated the statements in parallel poetic lines. See Chap. III, p. 50.

[146]Ps 45:4, 6; 1 Sam 17:37-40, 45-47, 48-50; 1 Sam 18:14, 30; 30:17; 2 Sam 3:1; 7:1.

[147]Exod 11:4; cf. Deut 32:51. The presence of Yahweh with his people is a central tenet stressed particularly in the 'P' redaction: Exod 25:8; 29:45, 46; Lev 26:11, 12; Num 5:3; 16:3; and in Ezek 43:7, 9.

presence for Israel. The Dtr placed the words of assurance in this regard in the form of a prophetic oracle:[148]

> . . . and I will dwell among (בתוך) the children of Israel, and will not forsake my people Israel (1 Kgs 6:13).[149]

and as an affirmation spoken by the people:

> Today we know that the Lord is in the midst of (בתוך) us, . . . (Josh 22:31).[150]

The use of the phrase בתוך to indicate the relationship between Solomon and the people of Yahweh seems to indicate that the king, by his

---

[148]The use of a prophetic speech form interrupting a narrative report is one of the techniques common to the Dtr: 1 Sam 15:10; 2 Sam 7:4; 1 Kgs 12:22; 13:20-21; 16:1, 7; 17:2, 8; 18:1, 31; 19:9; 21:17, 28; 2 Kgs 20:4.

[149]Because of the oratorical style and the peculiar Deuteronomistic themes in the speech 1 Kgs 6:11-13, we attribute this text to the Dtr author. The position of this speech, interrupting the annalistic description of the temple, provides insight into a rhetorical technique of the author. 1 Kings 6-7 contain a continuous and detailed account of the building operations. The divine oracle placed within the annalistic report effectively foreshadows the completion of the temple and Yahweh's taking up residence there. A deuteronomistic text, 1 Kgs 8:1-13, follows upon the annalistic report. There a number of the traditional symbols for the divine presence are brought together: the ark, vv 6-8; the tables of the covenant, v 9; the cloud, the Glory of Yahweh, vv 10-11. Significantly, this section of 1 Kings 8 terminates with the words of Solomon: "I have built thee an exalted house, a place for thee to dwell in for ever" (v 13) as a summation of the context developed in the preceding verses and foreshadowed in 1 Kgs 6:11-13.

[150]Another term frequently used to express the same concept is בקרב. In the earlier traditions, the presence of Yahweh is a matter of particular concern, as we hear in the expression: "Is the Lord among us (בקרבנו) or not?" (Exod 17:7; cf. 33:3, 5; 34:9; Num 11:20; 14:42).

The concern that the Lord may not be present with his people is reflected likewise by the Deuteronomist in Deut 1:42 and 31:17. The term בקרב is used in these instances. The Deuteronomist refers to the divine presence in yet another context. Expressed by the phrase בקרב, the Deuteronomist identifies Yahweh as the God, distinct from other gods, who is among his people: Deut 6:15; 7:21; Josh 3:10; 1 Sam 4:3. Because of the belief that Yahweh was present with Israel, the prophets drew upon the tradition in polemic against false hope, so, Mic 3:11b; or as basis for trust, so, Hos 11:9 and Jer 14:9b.

position of authority and responsibility, functions as a form of presence in place of God for the people. This was the precise role of Solomon according to the Deuteronomist. We have already seen this in the role of Solomon as leader in the wars of Yahweh, and we will consider other official functions in which the king mediates for the people in our investigation of the language used in the remainder of the dream text.

Interestingly, this particular idea is not repeated in the DtrH in regard to any other king. In fact, the phrase is applied to a king's relationship with his kingdom in only one text in Isaiah. The use in Isaiah is enlightening for our study.

The situation behind the oracle in Isaiah is the attempt to remove Ahaz, a Davidide, from the throne in Judah. The oracle spoken to Ahaz describes the attempted usurpation:

> Let us go up against Judah . . .
> and let us conquer it for ourselves, and
> set up the son of Ta'be-el as king in the midst of it (בתוכה)
> (Isa 7:6).

In this context, the phrase בתוך applies to the relationship between king and the kingdom. That relationship is perceived as a great evil which the oracle, in fact, condemns. The evil attacked is undoubtedly the attempt to put upon the throne of Judah one who could not legitimately function as Yahweh's representative for his people because he was not from the family of David.

Looking back to the dream, we understand that the narrative serves the function of making operative for Solomon and for all succeeding descendants of David the promise made to David. Only one from David's family possesses the divinely given right to act authoritatively for the nation composed of Yahweh's people. Solomon, as a legitimate son of David, is presented as being "in the midst of" the people. Because he is a son of David he lawfully reigns over the people and thus represents Yahweh to them by his demeanor and his conduct.

Two models of the king as he functions in society have been presented in the formulae צאת ובא (going out and coming in) and בתוך (in the midst of). Each of these formulae contribute an important facet to the multi-dimensional role of the Israelite king among the people of Yahweh. The complete design for kingship from the perspective of the king's role among the people of Yahweh will emerge when what has been presented here is combined with the aspects of that role that are named in subsequent verses to be discussed in Chapter V.

DEUTERONOMISTIC ELEMENTS

The Dtr explicitates every aspect of kingship; no dimension is taken for granted. Solomon's kingship obtains its legitimacy from the kingship of David. Therefore, Solomon must explicitly be shown to be the legitimate successor to David. The Dtr articulated Solomon's legitimacy in two separate phrases, both of which are crucial in the context that combines the oracle to David in 2 Samuel 7 with the inauguration of Solomon's reign in 1 Kings 3. The link between David and Solomon is made explicit in the expressions:

> a son to sit upon his throne (1 Kgs 3:6d);
> you have made your servant king in place of David (1 Kgs 3:7a).

The first of these formulae: "a son to sit upon his throne" (בֵּן יֹשֵׁב עַל-כִּסְאוֹ)[151] culminates a series of queries about who will succeed David as king. The actual event of Solomon's enthronement comes about in the course of the narrative not abruptly or unexpectedly. The event is promised, then progresses to fulfillment in a sequence of dramatic moments.[152]

Bathsheba provokes from David the promise that Solomon would be the successor to the throne.[153] Three times the promise is repeated:

---

[151]The expression יֹשֵׁב עַל-כִּסֵּא is an expression for "reigning," which could apply to Yahweh: Isa 6:1; 2 Kgs 22:19; as well as to any king who is currently upon the throne: 1 Kgs 16:11; 22:11; 2 Kgs 10:3, 30; 11:19; 13:13; 15:12.

It is used in Jeremiah to designate that king who provokes the judgment of the prophet: Jer 13:13; 17:25; 22:2, 4, 30; 29:16; 33:17; 36:30.

[152]The significance of this phrase in determining that the theme of the Succession Narrative is the question about the successor to David has been proposed by L. Rost ("Thronfolgegeschichte," in *Das Kleine Credo*, 191-244, esp. 194-95, 200, 207, etc.).

Against this, others argue that the succession element is secondary to the story of Absalom's revolt. So, L. Delekat, "Tendenz und Theologie der David-Salomo-Erzählung," in *Das ferne und nahe Wort*, 26-36; and J. W. Flanagan, "Court History or Succession Document? A Study of 2 Samuel 9-10 and 1 Kings 1-2," *JBL* 91 (1972) 172-81.

[153]Such a promise had apparently been announced to Bathsheba by the prophet Nathan at the time of Solomon's birth, or at least the narrative is so structured as to imply this. See 2 Sam 12:24-25.

> Solomon your son shall reign after me, and he shall sit upon
> my throne (1 Kgs 1:13, 17, 30).

At that time, Adonijah an elder son of David had taken the crown by force. In face of Adonijah's act, both Bathsheba and Nathan inquire from David:

> who shall sit on the throne of my lord the king
>   (1 Kgs 1:20, 27).

At one point in the dialogue, Nathan repeats the words of the promise substituting the name of Adonijah for Solomon. Nathan asks:

> have you said, "Adonijah shall reign after me, and he shall sit
> upon my throne (1 Kgs 1:24)?"[154]

David finally expresses his will that Solomon should be crowned as the legitimate heir:

> (Solomon) shall sit upon my throne (1 Kgs 1:35).

When Solomon had been anointed, word was carried to David that

> Solomon sits upon the royal throne (1 Kgs 1:46).

David, in turn, praised God:

> Blessed be the Lord, the God of Israel,
> who has granted one[155]
> to sit on my throne this day . . . (1 Kgs 1:48).

In the transition from the court history of David to the history of Solomon, the way is clearly marked to prepare for this particular son to reign. The central issue that a son sit upon David's throne echoes throughout the verses like a refrain preparing the reader for the event. Even after the ritual of coronation, related in great detail in 1 Kgs 1:32-40, had been enacted, the Deuteronomist does not loose sight of the central concern. As part of the death notice of David, it is again proclaimed with great finality and triumph:

> And Solomon "sat upon the throne" of David his father
>   (1 Kgs 2:12).

---

[154]The language of this question is identical with the statements in 1 Kgs 1:13, 17, 30.
    [155]RSV reads with LXX "one of my offspring." The Hebrew rendering with a participial construction suffices to express the intended meaning.

At this point in the narration, Solomon's dream is placed as the climax culminating the series of movements to this point and acting as the transition to what follows. This criterion alone suggests that 1 Kings 3 is the composition of the Deuteronomist. By the use of the precise phrase, ישב על-כסא, the Deuteronomist picked up a theme from the Succession Narrative and with it announced the fulfillment of that theme in Solomon. The theme continues through the history of Solomon as a thread tying together the components of the narrative.[156]

In the dream text, the point is made that "the son who will sit on the throne" has been given to David. The point is minor but, in fact, a bridge is drawn from the promise made to David in 2 Samuel 7, especially v 12. The Nathan promise is thus balanced with the dream narrative in a pattern of promise and fulfillment. Lines of continuity are drawn to the dream of Solomon from the Davidic promise as well as from the Succession Narrative.

The second expression, "You have made your servant king in place of David my father," reiterates the event of Solomon's enthronement in succession to David. The expression מלך תחת literally means, "reigning in succession to another."

In a number of texts we have pointed out in the transition from David to Solomon, this expression occurs together with the statement ישב על-כסב. The combined formulae make up the promise that is reiterated several times in the discourse between David and both Bathsheba and Nathan:

Solomon your son *shall reign after me,*
and he *shall sit upon my throne.*[157]

In the four times this double expression is repeated, the formula reads ימלך אחרי, the adverbial אחרי substituting for תחת, which is used, however, in David's command to the priest and prophet that Solomon should reign:

. . . and he shall come and *sit upon my throne*
for he shall be king in my stead . . . (ימלך תחתי)
(1 Kgs 1:35).

In any case, the minor variation does not affect the intended meaning.

---

[156] 1 Kgs 2:24; 5:19 (Eng 5:5); 8:20, 25; 10:9.

[157] 1 Kgs 1:13, 17, 30; and with Adonijah substituted for Solomon in 1 Kgs 1:24.

Greater importance must be given to the two different circumstances presented by the two different expressions--"a son to sit upon the
throne," and "reigning in place of." Solomon has assumed the throne and
he legitimately succeeds David. The one circumstance is distinct from
the other. Solomon could have attained the throne as Adonijah tried,
apart from divine will.

Both circumstances are emphasized in the events that lead up to
Solomon's kingship, and both circumstances are included in the dream and
culminate there. In the dream, however, it is not David who legitimates
the reign of Solomon as in the narrative to this point. The verb מלך in
v 7, in the *hifil* form, makes unmistakeably clear that the legitimacy of
Solomon is the work of God: Yahweh has made Solomon king. In this
slight emphasis, we note the hand of the Deuteronomist composing the
dream narrative in continuity with the Davidic promise and to stress his
theological viewpoint concerning the kingship of Solomon.

The dream narrative, to be sure, focuses upon the one event of
Solomon's legitimate kingship. That this is the occasion which the author
intended to present, we can be certain, for precisely at this point in the
dream narrative, we find the temporal expressions so characteristic of the
Deuteronomist-- כירם הזה and ועתה. Each of the expressions ישב
על-כסא (sit upon the throne) and מלך תחת (reign in succession to) is
defined temporally:

a son sits upon the throne "*as it is this day*,"
"*and now*" you have made your servant king (1 Kgs 3:6-7).

The temporal phrase כירם הזה (as it is this day) occurs within the
deuteronomistic work only in speeches on the lips of Moses and Solomon.[158] The use of the expression in different contexts could have
different meanings. The writer does not believe that the expression
always carries the same connotation. To analyze the meanings, however,
would be beyond the scope of this study. Weinfeld states that speakers
employ this term when recalling past events with specific reference to
their own present time. The temporal allusion would be the day of the
speaker.[159] If we consider only the three uses of the expression put upon
the lips of Solomon, it is certain that Solomon makes no reference to the

---

[158]Other temporal expressions occur elsewhere: הירם/עד
הירם/הזה. The speeches of Moses where the phrase is used are: Deut
2:30; 4:20, 38; 6:24; 8:18; 10:15; 29:27 (Eng 28); and of Solomon, 1 Kgs 3:6;
8:24, 61.
[159]*Deuteronomy and the Deuteronomic School*, 175.

past as if that past had become present. The reference is to specific events within Solomon's reign--his enthronement and the temple dedication. Both of these events are high points in the history of Solomon and each is made present in the creation of the narrative. From this we may conclude that the dream narrative was written so as to create the effect that the event of Solomon's enthronement was happening at the time of the writing and of the reading. The temporal expression in the dream narrative makes the event of Solomon's coronation present in an all-encompassing sense. We the readers are made present with Solomon as he speaks; and Solomon is made to appear as if he is speaking at the time of the writing.

The phrase ועתה (and now), on the other hand, occurs in speeches throughout the DtrH. It is a rhetorical device used by the writer to make a transition.[160] The transition could be within orations from a historical survey to a contemporary situation.[161] Or, the transition could be from a presentation of a situation to a present circumstance regarding that situation.[162]

In the dream narrative, the phrase ועתה (and now) marks the transition within the response of Solomon from the recounting of the past, i.e., the relationship between Yahweh and David, to the present reality of Solomon's legitimation on the throne of Yahweh. With this rhetorical device, the deuteronomist has brought our attention from David and focuses it upon Solomon. The Dtr is saying that the remainder of the narrative will be directed to the reign of Solomon.

---

[160]See James Muilenburg, "The Form and Structure of the Covenantal Formulations," *VT* 9 (1959) 347-65. Muilenburg points out the significance of ועתה as a transition in the covenant texts: Exodus 19; Joshua 24 and 1 Samuel 12 (pp. 352-53, 359, 361).

[161]The transition from a historical survey to a contemporary situation through the use of ועתה occurs within significant Deuteronomistic speeches: Deut 10:12; 26:10; Josh 24:14; 1 Sam 12:2, 7, 13; 2 Sam 7:8; 1 Kgs 5:18 (Eng 4); 8:25, 26.

[162]Following ועתה, the present is usually set forth in an instruction, a command, or a question. Examples of these speeches are numerous. To cite only a few: Deut 4:1; 5:22 (Eng 25); Josh 9:23, 25; 22:4; Judg 9:16, 32; 13:4; 1 Sam 13:14; 15:3, 25; 23:20; 25:7, 26, 27; 2 Sam 2:6, 7; 7:25, 28, 29; 12:23, 28; 1 Kgs 1:12, 18; 2:9, 16, 24; 5:20 (Eng 5:6); 12:11.

V

Content of the Dialogue in
Verses 5b and 9-14

In our analysis of vv 6-8, we found that the content is expressed throughout in formulaic language deriving from tradition. We noted that the Dtr had appropriated expressions or motifs from the faith traditions of Israel and from royal and sapiential traditions and had so cast the formulaic language of these traditions to present a design for kingship which emphasizes the king's rulership among the covenant people.

In the present chapter, we will continue in the analysis of the content of the dialogue portion of the narrative. It is our intention to demonstrate that the content is built up from traditional elements, and that these elements have been selected because they contribute to the total picture of a *king under Torah*. In this section we will unfold the Dtr design for kingship in which are integrated (a) the earlier royal ideology, (b) traditions of Yahwism, and (c) the Dtr interest in Torah. Our task will be to demonstrate that these various traditions contribute to the deuteronomistic ideal of kingship.

IDENTITY OF THE DIALOGUE PARTNERS

The structural framework for the dialogue has been discussed above.[1] We demonstrated that two patterns--the interchange between the verbs "ask" and "give" and between the dialogic pronouns "I" and "you" --form the structure that gives internal unity to the narrative.

The first clue to the theological content is given in the use of the divine name *Elohim* in each of the two sections of the dialogue. At the beginning of v 5 and again in v 11, the dialogue is bound together by the

_____

[1]See Chap. III, pp. 43-46.

consistent use of the divine name *Elohim* in the question itself and again in the response to the question. We have argued that the title *Yahweh* was adopted for the hymn section because of the appropriateness of that name to the traditions of election and promise. So also is the name *Elohim* used in its particular context because of the association of this name with the tradition of blessings.[2]

The exchange between the names *Elohim* and *Yahweh* in the dream narrative has too facilely been explained as indication that several sources contributed to the present composition.[3] The writer suggests that the variation in the use of the divine names is for rhetorical effect and can throw light on the purpose of the historian in this particular narrative.[4]

The key to understanding the use of *Elohim* in the context of the dream is not so much in the name itself as it is in the combination of *Elohim* with the verb "give." According to tradition, *Elohim gives* all things for a blessing.[5] In contrast with the gifts of land and progeny which are the content of the promise spoken by *Yahweh*, tradition attributes to *Elohim* all other gifts. Elohim gives "life"--a child in birth,[6] and all things made.[7] When Isaac asks the blessings of the earth for Jacob, he calls upon *Elohim*:

> May *Elohim* give you the dew of heaven,
>   and of the fatness of the earth,
>   and plenty of grain and wine (Gen 27:28).

---

[2] It should be noted that the name *Elohim* is characteristic of biblical writings from the exilic and post-exilic periods. This is true of the 'P' redaction of the Tetrateuch, the Chronicler's history and wisdom literature. The emphasis on the general name for God in the later period may have influenced the fact that the Dtr demonstrates great freedom in fluctuating between the names *Yahweh* and *Elohim*: 2 Samuel 7; 1 Kings 8; and 2 Kings 17.

[3] This is particularly true of Gustav Hölscher, "Das Buch der Könige, seine Quellen und seine Redaktion," 158-213; and *Geschichtsschreibung in Israel*. See above, Chap. I, n. 81.

[4] Another example of a change in the divine name for rhetorical effect is in Gen 3:1-5. In their dialogue, the serpent and the woman speak of *Elohim*, whereas in the surrounding context the divine name is consistently *Yahweh Elohim*.

[5] Genesis 1; 9:3.

[6] Gen 30:6, 18; 48:9; 1:26-30.

[7] Gen 1:1-25; 9:3.

Indeed all material goods were recognized as being given by the hand of
Elohim, as the prayer of Jacob indicates:

> If *Elohim* will be with me . . .
>> and will *give* me bread to eat
>> and clothing to wear . . .
>> and of all *Elohim gives*
> I will give the tenth to you (Gen 28:20-22).

The theme *Elohim gives* is grounded in the tradition of creation. All of
creation, nature itself and material goods, come from *Elohim.* Therefore,
creation is uniquely related to *Elohim* as Creator.[8]

The Dtr effectively employed the traditional formulary "*Elohim
gives*" to establish a second basis for the relationship between the God of
Israel and the king. *Yahweh* is used in association with the traditions of
God's self-revelation in the choice of the Israelite nation and in giving the
promise to indicate a relationship rooted in *covenant.* *Elohim* is used in
association with God's self-revelation as Creator, in the giving of life and
of all blessings to indicate a relationship grounded in *creation.*

Whether the relationship of the king with his God is defined by
covenant or by *creation,*[9] the intention of the Dtr is to emphasize that

---

[8]Claus Westermann argues that the activity of the Creator God is a
steady and continual working for life. His action is that of *blessing.* See
"The Way of Promise through the Old Testament," in *The Old Testament
and Christian Faith* (New York: Harper & Row, 1963) 210ff; *Der Segen in
der Bibel und im Handeln der Kirche* (Munich: Chr. Kaiser, 1968) 40-42;
and "Creation and History in the Old Testament," in *The Gospel and
Human Destiny* (ed. Vilmos Vajta; Minneapolis: Augsburg, 1972) 11-38.
See also Patrick D. Miller, "The Blessing of God," *Int* 29 (1975) 247-51.

[9]Since the Old Testament recounts the story of a particular people
who had experienced God in their history, Old Testament theology has
been a theology primarily of a God who saves and judges. The God who
acts for Israel is the God of *covenant.* There is another view of a God
whose power reaches beyond the confines of Israel to the limits of the
universe. This is the creator God who exists and acts for life in fruitfulness and blessings. This God is known from observance of *creation.*
Though theology tends to stress the covenant god of the Old Testament,
the image of God as Creator is equally pervasive. Some argue that the
biblical tradition does not attempt to integrate the Creator God with the
God of Covenant nor to harmonize the creation event with the covenant
event. See Gerhard von Rad, "The Theological Problem of the Old Testament Doctrine of Creation," in *The Problem of the Hexateuch,* 131-43;
and *Old Testament Theology,* 1. 136-64. It must be recognized, however,

the king is related to God in a subordinate and dependent position. The nature of the king's relationship with God is the point being made by the Dtr in bringing together traditions rooted in *covenant* and *creation*. The Dtr stresses that Solomon sits upon the throne of Israel because the throne was given to him as the sign of Yahweh's fidelity to his promise to David and in fulfillment of the promise made to Abraham; and that Solomon receives all his blessings, both natural and material, not by virtue of his kingship, but from *Elohim*, the Lord of Creation.[10]

That Solomon receives all blessings from God is made explicit in the function of "*Elohim* gives" as a crucial structural element within the narrative. Each of the benefits of the king is contingent upon this statement. The king receives nothing on his own power or on account of his prestige or position. The theological principle being highlighted is that the abilities of the king to administer the kingdom as well as the rewards that come to the king, indeed, all the gifts he possesses are given by God. The king is, therefore, completely dependent upon his God.[11]

In this dialogue section of the dream, the dependence of the king upon the God of Isreal is confirmed through the use of a second divine name, that of *Adonai*. A discussion of this title will prepare us to address

---

that the biblical tradition in its canonical form does integrate creation and covenant. It is the God of Genesis 1 who covenants with Abraham and at Sinai. From another perspective, creation is closely tied to royal ideology (Psalm 72) and this latter early on with covenant (2 Sam 23:5). Since the Dtr relied mightily upon royal ideology for his materials, it is to be supposed that he was influenced by this royal and covenant tradition in making the link between covenant and creation.

[10]W. Zimmerli ("The Place and Limit of the Wisdom," 157) points out the significance of the phrase "Elohim gives" in the book of Ecclesiastes.

[11]This is a marked deviation from the understandings of the king himself being divine in the ancient oriental cultures. See Henri Frankfort (*Kingship and the Gods: A Study of Ancient Near Eastern Religion as the Integration of Society and Nature* [Chicago: University of Chicago, 1948]) for a description of the various ideologies of kingship and the distinctiveness of Israelite royal ideology. Because of the interest in this study, we point out that the Mesopotamian king, unlike other ancient oriental monarchs was tied to his god. He was not independent. On this, see Rene Labat (*Le Caractère religieux de la royauté assyro-babylonienne* [The Schweich Lectures of the British Academy 1945; London: Oxford University, 1948]34, 39-40).

the appropriateness of the king "asking" of God. In the transition the deity is identified as *Adonai*:

> And the request pleased *Adonai*
> because Solomon asked this thing (1 Kgs 3:10).

We are able to understand the significance of the title *Adonai* (Lord) from its repeated use particularly in the Amarna Royal Correspondence.[12] The Pharaoh/king who has placed another upon the throne and bestowed the power of jurisdiction over a given territory is always addressed as "Lord," while the prince/king whose authority is given acknowledges himself to be "servant" or "son."[13] A relationship such as this is based on a suzerainty treaty. The treaty partners are unequal, though both are kings.[14]

The tradition of a relationship between a superior and an inferior party is reflected in the early narrative accounts. In each case, Yahweh is addressed as *Adonai* and the subordinate partner refers to himself as "servant."

Such is the case on the occasion of the divine visitation to Abraham to announce the fulfillment of the promise that a son would be born to Abraham and Sarah.[15] In acknowledgment of his stance before the divine visitor, Abraham addressed the spokesman as "Lord" and referred to himself as "servant":

---

[12] *ANET*, 483-90. All of these letters were exchanged between the Egyptian Pharaoh and the princes of the Syro-Phoenician and Palestinian regions.

[13] See Dennis J. McCarthy, "Notes on the Love of God in Deuteronomy," 144-47; and F. Charles Fensham, "Father and Son Terminology for Treaty and Covenant," in *Near Eastern Studies in Honor of William Foxwell Albright* (ed. Hans Goedicke; Baltimore and London: Johns Hopkins, 1971) 121-35.

[14] For discussions on the suzerainty treaty and the Old Testament, see G. E. Mendenhall, "Covenant Forms in Israelite Tradition," *BA* 17 (1954) 50-76; now appearing in *BAR* 3 (1970) 25-53; Edward F. Campbell, "Moses and the Foundations of Israel," *Int* 29 (1975) 141-54; and "Sovereign God," *McCQ* 20 (1967) 176-81; and F. M. Cross, "The Ideologies of Kingship in the Era of the Empire: Conditional Covenant and Eternal Decree," in *Canaanite Myth and Hebrew Epic,* 268-71. For a view that is contrary to the work of the above-named scholars, see D. J. McCarthy, *Treaty and Covenant.*

[15] Gen 18:16ff. Cf. Judg 13:8, the announcement of the birth of the son Samson to Manoah and his wife. Manoah addresses God using the title *Adonai.*

> *Adonai,* if I have found favor in your sight,
> do not pass by your *servant* (Gen 18:3).[16]

The Yahwist narrator presents Abraham as one who is related to the God of promise in a covenant relationship in the position of the subordinate party. Abraham acknowledges his subordination and allegiance by the address *Adonai,* a title borrowed from the world of kings.

Another example in which the relationship between the two parties in dialogue is clearly outlined as being one of inequality is to be found in the case of Yahweh and Moses. Moses was visited by God with the invitation to be spokesman for Yahweh as a type of prophet.[17] This particular example is instructive in that Moses is being designated for a position of authority by his Sovereign Lord, thus providing another model in the biblical tradition analogous to that of the king enthroned by another king. Moses objects to the call as one who perceives the relationship between himself and the God of the Fathers as a relationship of "servant" and "Lord":

> Ah, *Adonai,* I am not eloquent, either heretofore or since you
> have spoken to your *servant*; but I am slow of speech and of
> tongue (Exod 4:10).[18]

By using the reference *Adonai* for God and "servant" for himself, Moses is acknowledging his dependence and submission to the God by whom the call to service is given. Moses acknowledges by his response and by the address *Adonai* that his relationship is one of covenant.

These examples of Abraham and Moses indicate that the titles "Lord" and "servant" had been adopted from the royal milieu of the ancient orient into the Israelite tradition as early as the Yahwist narrative. Both Abraham and Moses are presented as recognizing that they are in covenant in a relationship between unequals. It is, nonetheless, covenant, making dialogue possible.[19] The Dtr followed an already established

---

[16]On the difficulty of the three visitors being addressed in the singular, see Gerhard von Rad, *Genesis: A Commentary* (rev. ed.; Philadelphia: Westminster, 1972) 204-6.

[17]Exodus 3-4. See the discussions by Norman C. Habel, "The Call Narratives," 297-323; and W. Richter, *Die sogenannten vorprophetischen Berufungsberichte* (FRLANT 101; Göttingen: Vandenhoeck & Ruprecht, 1970) 57-133.

[18]It is significant that the address *Adonai* is used in the calls of both Gideon (Judg 6:13, 15); and Isaiah (Isa 6:1, 8, 11).

[19]Dialogue between a king and his patron-god is unknown in royal ideologies of the Ancient Near East. It is a significant feature of Israel's

Israelite tradition in his presentation of Solomon in dialogue with Yahweh.[20]

On account of the dream narrative being dialogue, the Dtr introduced the title *Adonai* in the transition statement, as if Solomon had
addressed God by this title.   Besides being the address for Yahweh as
covenant partner in the Israelite tradition, the title introduces into the
narrative an intimation that the relationship between Yahweh and Solomon may be severed.   The relationship founded on covenant promise or on
creation depends solely on the graciousness of God and therefore derives
its permanence from the fidelity of God.   The relationship founded on
suzerainty is different, for that relationship depends upon the loyalty of
the inferior partner.   Thus the title *Adonai* introduces into the narrative
an alternative understanding of the relationship between Solomon and
God.   It hints of a new theological focus in royal theology, one that is
achieved by the Dtr precisely by such juxtaposition of traditions.

It should be noted that when Solomon addresses Yahweh, the God
of Promise, the king refers to himself as "servant" (1 Kgs 3:7, 8); so also,
when the king asks from *Elohim,* the God of Creation (1 Kgs 3:9). This is
another example of the Dtr's technique of "opposition of traditions" for
the sake of theological impact.   The meaning intended by the Dtr is
clear: the king is assured of the graciousness of God, but at the same
time acknowledges that a continuing relationship depends on his own
loyalty before God.   Thus, the king is presented as one who "asks"; he asks
as creature calling upon the Source of Blessings; he asks as the chosen
who can depend upon the fidelity of the God of Promise; and he asks as
servant before his Lord to whom he must demonstrate loyalty.

The presentation of the king as one who "asks" of God is not the contribution of the Dtr, but a reflection of royal ideology.[21]   That ideology is

---

tradition, however.   Two texts to be noted in particular are: Gen 18:22-
33, the account of Abraham's appeal for the people of Sodom and Gomor-
rah; and Exod 33:12ff, Moses' plea to know the presence of Yahweh with
his people.

[20] Other examples of dialogue are found in Josh 7:8-16; Judg 6:13-18;
and 13:8ff; also Isa 6:1-11.   It should be noted that, in every instance,
Yahweh is addressed as *Adonai.*

[21] In the royal tradition of the Mesopotamian cultures, a king owed
his kingship to a particular patron-god.   The continuation of the king upon
the throne depended upon the king's service to that god.   The relationship
of the king with his patron-god is illustrated in the intercession for the

apparent especially in the royal psalms that derive from the royal cultus of the early monarchy.[22]

In Psalm 2, a psalm used for a ritual of enthronement,[23] an oracle invites the king to "ask":

> Ask of me, and I will give the nations for your inheritance (Ps 2:8).[24]

The language of the oracle in Psalm 2, שְׁאַל מִמֶּנִּי וְאֶתְּנָה (ask of me, and I will give), is exactly that used by the Dtr to express the oracle that introduces the dialogue in the dream:

> Ask, what shall I give you שְׁאַל מָה אֶתֶּן־לָךְ (1 Kgs 3:5b)?[25]

---

help of the god before battle and the ardent praise offered in time of victory. See H. Frankfort, *Kingship and the Gods,* 262-74.

[22]On the royal psalms, see: Keith R. Crim, *The Royal Psalms* (Virginia: John Knox, 1962); Hans-Joachim Kraus, *Worship in Israel: A Cultic History of the Old Testament* (trans. Geoffrey Buswell; Virginia: John Knox, 1965) Chap. 5; A. R. Johnson, *Sacral Kingship in Ancient Israel* (2nd ed.; Cardiff: University of Wales, 1967); and J. H. Eaton, *Kingship and the Psalms* (SBT 2nd series 32; London: SCM, 1976).

[23]So, Keith Crim, *Royal Psalms,* 71-75; Artur Weiser, *The Psalms: A Commentary* (Philadelphia: Westminster, 1962) 109; S. Mowinckel, *The Psalms in Israel's Worship* (Nashville: Abingdon, 1962) 1. 47; H.-J. Kraus, *Psalmen I* (Neukirchen-Vluyn: Neukirchener, 1966) 11-22; and W. H. Brownlee, "Psalms 1-2 as a Coronation Liturgy," *Bib* 52 (1971) 321-36.

[24]The words "ask" and "give" occur frequently in the royal psalms. See Pss 20:4, 6; 21:3, 5; 18:36, 41, 48. In Ps 18:4 and 7, the verbs "call" (קרא) and "cry" (שׁוע) convey the idea of asking.

According to Westermann, שׁאל in cultic usage is connected with the priest's administration of oracles: "Die Begriffe für Fragen und Suchen im Alten Testament," *KD* (1960) 2-30.

[25]With this text and that in Ps 2:8, we compare a text from the Ugaritic epic of Anat and Aqhat. The goddess Anat promises life to Aqhat in exchange for his bow:
Ask life, O young man Aqhat,
ask life and I will give it to thee
everlasting life and I will send it to thee.
(Quoted from Charles H. Gordon, *Ugaritic Manual* [1955] 183, in F. Charles Fensham, "Ps 21--A Covenant Song?" *ZAW* 77 [1965] 201).
With this Ugaritic text, in turn, we compare Ps 21:5:
He asked life of you
You gave it to him
length of days forever and ever.

The Dtr borrowed the oracle from the royal tradition and adopted it so that the object of the request could be expressed by Solomon. This question, as each element that was taken from tradition for the composition of the dream, belongs to the traditional language of Israel.

The formulaic nature of the question becomes apparent when we consider another use by the Dtr. It is found within the prophetic narrative at the transition from Elijah to Elisha (2 Kings 2). On the day that Elijah will be taken from the earth, he invites Elisha to make a last request with the words: "Ask, what I shall do for you . . ." (שאל מה אעשה-לך).[26] Here, the formula is not spoken by God; it has been taken from its setting and used in a new context by the Dtr who delights in the creative use of formulaic language.

In the dream narrative, the formulary placed on the lips of God and inviting the king to demonstrate his dependence, reflects a royal ideology, probably that of the king in relation to this patron-god.[27] This is one part of the image of the king in his stance with God. The picture of the king "asking" will be more complete when it has been enhanced by a tradition of Moses. The clue to that Mosaic tradition is presented in the question by Solomon:

who is able to govern your people, this burden מי יוכל
לשפט את-עמך הכבד הזה (1 Kgs 3:9d)?

In context, this question follows from Solomon's request that God give him ability to govern (v 9bc). The question mentions the particular people to be governed who, earlier in the narrative, had been described as "a chosen people," "a numerous people," and a people "not able to be counted" (v 8). These descriptions or definitions of the people seem to be reflected in the question posed by Solomon in the words "your people" and "this burden." The key to the Dtr's purpose in the use of the question, however, is not in the multitude of the people alone, nor in the task "to govern" alone. The

---

[26]2 Kgs 2:9. Except for the substitution of the verb עשה for נתן, the formulation is exact. The exchange between these verbs is a common phenomenon, as the glaring example in the dream itself illustrates:

behold, I now *do* . . .

behold, I *give* . . . (v 12ab).

[27]The task of the king was to attend to the service and reverence for the patron-god in the kingdom belonging to that god. Illustrative of this dimension of royal ideology are the texts of Hittite prayers of the king to his patron-god. See *ANET*, 396-401; O. R. Gurney, *The Hittites* (Baltimore: Penguin, 1954) 139-44.

clue to the interpretation of the question is found in the expression "this burden" (הכבד הזה), which as the Dtr uses the phrase seems incomplete.[28] But intentionally, I believe, the phrase is incomplete, since it was meant to identify two Mosaic traditions: one concerning the task לשפט, and the other, concerning the people עמך.

The Dtr borrowed from the tradition of Moses as שפט (judge) as this is reported in Exodus 18. According to that tradition, Moses apparently carried out this task alone. It was at the suggestion of his father-in-law that Moses appointed others to assist him in the execution of that charge. In words significant for our study, the father-in-law says:

> You and this people with you will surely wear yourselves out,
> for the thing is a burden (כבד) to you; you are not able
> (לא-תוכל) to perform it alone (Exod 18:18).[29]

In this tradition, it is the charge of judging (שפט)[30] which is a burden (כבד) to Moses and which he is not able (לא-יוכל) to perform alone. It would seem that the Dtr meant to reflect exactly this tradition. He has expressed the question precisely in the language given here.

There is, however, a second Mosaic tradition about the distribution of the spirit which is upon Moses to seventy elders who will support Moses in his charge.[31] In this narrative account in Numbers 11, the task of Moses is not specifically named. It can be concluded from the content that the task is a kind of administration that places responsibility upon Moses for the well-being of the people.

The people are presented complaining because they are given only manna for food, whereas they had formerly enjoyed meat in the land of Egypt (Num 11:1-9). In face of this discontent among the people, Moses complains before Yahweh about the people given to his charge and their continual troublesomeness. Moses laments that he could never provide meat sufficient for the great number of people. Moses addresses Yahweh with the words:

---

[28]RSV does not translate this expression but includes the idea by saying: "Who is able to govern this thy great people?"

[29]Cf. v 22.

[30]The verb שפט is used in the narrative in vv 22 and 26.

[31]Num 11:16ff. See Brevard S. Childs (*The Book of Exodus. A Critical Theological Commentary* [Philadelphia: Westminster, 1974] 321-26) for a discussion of the relationship between Numbers 11 and Exodus 18. Both Numbers 11 and Exodus 18 are reflected by the Dtr in Deut 1:9-18. We will discuss this latter text in another context. See below, pp. 143-45.

I am not able (לא־אוכל) to bear all this people alone, for
they are a burden (כבד) for me (Num 11:14).[32]

In this tradition, the כבד is the people so understood on account of their
numerousness as well as because of their discontent.

These Mosaic traditions address two different situations. In both,
however, the same language is used to present the problem. The Dtr
adopted the language from these traditions for the statement of the
question put upon the lips of Solomon. It is indeed traditional language.

Having looked at the two Mosaic traditions, we are certain that the
Dtr intended to be ambiguous in his attribution of "this burden," thereby
retaining the synthesis of the two traditions. There are two explanations,
of which we are aware, to account for the intentional ambiguity. On one
side, the Dtr wished to define the task of the king not exclusively as that
of judge or solely as administrator, but rather as a combination of both.
On the other, the Dtr desired that the king be perceived as one who
continues in the line of Moses as leader for the chosen people.

In this discussion about the king who "asks" we have noted that the
image of the king in this stance is a summary of several traditions, all of
which contribute to the identity of the king in Israel. The Dtr borrowed
from the royal theology of the Judean court which, in turn, reflects the
ideology of kings who are dependent upon a patron-god for the continuation of kingship. The Dtr integrated the tradition, presented in the
Yahwist narrative, of Abraham and Moses who address Yahweh as *Adonai*
thereby indicating relationship based on the Lordship of Yahweh and the
servanthood of the king with the consonant possibility of the termination
of the relationship. Finally, the Dtr drew upon the tradition of Moses as
judge and administrator with the concern for the people of God conveyed
in that tradition.

The king, being identified by the Dtr, is described in language from
several images. The Dtr *novum* of kingship emerges out of the combination of this diversity of streams of tradition.

We have been looking at the image of the dialogue partners as this
is presented by the Dtr. God is identified essentially as the one who gives
every gift, even those which oriental potentates are thought to obtain by
divine right. *Elohim* thus is identified as the Lord of Creation, the Creator whose graciousness is dependable. The king is cast as heir to royal
ideologies and leader in the line of Moses. From royal tradition, we

---

[32]Cf. vv 11 and 17. In these verses the message is the same, though
the choice of language differs.

obtain the picture of the king who must acquit himself to the whim of his patron-god and the king who is bound by treaty to a sovereign king. The Mosaic tradition offers an image of the leader as judge and administrator.

In the next section of our discussion, we will focus upon the gifts for which the king asks and those which *Elohim* gives. We will locate the gifts in tradition and consider how these requests informed by tradition contribute to the deuteronomistic picture of kingship.

THE GIFTS REQUESTED AND THE GIFTS GIVEN

Because of the internal structure of the narrative, it is possible for us to outline the content of the request as it is formulated by the Dtr.

Solomon asks for "an attentive heart" (לב שמע) that he might govern (לשפט) and that he might understand right from wrong (להבין טוב לרע).[33] Solomon's request is then restated by God: ". . . you asked understanding" (הבין) "to discern justice" (לשמע משפט).[34] Finally, God answers by saying that he is giving Solomon "a wise and intelligent heart" (לב חכם ונבון).[35]

If the Dtr is consistent in his methodology, and we suspect that he is, each of these expressions is adopted from tradition and each contributes to an understanding of the role of the king as this is being defined by the Dtr.

Solomon asks, first of all, for "an attentive heart to govern." This formulation derives its substance from the royal scene in Egypt.[36] There is available to us a very ancient collection, indeed, one of the oldest

---

[33] 1 Kgs 3:9.

[34] 1 Kgs 3:11.

[35] 1 Kgs 3 12.

[36] S. Herrmann (*Die Königsnovelle*, 57a), in his comparative work with the Königsnovelle, argued that there was no evidence in Egypt for the concept of a לב שמע. He asserted that the concept derived from Israel itself. He says: "aus der Mitte israelitischen Wesens kommt und ohne Parallele ist . . ." (It comes from the very center of Israelite being and is without parallel.)

H. Brunner ("Das hörende Herz," *TLZ* 79 [1954] cols. 697-700), offered the corrective by pointing out that the concept is indeed Egyptian with parallels in wisdom instructions and in the books of the dead. Brunner states that the heart of a person is the organ with which he receives the divine commandments, comprehends them indeed, that with which he also receives personal instructions.

collections of wisdom instructions.[37] The collection contains the instructions of a vizier[38] to his son who is being prepared to succeed his father
as a public official in the capacity of vizier. The instructions challenge
him "to hear"; and he learns that the "*heart* brings up its lord as one who
hears or as one who does not hear."[39]

In Egyptian culture, the order of the state and society resides in
the Pharaoh. The word of the Pharaoh is, therefore, directed to the good
of the state and society. It is the law to be heard/obeyed.[40] The instruction makes the point that the heart plays a central role in regard to
whether the official lives in accord with the divine order in the society or
not. The heart determines whether the official heeds the word of the
Pharaoh or not.[41]

Surely the Dtr appropriated this royal tradition of Egypt that he
might include the image of the king in a stance of attention to the Torah,
the word of Israel's King for the order of the covenant community.

---

[37] These are the instructions of Ptah-hotep, vizier of King Izezi,
from the 3rd millennium. The teachings, addressed to his son and designated successor, provide guidelines regarding the actions and attitudes for
a successful official of state. See the content of the instructions in
William McKane (*Proverbs: A New Approach* [OTL; Philadelphia: Westminster, 1970] 51-57; and the translation of the text in *ANET*, 412-14.

[38] The role of the Vizier will be discussed in an Excursus. See pp.
146-52.

[39] *ANET*, 414ab. Because of the charm of the instruction which is
expressed out of a play upon the word "hear," we quote the instruction in
full: "To hear is of advantage for a son who hearkens. If hearing enters
into a hearkener, the hearkener becomes a hearer. . . . To hear is better
than anything that is, (and thus) comes the goodly love (of a man). . . . It
is the heart which brings up its lord as one who hears or as one who does
not hear. The life, prosperity, and health of a man is his heart. . . ."

[40] In Egyptian thought, this order is a static reality residing in nature
and in society and embodied in the Pharaoh. It is an order established
from the day of creation. To insure the continuation of this divine order,
every official was trained so that, as a result of his instruction, he will
participate in this order by acting in harmony with it. See the discussion
on Maat in McKane (*Proverbs, 57-65*), and H. Frankfort (*Ancient Egyptian
Religion. An Interpretation* [New York: Columbia University, 1948] 43-
44).

[41] The heart has sometimes been considered a form of conscience.
See the discussion and the bibliography suggested by Manfred Görg (*Gott-
König-Reden in Israel und Agypten* [BWANT 105; Stuttgart: W.
Kohlhammer, 1975] 85-86).

Implied in the request for לב שמע (an attentive heart) is the desire to obey the God-given directions for life.

Because we have located the tradition in an ancient Near Eastern royal ideology, we must not think that לב שמע is foreign to the Israelite tradition. Israel's own wisdom instructions contain exhortations about the role of the *heart* and *hearing* for grasping and responding to the words of authority.[42] The congruence of these organs is apparent in the parallel structure of the instructions:

> Incline your *ear*, and *hear* the words of the wise
> and apply your mind (לב) to my knowledge (Prov 22:17).

> Apply your mind (לב) to instruction
> and your *ear* to words of knowledge (Prov 23:12).

> *Hear*, my son, and be wise
> and direct your mind (לב) in the way (Prov 23:19; cf. 5:2,
>   12-13).

In these proverbial sayings, we come closest to the meaning of the expression לב שמע as it was spoken by Solomon. The concept belongs to Israel's own wisdom tradition. It is a quality that enables a person to both hear and accept the words of another. Appropriately, the Dtr put the request for this quality upon the lips of Solomon that the king may be understood to be one who has the capacity and the desire to live in accord with Torah.

Because Solomon is king, his accord with Torah has ramifications beyond himself for the good of the entire kingdom. He, therefore, requests this quality that he might effectively function as king. He asks for the "attentive heart" for the specific task of "governing" (לשפט).

The naming of the task reflects the same Egyptian ideology; for, the function of the vizier in society was specifically that of a governor, whether in the capacity of a judge or an administrator, but a rulership through which the vizier acted to preserve justice in society. There are ancient texts that give some indication of the role of this official. One vizier declares in his autobiography:

---

[42]In the biblical writings, "heart" is the center of all human capacity. See R. C. Dentan, "Heart" in *IDB*, 1. 549-50; A. R. Johnson, *The Vitality of the Individual in the Thought of Ancient Israel* (Cardiff: University of Wales, 1964) 75-87; and H. W. Wolff, *Anthropologie des Alten Testaments* (Munich: Chr. Kaiser, 1973) 68-95.

> I raised justice to the height of heaven. . . .
> When I judged the petitioner, I was not partial.
> I did not turn my brow for the sake of reward. . . .
> I rescued the timid from the violent. . . .[43]

An installation text specifies the duty of the vizier:

> Pass over no petitioner without hearing his case. . . .
> Show anger to no man wrongfully and be angry only at that
> which deserves anger. . . . The distinction of a prince is that
> he does justice. . . . What one expects of the conduct of the
> vizier is the performance of justice.[44]

The vizier, the Pharaoh's deputy and chief justice, is instructed explicitly
to receive any petitioner; the emphasis is upon the duty to be just in the
carrying out of his leadership.

The designation of the king as שפט [45] is consonant with the descriptions of the king's role in biblical tradition as well. When Solomon

---

[43]Taken from the autobiography of Rekh-mi-re, vizier during the
reign of Thut-mose III: *ANET*, 213a.

[44]Translation by Keith C. Seele, in Georg Steindorff and K. C.
Seele, *When Egypt Ruled the East* (Chicago: University of Chicago, 1942)
Cf. *ANET*, 213b.

[45]In western semitic dialects, the terms שפט/דין and שפט/מלך
are used in parallelism. The function of judging is thus understood to have
been associated with kingship. See the Ugaritic parallels of Prince Yamm
and Judge Nahar in *ANET*, 129-31; and the designation of Baal as both
"king" and "judge" in G. R. Driver, *Canaanite Myths and Legends* (Edinburgh: T. & T. Clark, 1956) 90-91, l.32. See F. C. Fensham, "The Judges
and Ancient Israelite Jurisprudence," *Die Ou Testamentiese Werkgemeenskap in Suid-Afrika* (Papers read at the 2nd Meeting held at Potchefstroom 2-5 February, 1959) 17, 20; and T. Ishida, "The Leaders of the
Tribal Leagues 'Israel' in the Pre-monarchic Period," *RB* 80 (1973) 517-20,
for a consideration of extra-biblical literature.

Some argue that originally the role of the "judge" was simply to lead
and that the function of judicial leader was a later development: so, H.
W. Hertzberg, "Die Entwicklung des Begriffes משפט AT," *ZAW* 40 (1922)
256-61; W. Richter, "Zu den 'Richtern Israels'," *ZAW* 77 (1965) 40-72; and
George Mendenhall, " 'Vengeance' of Yahweh," in *The Tenth Generation*
(Baltimore: Johns Hopkins, 1973) 84.

Others contend that primarily "to judge" meant the administration
of justice: so, A. van Selms, "The Title 'Judge'," in *Die Ou Testamentiese
Werkgemeenskap in Suid-Afrika*, 48; and Ludwig Köhler, "Justice in the
Gate," in *Hebrew Man* (London: SCM, 1956) 149-75.

requests the "attentive heart" for the task of "governing," he is naming the duty of the king as it was understood in practice. To illustrate: Micah calls the king "the ruler (שפט) of Israel" (Mic 4:14). Elsewhere the designations מלך and שפט are used in parallel structure;[46] as are the titles "prince" and "judge."[47]

The obvious congruity between מלך and שפט is reflected in the deuteronomistic understanding of kingship. Samuel is asked to appoint a king (מלך) to judge (לשפט).[48] When Jotham, the son of Azariah, assumed leadership in place of his leprous father, the Dtr reports that he "was over the household,[49] governing (שפט) the people."[50]

"To govern" (לשפט) derives from the tradition of kingship as it was known in Israel. One specification of the task לשפט is made by the Dtr at 1 Kgs 3:9c in the elaboration of that task with the words "to understand (the difference) between good and evil" (להבין בין טוב לרע).

The formulation of this new statement belongs to the store of traditional language. We illustrate the formulaic nature of the phrase בין טוב לרע by reference to two uses in biblical tradition where it has no particular attribution but simply connotes decision or valuation.

The first is found in the scene of Barzillai, a wise man, who had learned from long years of experience what choices were best for life. This wise man describes his approaching death with a series of questions, one of which concerns his ability to continue to make the right choices: "can I discern what is pleasant and what is not (האדע בין-טוב לרע)?"[51]

---

[46]So, Hos 7:7; 13:10; cf. Ps 2:10; Prov 8:15-16.

[47]So, Amos 2:3; Mic 7:3; Zeph 3:3; cf. Exod 2:14. In a number of instances, the three titles--king, judge, and prince--are treated as equivalents. See Hos 13:10; Ps 148:11; Prov 8:15-16.

[48]1 Sam 8:5b and 6.

[49]The title "over the household" is noteworthy since it is one of the titles that appears in the lists of officials in the court: so, 1 Kgs 4:6; 16:9; 18:3; 2 Kgs 10:5; 18:18, 37; 19:2. This office is described as being comparable to that of the vizier by Joachim Begrich, "Söfēr und Mazkīr; ein Beitrag zur inneren Geschichte des davidisch-salomonischen Grossreiches und des Königreiches Juda," ZAW 58 (1940-41) 26-27; and, Roland de Vaux, "Titres et Fonctionnaires Égyptiens a la Cour de David et de Solomon," RB 48 (1939) 402. Significant is the use of the title in Isa 22:15 and Gen 41:40, two texts the context of which pattern the installation rite as we know it from the Egyptian texts of the vizier's installation.

[50]2 Kgs 15:5b.

[51]2 Sam 19:36. R. Gordis treats this text in his discussion of the

A second text comes from the priestly tradition. This text reflects the priest's function to decide what is suitable for the service in the sanctuary, be it the people who will participate or the animals to be used in the sacrificial offerings. A levitical law states that the tithe which belongs to the Lord is not to be valuated: "A man shall not inquire whether it is good or bad ... (לא-יבקר בין-טוב לרע)."[52]

The technical phrase בין-טוב לרע indicates decision-making, i.e. discerning what is good/right from what is evil/not right. It is formulaic and applicable in different circumstances, whenever the situation is one of decision, be it choices of the wise man, the decisions of the priest, or the judgments of the leader. It has been appropriated to the description of the king's role specifically to indicate the responsibility of the king for making choices on the basis of Torah. Especially in the practice of judging cases, the king is charged to decide whether the situation is in accord with Torah or whether it violates Torah. He must decide בין-טוב לרע.

The biblical tradition provides ample evidence that one specification of the king's leadership was executed in the giving of justice to all who "had a suit (ריב)" and came "before the king for judgment."[53]

There is the example of David pronouncing judgment and sentence in a case of theft.[54] The case is related within the history of David as an allegory for David's own actions, but is significant as an illustration that the king acted as judge in accord with the customary law of the land.[55] The case of the woman of Tekoa is recorded in the Succession Narrative likewise for the purpose of calling attention to David's own actions. In its own right, however, this narrative presents a woman who comes to appeal

---

phrase "knowledge of good and evil." See Robert Gordis, "Knowledge of Good and Evil in the Old Testament and the Dead Sea Scrolls," in *Poets, Prophets, and Sages: Essays in Biblical Interpretation* (Bloomington: Indiana University, 1971) 198-216. His argument is that "knowing good and evil" means "sexual knowledge and experience" (204). It should be noted, however, that the text does not read ידע טוב ורע, a technical phrase in its own right, but בין-טוב לרע "good from evil" or "between good and evil" as the texts in our discussion indicate.

[52]Lev 27:33; cf. 27:10, 12, 14.
[53]2 Sam 15: 2, 6.
[54]2 Sam 12:5-6.
[55]The situation corresponds with that addressed in Exod 21:37; 22:2-3 (Eng 22:1, 3-4).

to the king in the situation of a family blood feud.[56] The case had apparently been decided in a familial decision (v 7), and is now being appealed
to the king.[57] Elsewhere in the historical books, there is the difficult
case of the two women which was brought before Solomon for a decision;[58] and that of the woman separated from her land during a period of
famine, who, upon her return, "went forth to appeal to the king for her
house and her land."[59]

The king's responsibility, as this is witnessed particularly in the
descriptions of the kings handling cases, must be informed by Torah. His
is the charge to decide for or against a party in the light of Torah. For
the Dtr, as well as in the tradition borrowed by the Dtr, kingship in Israel
obtains its meaning only in the light of Yahweh's covenant with his people
and the directives for keeping that covenant.

A further refinement to kingship is introduced by the Dtr in the
restatement of Solomon's request spoken by God: "you asked for yourself
understanding to discern justice" (הבין לשמע משפט).[60] This expression
derives from Israel's own tradition especially as the tradition is reflected
in the wisdom instructions.

The term "understanding" in wisdom is applied to an individual who
is able to be instructed and counseled[61] and to one who is open to rebuke
and correction.[62] The appellation accordingly suits the king being defined
as one who desires to heed the God-given directions for the keeping of
covenant.

According to the Dtr articulation, however, the "understanding" is
directed to a specific end--"to discern justice" (לשמע משפט). The practice of justice and one's loyalty to covenant are an issue in royal theology.[63] We quote two proverbs that address this issue:

---

[56]2 Sam 14:4-11.

[57]The sentence issued for this crime is in accord with the customary
law code: see Exod 21:12. However, the circumstance of the last male in
the family facing death warranted appeal to the highest court which was
the king. This was one of those situations "too difficult" to be handled in
the local court: see Deut 17:8; Exod 18:22.

[58]1 Kgs 3:16-28.

[59]2 Kgs 8:3. For a statement about the interface of King-Land-
Torah, see W. A. Brueggemann, *The Land* (Overtures to Biblical Theology;
Philadelphia: Fortress, 1977) 71-106.

[60]1 Kgs 3:11c.

[61]Ps 32:9; Prov 1:2, 6; 8:8-9.

[62]Prov 17:10; 19:25.

[63]See H. A. Kenik, "Code of Conduct for a King."

Evil men do not understand justice (לא-יבינו משפט)
but those who seek the Lord understand it completely
(Prov 28:5; cf. Job 32:9).

A righteous man knows the rights of the poor;
a wicked man does not understand (לא-יבין) such knowledge
(Prov 29:7).[64]

The one who "understands justice" is "righteous"[65] and "seeks the Lord,"[66] both designations implying covenant. Conversely, being in covenant means "understanding justice" and "knowing rights of the poor."

The formulation הבין לשמע משפט provides one more refinement of kingship that was known in Israel's tradition. It locates a duty of kingship in the leadership tasks that look to the rights of individuals in the covenant community. Not only as judge, but also in the administration which attends to societal abuse and provides for needs of individuals, the king's actions preserve the order and harmony in society when they correspond with the God-given words for life--the Torah.

The importance of "doing justice" as a rubric for kingship is apparent in the Dtr's own ascriptions. Transitions into the reigns of both David and Solomon are introduced similarly. First, there is a summary statement about kingship, then an enumeration of the court officials, and finally the historical report itself. Introductory to the succession narrative of David, the Dtr reports:

---

[64]Both Proverbs 28 and 29 come from what has been called the legal collection by Udo Skladny, *Die ältesten Spruchsammlungen in Israel* (Göttingen: Vandenhoeck & Ruprecht, 1962) 66-67. Skladny points out that this collection has a correspondence with the instructions for princes, the *Regentspiegel*, found in the texts 2 Sam 23:1-7; 1 Kgs 3:4-15, and Psalm 101. While Skladny does not elaborate upon the nature of that correspondence, we acknowledge his insight which touches upon the present investigation of 1 Kgs 3:4-15.

[65]"Righteousness" is a key term for expressing the notion of relationship especially as this relational bond exists between God and man in covenant. See G. von Rad, " 'Righteousness' and 'Life' in the Cultic Language of the Psalms," in *The Problem of the Hexateuch*, 243-66.

[66]This formulary has a cultic usage for inquiring of the deity through a prophet (1 Kgs 22:5; 2 Kgs 3:11; 8:8; 22:13). The covenant partner turns to Yahweh in some distress. So, C. Westermann, "Die Begriffe," 20.

> So David *reigned* over all Israel;
> and David *administered justice* and equity
>   to all his people (2 Sam 8:15).

This is phrased in the Dtr's formulation: David rules (ימלך) and he prac-
tices justice (עשה משפט). The second text to which we refer introduces
the history of Solomon:

> And all Israel heard of the judgment which the king had
> rendered, . . . they perceived that the wisdom of God was in
> him, *to render justice,* King Solomon *was king* over all Israel
> (1 Kgs 3:28-4:1).

Here too, the Dtr says simply: Solomon was king (מלך) and he renders
justice (לעשות משפט).

The Dtr's ideal of kingship incorporates many dimensions. The king
models the vizier whose "attentive heart" enables him to heed the divinely
given directives for life. This stance of the king is crucial, since it provides for the king to be leader (לשפט) in the covenant community. As
leader among the people of God, the king decides cases or makes judgments in the light of Torah; and he administers the kingdom, protecting
the rights of individuals, in the light of Torah. In summary, the king, as
the Dtr defines his role, is charged with keeping the kingdom as the
covenant community of Yahweh.

The response to Solomon is spoken by God with the assertion:

> I give you *a wise and intelligent heart*
> לב חכם ונבון (1 Kgs 3:12b).

A quality of kingship is contained in the gift of Elohim; it is one that
closely relates to the quality expressed as לב שמע.

The wisdom instructions in the biblical tradition provide some
information about the meaning of the gift. The terms of the expression
are often used in the instructions in parallelism indicating their congruence:

> The intelligent mind (לב נבון) acquires knowledge
> and the ear of the wise (חכמים) seeks knowledge
>   (Prov 18:15; cf. 1:5).

> Even a fool who keeps silent is considered wise (חכם)
> when he closes his lips,
>   he is deemed intelligent (נבון) (Prov 11:28).

> The wise of heart (חכם-לב)
>   is called a man of discernment (נבון) (Prov 16:21a).

Whoever is wise (חכם)
>let him understand these things;
whoever is discerning (נבון)
>let him know them . . . (Hos 14:9).

Woe to those who are wise (חכמים) in their own eyes,
and shrewd (נבנים) in their own sight (Isa 5:21; cf. Isa 29:14)!

As in the formulary לב שמע, there is a two-pronged emphasis in the juxtaposition of these terms. The חכם is one who hears,[67] and is, therefore, one who is receptive to instructions,[68] to advice,[69] to admonition,[70] and to commandments.[71] נבון, on the other hand, describes one who has knowledge[72] and wisdom,[73] and who translates the acquired skill and learning into speech.[74] How appropos! The king acts most effectively by his choices spoken in judgment or administration.

The content of the formulary לב חכם ונבון then embraces the two-faceted responsibility of the king: the king is obliged to be obedient to the word of the divine ruler, and he is charged to act in accord with that word in an administration of justice.

The significance of the formulary becomes most apparent, however, in the contexts where it occurs as a technical term. The Dtr himself made the expression formulaic within the DtrH; outside the DtrH, the expression is used as a technical term only in the Joseph Story.[75]

The technical expression may well derive from the tradition of the vizier, though we have no evidence to substantiate this suspicion. The formulary is applied to Joseph, to be sure, in the texts which describe his installation as an official in the Egyptian court.[76] The representation of Joseph is such that the position held by him appears to be that of the vizier. The granting of authority to Joseph was on account of his attribution, נבון וחכם.

---

[67]Prov 1:5, 33; 8:6, 33, 34; 12:15; 13:1, 18; 15:31; 19:27; 23:19.
[68]Prov 13:1; 19:20.
[69]Prov 12:15; cf. 26:12.
[70]Prov 15:31.
[71]Prov 10:8.
[72]Prov 18:15; 15:14; 14:6; 19:25; cf. 1:5.
[73]Prov 10:13; 14:33.
[74]Prov 12:18b; 13:14; 14:3; 15:2, 7, 12; 16:21, 23; 17:28; 25:12.
[75]The formulation is not exact in that the terms of the expression are reversed within the Joseph narrative (Gen 41:33, 39). This inversion of terms, however, does not influence the basic meaning nor deny the traditional basis of the expression.
[76]Gen 41:33-45 and 45:8b-13. Cf. Isa 22:15-25.

Because Joseph had shown himself to be נבון וחכם, Pharaoh "set him over the land of Egypt."[77] Joseph was given the position second to that of Pharaoh: "only as regards the throne will I be greater than you" (Gen 41:40); and, Joseph rode the "second chariot" (Gen 41:43). This second position in Egyptian rulership, the greatest of Egyptian officials, belongs to the vizier. The description of the installation (Gen 41:42-43), the titles bestowed on Joseph (Gen 45:8-9), as well as the task assigned to him (Gen 41:25-36)[78] suggest that Joseph is presented as one who held the title of the Vizier when he administered the land of Egypt. His primary task demanded that he distribute provisions in justice. His concern was for the life of all the people--the rich and the poor, the peoples of the land and the sojourners. No one was to have more than his share, but the food was to be used sparingly and distributed equitably, "that many people should be kept alive" (Gen 50:20). Joseph was charged to preserve life in the land in accord with the decree of the Pharaoh; he possessed those attributes, נבון וחכם, that enabled him to act for the people as an obedient servant of Pharaoh, thereby preserving in society the order and life inherent in the will of Pharaoh.

Joseph, so imaged, indicates that the model of the vizier was known and applied during the early monarchy. The viziership is evident in the formulaic attribution נבון וחכם and in the vestiges of the installation of a vizier in the description of Joseph's position.

Because the task of the vizier proved useful and because the vizier's position was second to the Pharaoh/god, it is highly probable that the viziership supplied a useful analogy for speaking about the king in the very early monarchy. Throughout the monarchy, the tension between kingship and Yahweh, the sovereign king, never lessened. The king in the model of the vizier offered one solution to the difficulty. It allowed for the king to be deputy and chief justice for Yahweh. It provided for the king's obedience to the divinely given directives for living in covenant.

A direct reference to the analogy between the king and the vizier[79] is not made, except perhaps in the example of Joseph as vizier.

---

[77] Gen 41:41, 43; cf. vv 33, 45. The one who held the office of vizier was the chief administrator in the realm.

[78] Joseph was given charge of the food supply that all peoples might have adequate provisions during the time of famine.

[79] This analogy had been noted by Begrich in his study on the Israelite officials ("Sōfēr und Mazkīr," 28). Begrich contends that because the highest position, that of the vizier, is lacking among the officials listed in Israel, the position of the vizier was probably understood to be held by the

Even less direct are the numerous directives for the king in his rulership that derive from the tradition of the vizier. It is the Dtr who made the explicit application of חכם ונבון, an attribution of the vizier, to kings for Israel. Once the analogy had been drawn, the formulaic חכם ונבון became applicable for other situations by the Dtr.

One of those uses by the Dtr is located in Deut 1:9-18. This text is highly significant because it ascribes to Moses functions correlative to those charged to kings in the dream narrative. Thus, the two texts--Deut 1:9-18 and 1 Kgs 3:4-15--present the qualifications for leadership in two different eras of Israelite life. This becomes apparent in the structuring of the texts into the DtrH. Deut 1:9-18 introduces the account of Moses' leadership among the people; 1 Kgs 3:4-15 introduces the deuteronomistic interpretation of the king's leadership among the people. Each of these texts is deliberately positioned in the history to lead into the respective reports of Moses and of Kings. At the same time, the texts create a parallelism between the tradition of Moses' leadership and that of the tradition of kings.

We will draw the parallelism between the texts, but first, we comment upon the content of Deut 1:9-18.[80] Moses is presented complaining to the people that he is not able to bear them alone,[81] on account of their weight, their burden, and their strife.[82] The burden of which Moses speaks is the great multitude of people, the fruit of the promise:

> you are this day as the stars of heaven for multitude
> (Deut 1:10-11, esp. v 10b).

---

king. Cf. Tryggve Mettinger, *Solomonic State Officials: A Study of the Civil Government Officials of the Israelite Monarchy* (Lund: CWK Gleerups, 1971).

[80] Deut 1:9-18 is recognized as a composite account of Exod 18:13-27 and Num 11:14-17. Vv 9-12 compare with Numbers 11, and vv 13-17 with Exodus 18.

[81] Deut 1:9; cf. Num 11:14, 17; Exod 18:18b. The challenge as it is presented in the Numbers and Exodus tradition provides the setting for the report about the distribution of authority in Deuteronomy. In Numbers, the gift of the spirit qualifies the seventy elders and officers to perform Moses' function (Num 11:17). In Exodus, Moses chooses men to assist him in the judgment of cases (Exod 18:21, 25).

[82] Deut 1:12; cf. Num 11:11c; Exod 18:18b. In the Numbers tradition, the difficulty which Moses laments is the peoples' demand for meat; in Exodus, it is the challenge of judging so many people that is burdensome.

The people are told to choose from among themselves men who are "wise, intelligent and experienced" (חכמים ונבנים וידעים),[83] and Moses will appoint them as officials.[84] Something new is added to the tradition about those who will assist Moses. They are distinguished by qualities that derive from the royal tradition based on the tradition of the vizier in the Egyptian society. The speech of Moses continues with the report that he charged the judges "to hear" whatever cases were brought to them and "to judge righteously."[85] Moses then directs the judges in words that echo the decrees issued by the Pharaoh when he installed his vizier:

> You shall not be partial in judgment; you shall hear the small
> and the great alike; you shall not be afraid of the face of man
> ... (Deut 1:17a).[86]

Finally Moses gives the charge that the judges are to bring to him "the case that is too hard" for them.[87]

The account in Deut 1:9-18, so obviously composed from selected traditional elements of Exodus 18 and Numbers 11, reveals the hand of the Dtr in the shape given to the traditions in the articulation of the

---

[83]Deut 1:13, 15. With the designation of the chosen, we compare the qualifications of those chosen by Moses in Exod 18:25. They are to be "able men," a term implying men in battle. See Judg 20:44, 46; 2 Sam 11:16; 2 Kgs 24:16; Pss 76:6 (Eng 76:5); 60:14 (Eng 60:12)//108:14 (Eng 108:13).

[84]Deut 1:13b and 15a name the officials as "rulers, captains, and officers." Here the Dtr account remains faithful to the tradition in Exod 18:25 that the chosen men are military leaders. See Henri Cazelles, "Institutions et Terminologie en Deut. I 6-17," in *Volume du Congrès 1965* (VTSup 15; Leiden: E. J. Brill, 1966) 97-112.

[85]Deut 1:16. The injunction of Moses to these chosen corresponds with the law applying to judges in the Deuteronomic Code: Deut 16:18-19.

[86]With this compare the injunction for the vizier: "The abomination of the god is partiality." (*ANET*, 213).

[87]Deut 1:17b. This element is common to the traditions about judging: Exod 18:22, 26; 17:8-13; 1 Kgs 7:7. Apparently, only those cases which could not be settled in the family or tribe were brought before an assembly of elders who had been designated to hear cases; or before the king, in the time of the monarchy. See D. A. McKenzie, "Judicial Procedure at the Town Gate," *VT* 14 (1964) 100-104; and John M. Salmon, "Judicial Authority in Early Israel: An Historical Investigation of Old Testament Institutions" (Diss., Princeton Theological Seminary, 1968).

passage,[88] and particularly, in the addition of the distinguishing formulary
חכם ונבין וידע .[89]   The shape given to the traditional elements
becomes evident in a comparison of the Deuteronomy passage with the
dream narrative in Kings:

Setting   *Setting*
Moses speaks to the people   Dialogue between God and Solo-
                                        mon

Content   *Content*
Moses decries his burden (9,12)   Solomon questions his burden (9d)
burden = multitude of people   burden = multitude of people and
    (10-11)   task (8b)
people choose wise, intelligent   God gives Solomon a wise and in-
    and experienced men;   telligent heart (12b)
Moses appoints them (13-15)
judges are charged to judge righ-   Solomon asks for the ability to
    teously (16)   govern in justice (9bc; 11d)
Moses gives instructions for judg-   God charges Solomon to keep
    ing (17)   Torah (14)

The Dtr shaped the components of these texts according to a common
structure. Both passages focus upon the task of leadership in accord with
divine law; both texts hold a key position at the head of the respective
reports of Moses and the Kings; and in both, the qualifications of the
leaders who will so acquit themselves among the people of Yahweh are
expressed in the formulaic (וידע) חכם ונבון .

The Dtr applied to the leaders of the people in the Mosaic era the
characteristics of leadership that traditionally derive from the royal
tradition. This is the narrative technique of the Dtr. This theologian
expressed his theological point of view by skillfully structuring into each
narrative components drawn from tradition that contribute to the point
being articulated.

Another use of the formulary by the Dtr applies the formulary
חכם ונבון not to kings and not to other leaders of the people, but
purposefully to all the people of the land:

---

[88]This text falls into the category of passages created by the Deuteronomist. It is set in the style of a speech, composed out of traditional
elements and fashioned to present a specific theological point of view.

[89]The term דעת/ידע is more redundant than additional. Note the
parallelism of חכם and דעת in Prov 2:6, 10; 3:19-20; 14:6; 22:17; 24:5;
30:3. דעת is often the result of "being wise": Prov 10:4; 15:2, 7; 18:15b;
21:11; as well as of "being intelligent": Prov 15:14; 18:15a.

Notice the use of דעת in place of נבון in 2 Chr 1:10, 11, 12.

the peoples . . . when they hear all these statutes, will say,
'Surely this great nation is a wise and understanding people
(עם-חכם ונבון)' (Deut 4:6b).

The formulary to this point had applied to leaders charged with the leadership among Yahweh's people. In the execution of leadership, both judges
and kings were obliged to act in conformity with the God-given directives
in Torah.

But the theological focus of the DtrH is that everyone is subject to
the law of Yahweh; everyone is charged to keep and do the statutes;
everyone is responsible for obeying the Torah and for acting in accord
with its directives. The formulary, חכם ונבון, from the royal tradition implies this obligation to heed and to obey. This formulary served
the Dtr purpose to affirm that not only the leaders are subject to Torah,
but that everyone in the land is so responsible.

That our interpretation of the application of the formulary is correct is affirmed by the Dtr himself. He says that keeping Torah is
חכמתכם ובינתכם:

Keep them and do them; for that will be your wisdom and
your understanding in the sight of the people (Deut 4:6a).

In this discussion on the formulaic חכם ונבון, we have demonstrated that the expression derives from the tradition of the vizier who
was obliged to heed the decrees of the Pharaoh and to act in accord with
those decrees in his administration of justice. This tradition influenced
the formulation of royal theology in the early monarchy, but was not ex-
plicated until the work of the Dtr. The Dtr made the analogy of the king
with the vizier explicit in the attribution of the formulaic חכם ונבון
to Kings in the person of Solomon. The Dtr, moreover, applied the attribution to the Israelite leaders in the era of Moses, and indeed, to the
people themselves, for everyone--leaders and people--were charged to
"heed the statutes and ordinances and to do them" (Deut 4:1) and passim.

Excursus: Egyptian Vizier and
Israelite King and Prophet

In Egyptian society, the Vizier held the highest position, second only
to Pharaoh himself. The Vizier was commissioned by Pharaoh with the
administration of justice in the land. His authority was unquestioned.
Yet, the Vizier's authority was limited by the will of the Pharaoh, for the
Vizier was charged to act in accord with the words of the Pharaoh-god by

which Maat was established. Thus, the Vizier functioned as the deputy of the Pharaoh and the chief justice in the land.

At the time of the Vizier's installation, the Pharaoh addressed the Vizier with the directive that the Vizier was to act in accord with the decrees of the Pharaoh. The word of the Pharaoh was the law of the land.[90] The decrees spoken by the Pharaoh were the law that determined the Vizier in his tasks:

> Would that thou mightest act in conformance with what I say! Then Maat will rest in her place.[91]

> See to it for thyself that all (things) are done according to that which conforms to law. . . . This is the instruction and thus shalt thou act: . . .[92]

The purpose of the Vizier's obedience to the decrees of the Pharaoh was that Maat, embodied in the Pharaoh, might be preserved in society through the Vizier's practice of justice.

There is an Egyptian text that records the words of the Pharaoh. This text provides an example of some of the directives by which the Vizier was charged to carry out his administration in society.

> Behold, it is the official's place of refuge to act in conformance with the regulations. . . . (The) abomination of the god is partiality. This is the instruction and thus shalt thou act:

>> Thou shalt look upon him whom thou knowest like him whom thou knowest not, upon him who has access to thee like him who is far away. . . .

> Behold, thou shouldst *attach* to thy carrying out this office thy carrying out of justice.

---

[90]No law codes have been found for ancient Egypt because pharaonic Egypt operated on the basis of topical justice originating in the word of the god-king. See *ANET*, 212. In ancient kingdoms each king issued decrees on the day of his coronation to establish a new era of justice. These royal decrees were the most common form of law. See James A. Sanders, *Torah and Canon* (Philadelphia: Fortress, 1972) 27; and, Dennis J. McCarthy, Review of *Deuteronomy and the Deuteronomic School, Bib* 54 (1973) 449.

[91]Taken from the autobiography of Rekh-mi-re, vizier during the reign of Thut-mose III: *ANET*, 213a, l. 14.

[92]A text from the installation of a vizier during the time of Thutmose III: *ANET*, 213b, ll. 5, 13.

> Behold, what is desired is that the carrying out of justice be
> the produce of the vizier. . . .[93]

The will of the Pharaoh for justice-order-peace determined the Vizier in
his rulership. In another text, the Vizier's declaration of his faithful
compliance with the Pharaoh's decrees echoes the directive that he act in
accord with regulations, the most explicit of which is impartiality. Thus
the Vizier confesses:

> (*I acted*) in conformance with that which he had ordained.... I
> raised justice to the height of heaven; I made its beauty
> circulate to the width of the earth. . . .
> When I judged the petitioner, I was not partial. I did not turn
> my brow for the sake of reward. I was not angry (at *him who
> came*) as (a petitioner)
>> nor did I *rebuff* him (but) I tolerated him in his moment
>> of outburst.
> I rescued the timid from the violent. . . .[94]

In these texts from the Egyptian royal sphere, we have noted the correlation between obedience to the law of the king-god, and the assignment to
preserve justice in the land through administration and judgment. In
ancient Egypt, the tasks for the order in society were delegated to the
Vizier whose position was second only to Pharaoh. In the Pharaoh-god
alone resided the power for harmony in nature and for order in society.
For this reason, the decrees of the Pharaoh established the limits for the
performance of the Vizier that "Maat will rest in her place."

Klaus Baltzer has recently introduced a study that argues for a
correspondence between the office of the Vizier and that of the
prophet.[95] His argument is based on the form of the "biography" found in
Egyptian installation texts and the call narratives of the prophets.
Baltzer contends that the call of the Judges (Gideon, Debora, and Samuel)
as well as the Last Words of David in 2 Sam 23:1-7 are examples of the
"biography," and indeed, indicate an office that anticipates that of the
prophet in the Israelite tradition. Baltzer traces an office analogous to
that of the Vizier from the Judges through the charismatic leaders of the
Northern Kingdom to the classical prophets. The comparison holds except

---

[93]*ANET*, 213b.
[94]*ANET*, 213a.
[95]*Die Biographie der Propheten* (Neukirchen-Vluyn: Neukirchener,
1975); also, "Considerations Regarding the Office and Calling of the
Prophet," *HTR* 61 (1968) 567-81.

for the period of the monarchy when there are two offices that could be
identified with that of the Vizier. Baltzer stresses that, during the four
centuries of the monarchy, there was tension between the king and the
prophet. He asserts, nonetheless, that the prophet holds a position above
that of the king. He draws this conclusion on the basis of word study.
The prophet identifies himself as "servant" and therefore as the one who
stands in the service of Yahweh. The king, on the other hand, is called
"ruler" (נשיא), or "leader" (נגיד) from among the people.[96] Baltzer
argues in favor of the prophet as being second to Yahweh because the
prophet is responsible for the whole world; he possesses jurisdiction over
all the nations. The king's rule is limited to that of Israel; his is not a
universal reign, and therefore, he cannot be taken seriously to have held a
position like that of the Vizier. For his argument, Baltzer also studied the
titles of the Vizier. He claims that these can be associated with the
charges given to the Judges and later to the prophets.

It is problematic, we believe, to attempt to draw out a clear cut
analogy between an office in the Egyptian culture and that in Israel. The
borrowings from Egypt, or from any other culture in the ancient oriental
world for that matter, are not such that Israel appropriated *in toto* any
particular pattern for the description of its officers. Israel's theologians
borrowed from many royal ideologies and in various degrees. The domi-
nating influence was always the elements that served best to express the
reality in Israel which needed to be expounded. Israel borrowed poetic
components, metaphors, motifs and expressions. These obtained meaning
only in the new context of Israelite kingship.

In this study, we have argued that many motifs from the literature
of the vizier influenced the expression of kingship for Israel in the early
monarchy and, most certainly, in the time of the Deuteronomist. This is
not to say that the pattern of the vizier provided Israel with its design for
kingship. Viziership offered one model; or better said, viziership provided
numerous motifs that helped to clarify the position and the task of the
Israelite king.

The primary function of the Vizier to preserve Maat in the land,
i.e. to guarantee the order in society through his decisions and actions in
accord with the decrees issued by the Pharaoh-god, is recalled in Israel's
wisdom tradition. There the king is named as the one whose decisions and

---

[96]Ibid., 92-93.

choices insure life in the nation.[97]   He judges against those who disrupt
the peace within society:

> A king who sits on the throne of judgment
> winnows all evil with his eyes (Prov 20:8; cf. 20:2; 14:35;
>   16:14a).

> A wise king winnows the wicked,
> and drives the wheel over them (Prov 20:6; cf. 6:16-19; 2:12-
>   15).

> take away the wicked from the presence of the king,
> and his throne will be established in righteousness (Prov 25:5;
>   cf. Ps 101:4-7).

And he acts in support of those who contribute to truth and equity:

> Inspired decisions are on the lips of the king;
> his mouth does not sin in judgment (Prov 16:10; cf. 16:15;
>   19:12b).

> Righteous lips are the delight of a king,
> and he loves him who speaks what is right (Prov 16:13; cf. Ps
>   101:5, 7).

> He who loves purity of heart,
> and whose speech is gracious,
> will have the king as his friend (Prov 22:11).

Israel's wisdom reflects the thought that the king is attuned to the divine
will in all things:

> The king's heart is a stream of water
>   in the hand of the Lord;
> he turns it wherever he will (Prov 21:1).

The king's own actions, moreover, accord with the divinely-given orders to
maintain the justice and righteousness upon which kingship is founded:

---

[97]It has long been recognized that kings throughout the ancient
Orient were charged with the preservation of order in society and that
judging was one means of fulfilling this charge: see H. Frankfort, *King-
ship,* 51-60; 148-61; 277-94; S. Mowinckel, *He That Cometh,* 21-95; Alfred
Jepsen, "צדק und צדקה im Alten Testament," in *Gottes Wort und
Gottes Land* (ed. H. G. Reventlow; Göttingen: Vandenhoeck & Ruprecht,
1965) 78-89; and H. H. Schmid, *Gerechtigkeit als Weltordnung. Hinter-
grund und Geschichte des alttestamentlichen Gerechtigkeitsbegriffes*
(BHT 40; Tübingen: J. C. B. Mohr [Paul Siebeck], 1968) 83-89; and
"Schöpfung, Gerechtigkeit und Heil," *ZTK* 70 (1973) 1-19.

It is an abomination to kings to do evil,
for the throne is established by righteousness (Prov 16:12).

Loyalty and faithfulness preserve the king,
and his throne is upheld by righteousness (Prov 20:28).

It can be said with certainty that the image of the king as the guarantor
of order-justice-truth in society is reflected in these texts contained in
Israel's royal wisdom collections. The image is like that of the Vizier
whose chief obligation was to act for the nation in accord with the established order residing in the word of the Pharaoh. The image is likewise
like that of the Mesopotamian king who was obligated to truth and justice
in his judicial activity.[98] Unlike the other oriental monarchs, the Mesopotamian king was not above the law. He was mightily concerned to
establish *kittum u mēšārum*. This idea expressed the total law which
safeguarded the eternal and immutable truths on which the cosmos was
founded. The king was not the source of the law; he was the agent of
Babylonian law on behalf of his master, the god. The king was no more
exempt from the law than any other person.

The Mesopotamian king and the Vizier held in common the obligation to word/law that was divinely given. It is not surprising, therefore,
that these images are recalled in the biblical tradition.

The early monarchy gathered to itself the content of various royal
ideologies of the ancient Orient. This is evident in the collections of
wisdom instructions.[99] This is evident in the royal psalms that were used

---

[98]For a discussion about the Mesopotamian king's obligation to law,
see, G. R. Driver and John C. Miles, *The Babylonian Laws*, Vol. I.: *Legal
Commentary* (Oxford: Clarendon, 1952) 21-23; E. A. Speiser, "Authority
and Law in Mesopotamia," *Supplement to the Journal of the American
Oriental Society* 17 (1954) 11-14; and D. J. McCarthy, *Treaty and Covenant*, 89-90.
[99]The court has long been accepted as the setting for the collection
and the use of literary wisdom. Proponents of this view include: Gerhard
von Rad, *Old Testament Theology*, 1. 429-32; and *Wisdom in Israel* (Nashville: Abingdon, 1972) 11-12, 15-23; Udo Skladny, *Spruchsammlungen*, 44-
66, 66-67, 80-82; Roland de Vaux, *Ancient Israel*, Vol. I: *Social Institutions* (New York: McGraw-Hill, 1965) 48-50; William McKane, *Prophets
and Wise Men* (SBT 44; London: SCM, 1965) 44-47; R. N. Whybray, *Wisdom in Proverbs: The Concept of Wisdom in Proverbs 1-9* (SBT 45; London: SCM, 1965) esp. 71; H.-J. Hermisson, *Studien zur israelitischen
Spruchweisheit* (WMANT 28; Neukirchen-Vluyn: Neukirchener, 1968) 94-
96; Roland E. Murphy, "The Wisdom Literature of the Old Testament," in

for the ritual celebration of kingship.[100] We prefer to speak about the patrimony from royal ideologies that influenced the Israelite royal tradition. From the literatures of the various royal ideologies, those motifs were appropriated that were applicable to the articulation of the unique kingship in Israel. Those motifs, expressions, metaphors, and images were borrowed that contributed to and were not contradictory with Israel's concept of kingship. In fact, the language from some literatures was dominant because the motifs there were especially suited to account for the phenomenon of a king who was subject to the directions of a Sovereign King.

THE GIFTS NOT REQUESTED AND THE GIFTS GIVEN

Our discussion continues with a consideration of a second group of royal benefits. These are structured into the dream narrative on the framework of the verbs "ask" and "give" in such a way that these benefits, which derive from a different royal ideology, might be shown to be distinct. The benefits named are hinged upon the negative aspect of the verb "ask": Solomon "did not ask" but "Elohim gives" also that which Solomon "did not ask":

> you did not ask *long life* for yourself
> you did not ask *riches* for yourself
> you did not for the *life of your enemies* (1 Kgs 3:11b).

A theological point is being made by the Dtr in the repetition of the phrase, "you did not ask. . . ." The fact is that the benefits that Solomon "did not ask" are not given for the asking; they are the consequence of a relationship with God by whose will the king reigns. These are the signs of kingship; they indicate that the king is favored by the patron-god and that therefore he is established upon his throne.

The Human Reality of Sacred Scripture (Concilium I/10; New York: Paulist, 1965) 126-40; "Assumptions and Problems in O. T. Wisdom Research," *CBQ* 29 (1967) 407-18; "Form Criticism and Wisdom Literature," *CBQ* 31 (1969) 475-85; and, Bruce V. Malchow, "The Roots of Israel's Wisdom in Sacral Kingship" (Diss., Marquette University, 1972).

[100]See J. H. Patton, *Canaanite Parallels in the Book of Psalms* (Baltimore: Johns Hopkins, 1944); Mitchell Dahood, *Psalms I: 1-50; Psalms II: 51-100; Psalms III: 101-150 (AB; Garden City: Doubleday, 1966-70)*; S. Mowinckel, *The Praise of God in the Psalms*; and, A. Johnson, *Sacral Kingship*.

The blessings of long life, of possessions, and of victory are cele-brated in the royal psalms of the early monarchy. The motifs are appro-priated from an ancient oriental royal ideology but given a new context so that these blessings are the signs of Yahweh's promise to the king and the indications of Yahweh's fidelity to the king in giving him the throne. In contrast to the requests of Solomon in the previous section--requests that emphasized the obedience of the king, these favors highlight the loyalty of Israel's God to his promise to the Davidic family. They are the indi-cators that God favors the king and that the throne is secure.

Long Life

Kingship and nature were integrally bound in ancient oriental royal ideologies. The seasons of the year and the fertility in nature correspond with the reign of the king. In cultic practice, yearly fertility rites in which the king played a central role insured continuity in the seasons and the fruitfulness in nature. The "long life" of the king, i.e., his permanence on the throne, guaranteed the perpetuity of the natural and cosmic forces. Thus the king upon the throne preserved the order in the universe; it indicated that the king remained in accord with the god by whose favor he reigns.

Translated to the celebration of kingship in the Israelite royal tradition, the motif of a "long life" was used to indicate Yahweh's choice of the king and his favor in the covenant promise. The motif occurs in the context of covenant; it was appropriated as another way to express Yah-weh's covenant with the king.

In Psalm 89, the theme of an enduring reign is expressed by com-parison with the permanence and continuity observable in nature. Like the forces in nature, so will Yahweh's fidelity to his promise be observed:

> His line shall endure forever,
> his throne as long as the sun before me.
> Like the moon it shall be established for ever;
> it shall stand firm while the skies endure (Ps 89:36-37;
>   cf. 2 Sam 7:16; Jer 33:20-21).

> I will establish your descendants for ever,
> and build your throne for all generations (Ps 89:4; cf. 2 Sam
>   7:11b-12; Ps 132:11).

> I will establish his line for ever
> and his throne as the days of the heavens (Ps 89:29).

The Israelite view of kingship clearly focuses upon the initiative of Yahweh. The king reigned by divine promise and he continued on the throne
as a sign of Yahweh's fidelity to his promise. Yahweh alone gives kingship
and Yahweh alone preserves the king upon the throne. Therefore, the king
asks for the permanence of his reign from the one who is able to give it.
He asks in language paralleled in the Ugaritic mythology of kingship:

> (The king) asked life of thee;
> thou gavest it to him,
> length of days for ever and ever (Ps 21:5).[101]

Or, the people might ask Yahweh for the king's longevity upon the throne:

> Long may he live (Ps 72:15).

> Prolong the life of the king;
> may his years endure to all generations!
> May he be enthroned for ever before God (Ps 61:6-7a).[102]

The "long life" of the king upon the throne is an indication that Yahweh is
faithful to his promise to the king. It is sign that Yahweh gives the throne
and it is assurance that Yahweh is with his chosen king.

The psalms we have quoted here provide ample evidence that in
royal tradition an enduring reign was a manifestation of covenant and
attested to Yahweh's fidelity. A long life was celebrated because this
blessing was interpreted as a sign of Yahweh's graciousness to his chosen
and faithful king. It is this tradition of a long reign which the Dtr received from royal tradition and applied to Solomon in the dream narrative. It is a tradition that is made to focus upon the fidelity of Yahweh to
his promise and which contrasts with the benefits which Solomon had
asked. These latter focus upon the obligations and responsibilities of the
king; the former stresses the promise that can be trusted.

---

[101]With this compare a text from the Ugaritic epic of Anat and
Aqhat:
> Ask life, O young man Aqhat,
> ask life and I will give it to thee
> everlasting life and I will send it to thee.
See above, n. 25. The covenant context for Psalm 21 had been established
by F. Charles Fensham, "Ps 21," esp. 197.

[102]With this psalm, compare Prov 9:11:
> For by me your days will be multiplied
> and years will be added to your life.

Riches

Another sign of kingship is great possessions. This is true in Canaan-ite royal ideology,[103] and it is true in the royal theology of Israel. Since riches indicate the divine favor, this motif very suitably expressed the giving of kingship which was an indication of divine favor. We find in the early narratives of Israel that the abundance and prosperity of the Patri-archs was indicative of Yahweh's blessing and his promise.[104] The royal psalms declare that the kings, in like fashion, are the recipients of great blessing because of God's favor:

May gold be given to him! . . .
May there be abundance of grain in the land;
on the tops of the mountains may it wave;
may its fruit be like Lebanon;
and may men blossom forth from the cities
    like the grass of the field (Ps 72:15a, 16).

The possessions and wealth that come to the king as an indication of the divine favor are expressed in the image of the fruitfulness of nature and in material prosperity. These riches are the sign of Yahweh's gracious-ness; when they are given there is indeed covenant between Yahweh and the king.

Words of thanksgiving praise Yahweh because he has kept his promise:

Thou dost meet him with goodly blessing;
thou dost set a crown of fine gold upon his head (Ps 21:4).

His glory is great through thy help;
splendor and majesty thou dost bestow upon him (Ps 21:6).

Many possessions and great wealth manifested God's special love for the possessor; it evidenced a relationship in covenant between Yahweh and the blessed king. It is this understanding of material blessings from the royal tradition which the Dtr employs to express Yahweh's faithfulness to his king. It is Yahweh's fidelity which is being emphasized to contrast with the obligations for the service of the king which had been empha-sized in the counter-structure of "ask." The Dtr structured on the verb

---

[103] An example of the equation between kingship and riches is found in the tale of Keret. See, G. R. Driver, *Canaanite Myths*, 29; ll. i, 41-ii, 3.
[104] Gen 13:2, 5; 14:23; 26:12b-14.

"not ask" those blessings that signify Yahweh's faithfulness to his promise to the king.

Life of the Enemy

In Semitic royal ideology, a king attained the throne when he had defeated all opposing forces.[105] Thus, the defeat of the enemy was another sign of kingship and an indication of divine favor. The enthronement of the king followed upon his victory over the enemy forces of death, darkness, evil.

Vestiges of a ritual enactment of the king's victory over the enemy are present in the royal psalms. This is true especially in the psalms used for the event of the king's coronation.

By divine decree, the king is assured victory over the enemy. He is placed upon the throne with the promise that Yahweh gives the victory:

> You are my son, today I have begotten you.
> Ask of me, and I will make the nations your heritage,
> and the ends of the earth your possession.
> You shall break them with a rod of iron, and
> dash them in pieces like a potter's vessel (Ps 2:7-9).

Another psalm celebrates the designation of David as king and commemorates Yahweh's promise to defeat anyone who threatens his covenant with his chosen:

> I have found David, my servant;
> with my holy oil I have anointed him;
> so that my hand shall ever abide with him,
> my arm shall also strengthen him.
> The enemy shall not outwit him,
> the wicked shall not humble him.
> I will crush his foes before him
> and strike down those who hate him (Ps 89:20-23; cf. vv 24-25
> and 2 Sam 7:1b).

It is Yahweh who gives the victory, according to the application of the motif from the Semitic royal ideology to the royal theology in Israel. It is Yahweh who gives the throne, the sign of which is the defeat of all opposing forces.

---

[105]This is illustrated in the Ugaritic tale of Baal's victory over Prince Yamm: *Canaanite Myths*, 81-83, Part III; and over Mot: *Canaanite Myths*, 111-15; and in the Mesopotamian "Creation Epic": *ANET*, 60-72.

In another psalm, Yahweh promises the king that anyone who threatens the relationship between the king and himself will be destroyed. The defeat will be brought about through the actualization of the curses.[106]

> Your hand will find out all your enemies;
> your right hand will find out those who hate you.
> You will make them as a blazing oven when you appear.
> The Lord will swallow them up in his wrath;
>   and fire will consume them.
> You will destroy their offspring from the earth,
>   and their children from among the sons of men.
> If they plan evil against you,
>   if they devise mischief, they will not succeed.
> For you will put them to flight;
>   you will aim at their faces with your bows (Ps 21:9-13).

It is significant that these verses follow upon a statement which expresses covenant between Yahweh and the king:

> For the king trusts in the Lord,
> and through the steadfast love of the Most High
>   he shall not be moved (Ps 21:8).

The opposition to the king actually provokes the anger of the Sovereign Lord, Yahweh, with whom the king is joined in covenant.

The defeat of the enemy signified Yahweh's fidelity to his king:

> Great triumphs he gives to his king,
> and shows steadfast love to his anointed (Ps 18:51//2 Sam
>   22:51; cf. Ps 144:10 and 20:3, 6).

> May his foes bow down before him
> and his enemies lick the dust (Ps 72:9)!

In the biblical tradition, we observe that the "life of the enemy" and Yahweh's covenant with his king are closely related. In some psalms, the motif was used as a sign of Yahweh's fidelity to his promise; in others, the motif was expressive of the actualization of the curses on account of threat to Yahweh's covenant partner. In either case, the victory of the king was a manifestation of Yahweh's favor and fidelity to the king.

---

[106]Cf. Deut 32:41-42. For a discussion of the correlation between the content of these verses and the curses of vassal-treaties, see F. C. Fensham, "Ps 21," 198-200.

The Dtr borrowed the motif as it had been given to him in the biblical tradition. He tied it to the structure built by use of the verb "did not ask" as one of the signs of Yahweh's loyalty to his king. The "life of the enemy" as well as "long life" and "riches" metaphorically express kingship itself, and, therefore, Yahweh's fidelity to his chosen to whom kingship is given. The Dtr is focusing upon the dimension of royal theology which affirms Yahweh as the giver of kingship and as the sustainer of the king upon the throne. In these motifs hinged upon the verb "did not ask," the emphasis is upon the fidelity of Yahweh; the structural scheme of "ask" introduced those motifs that emphasize the responsibility of the king to live in accord with Torah. These are very different dimensions of royal theology, but dimensions that together express the design that is the deuteronomistic interpretation of kingship.

Riches and Honor

Apart from the blessings which we have shown to be attestations of Yahweh's loyalty, *Elohim gives* other blessings which Solomon did not ask. In the dream narrative, it is stated by Elohim that

What you did not ask I give you
both riches and honor (1 Kgs 3:13a).

The text implies a synonymity between "riches and honor" and "long life, riches, and the life of the enemy," for "riches and honor" are named as the object of "what you did not ask." Yet, the Dtr precisely distinguishes one group from the other in a separation made within the structure. In this discussion, we will demonstrate that the distinction between the two groups of blessings is intentional. Each group derives from a different royal ideology; but, more importantly, "riches and honor" represent the benefits deriving from being in harmony with creation; whereas "long life, riches, and the life of the enemy" signify the loyalty of Yahweh to a relationship founded on covenant promise. Neither group, we might add, is asked of God because both are indicative of God's graciousness: in one instance, it is Yahweh's graciousness to his chosen; in the other, it is God's graciousness toward his creature.

The expression "riches and honor" derives from the Egyptian ideology of kingship where Maat, the goddess of order-truth-justice, is portrayed with a symbol of life in one hand and a sceptre symbolizing wealth and honor in the other.[107] According to Egyptian belief, officials con-

---

[107]For a survey of these representations and an explanation of the meaning, see Christa Bauer-Kayatz, *Studien zu Proverbien 1-9* (WMANT

formed to Maat by heeding the directives of the Pharaoh thereby reaping
the prosperity that signified harmony with the order innate in creation
and expressed in the words of the Pharaoh. The symbols linked with Maat
indicate the order of creation residing in the Pharaoh and the order in
society that is maintained by the will of the Pharaoh. Thus, in Egyptian
culture, there is a congruence between the divine order in creation and
the decrees of the Pharaoh.

The language from the Egyptian ideology was applied in Israel's
sapiential tradition to "wisdom" personified as a goddess. Of Wisdom, it is
said:

> Long life is in her right hand;
> in her left hand are riches and honor (Prov 3:16).

The application is consistent, for when Wisdom speaks, she holds out the
promise of the symbols she holds:

> Riches and honor are with me,
> enduring wealth and prosperity (Prov 8:18).

In the sapiential tradition, however, "Wisdom" is not a mere substitution
for Maat. Wisdom has taken on the tradition that sets the context in faith
in Yahweh.[108] Thus Wisdom is correlated with "humility" and "fear of the
Lord":

22; Neukirchen-Vluyn: Neukirchener, 1966) 102-17; and M. Görg, *Gott-
König-Reden*, 105-11.

[108]We are of the opinion that the integration of didactic wisdom
with Yahwism was accomplished in a long process from the first days that
individual believers in Yahweh shared in the intellectual tradition of the
surrounding peoples. On this, see W. Zimmerli, "Concerning the Structure
of Old Testament Wisdom," trans. by Brian W. Kovacs, in *Studies in Ancient Israelite Wisdom* (New York: KTAV, 1976) 185-86; also, "Zur Struktur der alttestamentlichen Weisheit," *ZAW* 51 (1933) 177-204; and G. von
Rad, *Wisdom in Israel*, 61-64.

The integration evident in the literary collection in Proverbs began
with the involvement of Israel as a nation in the culture of the ancient
Orient. G. von Rad calls this the "freethinking era" (*Genesis*, 29), when
there was the possibility for an "intellectual creative upsurge" (*Old Testament Theology*, 1. 48).

There are some who define wisdom as a secular didactic phenomenon
which was interpreted according to Yahwism in stages and then only late
in Israelite history: so, Johannes Fichtner, *Die altorientalische Weisheit
in ihrer israelitisch-jüdischen Ausprägung* (BZAW 62; Giessen, 1933) 24-25;
R. B. Y. Scott, *Proverbs, Ecclesiastes* (AB 18; Garden City: Doubleday,

> The reward for humility and fear of the Lord
> is riches and honor and life (Prov 22:4).

These few sayings make us aware that, though the articulation for these blessings of creation was mediated to Israel through the intellectual resources shared in the ancient Orient, Israel applied this expression for the goods of creation to her own understanding of the order in creation which she expressed variously as "wisdom," "humility" and "fear of the Lord." Each of these designations are further equated with heeding the instructions and directives of one's teachers.[109] The proverbial tradition stresses that learning the teachings and directives for life holds out the promise of good fortune. *Life* is the reward for the person who heeds the teachings:

> for length of days and years of life
> and abundant welfare will they give you (Prov 3:2).

Honor is given to a person who listens to the instructions:

> you will find favor and good repute
> in the sight of God and man (Prov 3:4).

Riches are the consequences for observing the directives:

> your barns will be filled with plenty,
> and your vats will be bursting with wine (Prov 3:10).

Implicit in this interpretation of the motif--life, honor and riches--is a correspondence between obedience to authoritative directions for life and the evidence of life in the fruitfulness of creation. In Egyptian mentality, "riches and honor" and that highest form of good fortune, "life," were perceived as evidence of divine favor upon the one who lived in conformity with the normative order innate in creation. Because of the

---

1965) 17; R. N. Whybray, *Wisdom in Proverbs*, 7; Michael V. Fox, "Aspects of the Religion of the Book of Proverbs," *HUCA* 39 (1968) 55-69; and, William McKane, *Proverbs*, 11, 413-15.

Others stress the foreign element basic to didactic wisdom. These, however, affirm that Israel adopted concepts from this old wisdom only selectively and critically, allowing that the didactic wisdom received a new shape under the influence of Yahwism: so, H. Gese, *Lehre und Wirklichkeit*, 31; Udo Skladny, *Spruchsammlungen*, 94; H. H. Schmid, *Wesen und Geschichte der Weisheit. Eine Untersuchung zur Altorientalischen und Israelitischen Weisheitsliteratur* (BZAW 101; Berlin: Alfred Töpelmann, 1966) 148.

[109]Prov 1:7, 29; 2:5; 9:10; 15:33; 11:2.

perception of reality in Israel, the Israelite cannot be understood to be one who simply conformed to an imposed order. More appropriately, the Israelite learned from experience and from observation that God had put an order in creation, the purpose of which was life in society and in nature. The Israelite freely and responsibly chose to comply with God's order in creation. That this statement is true becomes evident in the fact that the mystery in creation was celebrated from early times.[110] The Israelite understood that to be on God's side, i.e. to comply with the givens in creation, was to affirm life.

The tradition that God is the source of the goods that come to an individual in consequence of conducting oneself to the full flowering of life is not the creative contribution of the Dtr. This tradition underlies the Yahwist theology of creation,[111] and indeed, the narrative of the Yahwist theologian; it is the supposition for the other narrative compositions in tenth century Israel;[112] as well as the dominant theme of Proverbs.[113]

When the Dtr states that "*Elohim* gives both riches and honor," this theologian is taking up traditional material from creation and royal theology.[114] This theology affirms the relationship of king and God founded on

---

[110]Pss 19:1-6; 104; 8.

[111]Genesis 2-3 presents man and woman in this very positive light. They are painted in their relationships: as creatures to God; as partners within society, exemplified in the model of the ideal community of marriage; and as kings having dominion over all other creatures and charged with the care and preservation of the earth.

[112]The presence of this theology of creation and the influence of sapiential thought in the literature of the tenth century has been studied extensively by Walter Brueggemann, "David and his Theologian," *CBQ* 30 (1968) 156-81; "Israel's Moment of Freedom," *TBT* (April 1969) 2917-2925; "Scripture and an Ecumenical Life-Style: A Study in Wisdom Theology," *Int* 24 (1970) 3-19; "Kingship and Chaos (A Study in Tenth Century Theology)," *CBQ* 33 (1971) 317-32; "On Trust and Freedom: A Study of Faith in the Succession Narrative," *Int* 26 (1972) 3-19; "Life and Death in Tenth Century Israel," *JAAR* 40 (1972) 96-109; and *In Man We Trust*.

[113]Creation as the theological basis for the sayings in Proverbs is the subject of the study by W. Zimmerli, "The Place and Limit of the Wisdom." See also, "Concerning the Structure."

[114]Cf. W. Richter, "Urgeschichte und Hoftheologie," *BZ* 10 (1966) 96-105; W. A. Brueggemann, "From Dust to Kingship," *ZAW* 84 (1972) 1-18; and H. H. Schmid, "Schöpfung, Gerichtigkeit und Heil," *ZTK* 70 (1973) 1-19.

creation; and it makes an assertion about the king's conduct and attitude toward his Creator as well as toward community, nature and the world. "Riches and honor" together with "life" symbolize the benefits that flow to the one whose conduct evidences the learning of "wisdom" and a "fear of Yahweh."[115]

In the dream, the Dtr set "riches and honor," benefits granted in consequence of life-affirming conduct, in correspondence with "long life, riches, and the life of the enemy," blessings that symbolize God's promise in covenant. Both traditions are oriented in kingship; and both traditions imply a behavior in the king that reverences the particular relationship, be it covenant or creation.

It is essential for the Dtr purpose that both traditions of royal theology be noted in order that both may be redefined in the light of Torah under the Dtr influence. The juxtaposition of the two sets of blessings, each associated with a distinct dimension of royal tradition, prepares for the climactic interpretation of both within the ambit of Torah.

In the dialogue thus far, the Dtr presented the king in his capacity as ruler-judge asking and receiving from *Elohim*. We have argued that the language put upon the lips of Solomon and of *Elohim* indicate that the Dtr borrowed language from the literature associated with the Egyptian vizier to image the king in the model of a vizier, to emphasize the subordination of the Israelite king to the Divine King.

The Dtr also presented the king "not asking," nonetheless, receiving blessings from *Elohim*. We have proposed that the theme of "not asking" is a theologically pregnant concept asserting that the benefits named are those that symbolize kingship which in the biblical tradition is given as the sign of Yahweh's fidelity to his covenant promise. These blessings-- long life, riches, and the life of the enemy--attest to God's fidelity to his promise made in covenant assuming also that the king walks faithfully before his God. The other group of blessings are given outright, indicating that the benefits rooted in creation are given by *Elohim*. They do not accrue to the king on account of his position as ruler, as in the Egyptian tradition; but they are given by the Creator to his creature. These goods --riches and honor--attest to life-affirming relationships in society and in

---

[115]See the sayings in Proverbs:
The blessing of the Lord makes rich (Prov 10:22a).
A faithful man will abound with blessings (Prov 28:20a).
Blessings are on the head of the righteous (Prov 10:6a).

the world. They signify that the individual conforms his conduct in a way that does not conflict with God's will for life.

The Dtr has thus far presented the ideal of kingship out of the combination of traditions from royal theology, but the image of the ideal king is not yet complete. To this point the Dtr has prepared the way for a new coloration upon the relationship of the king with God. Each image presented already hints at the necessary obedience of the king, whether in his capacity as ruler, as covenant partner, or as creature. There remains one point to be made by the Dtr theologian--the designation of the Torah as the one standard for obedience to Yahweh.

THE CONDITIONAL STATEMENT

The outright link of the blessings, associated in royal theology with covenant and creation, to Torah is made in the final statement of the dialogue:

> If you will walk in my ways,
> keeping my statutes and my commandments,
> as your father David walked,
> then I will lengthen your days (1 Kgs 3:14).

The form of this statement, in contrast to every other part of the dialogue, is without question deuteronomic. For this reason, the presence of this verse in the dream narrative has universally been considered a secondary element to a text which is perceived to be a literary unity from a royal coronation appropriated from royal tradition for use in the history.[116] We have demonstrated in our analysis of the structure, however, that the presence of this statement is vital to the design of kingship. It is one more formulary taken from tradition which contributes to the ideal of kingship being expressed out of a combination of elements from royal tradition, from the traditions of Yahwistic faith, and from the Dtr interest in Torah. We have shown, moreover, that v 14 together with v 6 forms an inclusio with a chiastic structure of opposing elements. The structure speaks to the integrity of the conditional form within the narrative; the content and form also are indispensable to the design for kingship, as our discussion will indicate.

---

[116]So, Noth, *Ü St.*, 67; and *Könige*, 44; Fichtner, *Das erste Buch*, 73; Gray, *I and II Kings*, 125; and Cross, "Themes of the Book of Kings," 287, n. 49.

The conditional statement occurs frequently within the DtrH.[117] As a form, with the presentation of a case in the protasis and a statement of reward or punishment in the apodosis, it is related to case law. The form was appropriated in deuteronomistic thought to introduce the curses and blessings within the scheme of the covenant form.[118] It was utilized to present either the threat or promise that is consequent upon the actions of Israel,[119] or of an individual being addressed in the historical account.[120] In the dream narrative, the statement of the situation is addressed to Solomon and holds out promise for the future. The apodosis states that God will issue the reward of a long life to the king who keeps Torah. The text reads: "then I will lengthen your days" (1 Kgs 3:14b). The reward "length of days" must be understood in association with the benefits, riches and honor, we have discussed above. The three blessings appear together in the grasp of the goddess Maat--a symbol for life in one hand and a sceptre representing wealth and honor in the other. In most Egyptian contexts, "long life" is given first place among the benefits flowing from Maat.[121] This concept was given the same high priority in its application to "wisdom" and "fear of the Lord" when appropriated into

---

[117]In the DtrH, the form is introduced sometimes by the particle אם and sometimes כי. The case in question is introduced with אם. See the study by Harry W. Gilmer, *The If-You Form in Israelite Law* (SBLDS 15; Missoula: Scholars, 1975) esp. 27-43.

[118]Deut 28:1, 15 introduce the blessing and curse sections of Deuteronomy respectively. Deut 30:4, 10^2 contain statements of reward in the apodosis. The two conditional statements in v 10 are introduced by כי; (cf. Deut 4:29) whereas the condition in v 4 is introduced by אם.

[119]See Josh 24:20; 1 Sam 7:3; 12:14-15, 25.

[120]1 Kgs 2:4; 6:12; 9:4-7; 11:38. It is significant that these particular texts all state a promise/reward in the apodosis. It is as if the Dtr made use of the conditional form with a consequent promise in an effort to highlight the possibilities and hope for the future, though in each case the reverse situation was actually effected in the outcome of history. See our statement regarding the use of the conditional form by the Dtr in Chap. IV, 77-81. We suggest that the historian used the conditional promise as a rhetorical technique to prepare the reader for the possibility of infidelity on the part of the kings concerned and to account for the fact that the kingdom had been destroyed.

[121]For a survey of the Egyptian texts which stress the importance of "life," see M. Görg, *Gott-König-Reden*, 105-11; and Bauer-Kayatz, *Proverbien*, 102-7.

the biblical literature.[122]   Those who seek wisdom and who live in the fear of the Lord by heeding instructions and keeping commandments have learned that life is theirs:

> do not forget my teaching . . .
> for length of days and years of life
> and abundant welfare will they give you (Prov 3:2).

> Hear, my son, and accept my words,
> that the years of your life may be many (Prov 4:10).[123]

The highest form of good fortune--a long life--comes from a conduct that is oriented to the affirmation and preservation of what is life-giving:

> By me (wisdom) your days will be multiplied,
> and years will be added to your life (Prov 9:11;
>   cf. 3:18a; 8:35).

> The fear of the Lord prolongs life,
> but the years of the wicked will be short (Prov 10:27;
>   cf. 14:27; 19:23; 22:4).

We have observed that this theme of "long life" is celebrated in both the royal sapiential and the royal cultic traditions.[124]   This theme is a viable tradition of royal theology that was received by the Dtr and re-applied to the keeping of Torah. In earlier royal theology, a "long life" was recognized as a sign of covenant loyalty, as well as one of the benefits given as a consequence for living in conformity with the harmony in creation by heeding the instructions and commandments of those who have learned from experience and observation. Royal theology is enhanced under the influence of the Dtr with a fresh application of the reward of a "long life." The "long life" which was a "given" for a life of fidelity in covenant and for living in accord with the harmony in creation is put under condition and is defined as a reward for keeping Torah.[125]

---

[122]On the theme of "life" in wisdom literature, see W. Zimmerli, "Structure of O. T. Wisdom," 192-98.

[123]Cf. Prov 4:22; 5:23b; 13:17; 16:27; 19:16; 21:21.

[124]See the theme of life in the royal psalms quoted above, 153-54.

[125]In the dream narrative, we observe the redefinition of royal tradition by Torah being dramatized. This Dtr royal theology is subsequently applied to kings throughout the Dtr history of kings, so that kings of Israel and Judah are judged in the light of the Torah given to Moses on Horeb.

A reverse integration of traditions is observable in the Book of Deuteronomy. There, the people of Israel who are the recipients of the Torah, share in the benefits that were celebrated in royal tradition. Thus

The protasis of the condition reads:

If you will walk in my ways
> keeping my statutes and my commandments
> as your father David walked (1 Kgs 3:14a).

This if-clause of the conditional statement is positioned chiastically against the opening lines of Solomon's prayer. In v 6, Solomon acclaims Yahweh's fidelity to covenant and notes that the fidelity depends upon David's loyal service: "because he walked before you. . . ." Over against the presentation of the promise made in covenant, the Dtr positioned the statement of his own theological insight. The Dtr uses his ideal king David as the model in both cases: David walked faithfully before Yahweh in accord with the instructions for kings; and David walked faithfully in accord with Torah. The reinterpretation of the pre-Dtr royal theology in the light of Torah is accomplished in the structural balance affected in the position of v 6 in opposition to v 14.

In pre-Dtr royal theology, the focus is upon Yahweh's promise spoken to a loyal follower: Yahweh "showed great loving kindness because David walked before you. . . ." This style of expression is not the same as the condition in v 14. The promise is predicated upon the assumption of loyal service. In v 14, the promise is given as a reward upon the condition that the king keeps Torah. In Deuteronomistic royal theology, the stress is upon the conduct of the king, and the promise follows as a reward or punishment consequent upon the particular conduct.

We still must verify that the content of the if-clause refers strictly to Torah. The formulary "walk in the way" (הלך בדרך) is a popular Dtr expression synonymous with keeping the Torah, and is found in those passages which are speeches of Moses or Dtr compositions. Throughout

---

the uniqueness of the Dtr theology of Torah is its coloration by royal traditions. Since to demonstrate this would be a study in itself, we illustrate simply with the blessing of "length of days." The theme of "life" which in wisdom literature was promised for listening and keeping the instructions of teachers is, in Deuteronomy, promised for heeding and doing Torah: ". . . Lay up these words in your heart and in your soul . . . and you shall teach them to your children . . . that your days and the days of your children may be multiplied in the land" (Deut 11:18-21; cf. 4:40; 5:16, 33; 6:2; 11:9; 17:20; 22:7; 25:15; 32:47). In Deuteronomy, there is one charge for the people: "to love the Lord their God, to obey his voice and cleave to him; for that means life and length of days" (Deut 30:20).

his address to Israel, Moses admonishes the people to obey the Torah by challenging them "to walk in the way of Yahweh."[126]

Usually this formulary is expanded with elaborations of what precisely constitutes "walking in the way." By "keeping my statutes and commandments" is only one of several Dtr expressions used to describe how one "walks in the way" and "keeps the Torah."[127] This formulary "keeping my statutes and commandments" (שמר חקי מצותי) is found only in those texts which are Dtr compositions.[128]

In the speech of Moses in the Book of Deuteronomy, there can be no doubt that the formulary "keeping my statutes and commandments" refers to the divinely revealed Torah. The core of Deuteronomy is the Torah;[129] all that introduces and follows the presentation of the Torah has the Torah as its focus. The various terms--statutes (חקים/ות), ordinances (משפטים), commandments (מצות), and testimonies (עדות)-- indicate the words of Yahweh which were spoken on Horeb,[130] and which were written for the instruction of the people.[131]

Outside of the Book of Deuteronomy but within the DtrH, the formularies occur in contexts where an explicit reference is made to the Torah, thereby leaving no question that "walking in the way" and "keeping my statutes and commandments" are synonyms for obeying the Torah.

David's last words to Solomon, which form part of the introduction to the Solomonic history, make explicit mention of the Torah. David admonishes his successor to:

---

[126]In speeches of Moses, the formulary occurs in Deut 8:6; 19:19; 26:17; 28:9; 30:16; cf. 5:30; 10:12; 11:22.

Elsewhere in the DtrH, the formulary occurs in the Dtr summary essay: Judg 2:22; in the Dtr introduction to the Solomon history: 1 Kgs 2:3; and in the Dtr account of Jeroboam's call to kingship in the northern kingdom: 1 Kgs 11:33, 38.

[127]Other formularies which define the way of walking are: "by fearing the Lord your God"; "by loving him"; "by obeying his voice/ commandments."

[128]See Deut 4:40; 10:13; 28:45; 30:10; 1 Kgs 9:6; 11:34, 38; 2 Kgs 17:13; the verb "do" replaces "keep" in Deut 27:10 and both "keep and do" are used in Deut 28:15; cf. 1 Kgs 8:61.

[129]Deuteronomy 12-25.

[130]Deut 4:13-14, 33, 36; 5:1; 6:1, 20, and passim.

[131]Deut 9:9-11; 10:1-5. The law vocabulary used in this text has been studied by B. Lindars, "Torah in Deuteronomy," in *Words and Meanings* (eds. P. R. Ackroyd and B. Lindars; Cambridge: University Press, 1968) 117-36; and G. Braulik, "Die Ausdrücke für 'Gesetz' im Buch Deuteronomium," *Bib* 51 (1970) 39-66.

> keep the charge of the Lord your God,
>> walking in his ways, and
>> keeping his statutes, his commandments, his ordinances,
>>> and his testimonies,
> as it is written in the law of Moses (1 Kgs 2:3).

The Dtr summary text in which is recounted the history of a sinful people contains the warning that had been spoken over and over again for the instruction of the nation:

> Turn from your evil ways and
> keep my commandments and my statutes,
> in accordance with all the Law (2 Kgs 17:13).

Just as the DtrH begins with covenant and law in the Book of Deuteronomy,[132] so the DtrH ends with the renewal of covenant and the acceptance of the Law by both the king and the people:

> And the king . . . made a covenant before the Lord,
> to walk after the Lord and
> to keep his commandments and his testimonies
>> and his statutes . . .
> to perform the words of this covenant
>> that were written in this book;
> and all the people joined in the covenant (2 Kgs 23:3).[133]

The formulae in the DtrH, "walk in his ways" and "keep his statutes . . ." have no reference other than the Torah given to Moses on Horeb; and, not surprisingly, the formulae occur in those texts which are clearly Deuteronomistic.

---

[132]Cf. the study of D. J. McCarthy, (*Treaty and Covenant*, 109-40), which shows Deuteronomy with its presentation of the Torah to be a literary composition in the form of covenant.

[133]The employment of covenant in the structure of the DtrH is instructive for interpreting the theological thrust of the historian. The covenant set forth in Deuteronomy is a conditional covenant with the people. In the dream narrative the conditional covenant is applied to Solomon and to all subsequent kings. In 2 Kings 17, the announcement is made that the covenant with the people and the king has been broken and the curses have been actualized. In 2 Kings 23, the king and the people renew covenant and promise obedience to the Law. Does not this suggest hope for the nation? The future is hopeful; depending on the response of the nation to Torah, there is the open possibility of life or of death.

On the renewal of covenant, see Klaus Baltzer, *The Covenant Formulary*.

In the dream, God's words, "If you will walk in my ways, keeping my statutes and my commandments" intend to oblige Solomon and all future kings to keeping the Torah. We have demonstrated that these formularies are Dtr expressions referring exclusively to Torah; and that they are set in a conditional statement, itself borrowed from law, to leave no doubt as to the legal implication. With this conditional statement and clear reference to Torah, all that pertains to the king, all traditions of royal theology are redefined within the ambit of the Torah.

The conditional statement in the dream has indeed been erroneously termed an additional element by those who do not understand the Dtr literary process and his intention. Without the conditional statement, the dream narrative lacks force and intention, for only in this final assertion does the Dtr thought come into full expression. The intention in the composition of the dream narrative is precisely to bring into harmony the diversity of traditions that make up royal theology with the Law of Moses. The Dtr has not worked out a refined systematic theology in which the royal and Yahwistic faith traditions are homogenized. The Deuteronomistic method sets traditions in opposition and in congruence; it contrasts and compares, for the purpose of dramatizing the theological point that what is of the people pertains to the king and what is of the king is applicable to the people. In this process neither the traditions of promise and blessing nor the emphasis on conditionality and law are muted. Thus, the DtrH holds in tension the promissory covenant and the conditioned covenant; the instructions and the Torah; David and Moses; a theology based on creation and a theology based on covenant.

By his methodology, the Dtr created a Dtr royal theology refined by content from covenant/law for his history of the Kings; and a Dtr theology of Yahwistic faith refined by content from creation/wisdom instructions for his report about the people of Israel about to enter the land. By this we mean that under the influence of the experience in exile, the Dtr reinterpreted the traditions of kingship and the faith traditions of the people to address the current existential situation of his contemporaries who were without temple, king, and land.[134]

---

[134]Cf. G. Minette de Tillesse, "Sections 'Tu' et Sections 'Vous' dans le Deuteronome," *VT* 12 (1962) 81-87.

DEUTERONOMISTIC ELEMENTS

Basic to the discussion in this paper is the intention to demonstrate that the dream narrative, 1 Kgs 3:4-15, is a literary unit composed by the Dtr out of traditional material which has been imaginatively and carefully shaped to make a theological point about kingship. We have confirmed the literary unity by noting the precise and deliberate literary structure which was enfleshed by traditions of kingship and Yahwism, and by illustrating how the traditional elements serve a single viewpoint regarding the king. We have, moreover, argued that in the Dtr perspective the king is cast into a role of subordination to the Torah.[135]

In addition to traditional elements, there are components in the narrative that serve no purpose other than connecting the traditional material into a whole. These were furnished by the Dtr. Because of the role that the connectives play in the history as a whole we consider the two clauses:

> so that no one like you has been before you
> and after you will arise no one like you (1 Kgs 3:12c)

> so that there has never been any one like you
> among the kings, all your days (1 Kgs 3:13c).

An expression like these occurs frequently in Assyrian royal inscriptions:

> The king . . . had had no equal (rival) . . .
> . . . there has been no (prince) equal to him.[136]

This evidence tells us that such superlative evaluations appeared in royal historical texts from at least the time of the Assyrian power and the fall of the Northern Kingdom. Notwithstanding this evidence, the use of such an expression within the DtrH itself will prove more beneficial for our purpose in showing that these connectives serve the theological thrust of the Dtr.

The first connective consists of two sections:

(1 Kgs 3:12c) וְאַחֲרֶיךָ לֹא-קוּם כָּמוֹךָ and כָּמוֹךָ לֹא-הָיָה לְפָנֶיךָ

---

[135]In the overall composition of the history, the Dtr intention is the reverse: to apply to the people under the law the traditions of promise and blessing associated with kingship, and therefore, supply the people in exile with encouragement for the future.

[136]*AR*, 55, #104; 57, #107; 60, #117; 72, #137. See also, Weinfeld, *Deuteronomy and the Deuteronomic School*, 359.

It is immediately apparent that the phrases are balanced chiastically. This literary expression is significant in that the balanced language pattern lends itself to easy repetition and memory.

In reference to Solomon, the formulary carries the weight of the key words, חכם ונבון:

> I give you a wise and intelligent heart
> so that no one like you has been before you
> and after you will arise no one like you (1 Kgs 3:12bc).

The chiastically phrased formulary serves the Dtr purpose by setting forth the Dtr appraisal of Solomon, and by thus indicating that the phrase חכם ונבון (wise and intelligent) expresses the characteristic endowment for which Solomon is distinguished in the DtrH.

The Dtr employed the same formulary in the case of Hezekiah and Josiah, the only two kings in addition to Solomon whose historical accounts can be considered a developed narrative presentation. To be sure, the Dtr interest in each of these kings is apparent though scholarship has not yet fully explored the importance of these narratives in the overall theological message of the DtrH. At this time, we only point out the use of the evaluative formulary to which is linked a key theological claim.

Concerning Hezekiah, the Dtr states:

> He trusted in the Lord the God of Israel
> so that after him there was none like him
>   among the kings   ואחריו לא-היה כמהו
> nor among those who were before him.
>   (2 Kgs 18:5)[137]   ואשר היו לפניו

The theme of trust (בטח), which is hereby pointed out as the distinguishing characteristic of Hezekiah in the mind of the Dtr, has only a faint echo elsewhere in the DtrH.[138] But that theme dominates the historical account of Hezekiah.[139]

---

[137]The second half of this formulary is used in the Dtr evaluation of Jeroboam: "you have done evil above all who were before you" (אשר-היו לפניך), 1 Kgs 14:9.

[138]Deut 28:52.

[139]2 Kgs 18:5, 19, 20, 21, 22, 24; 19:10. The theme of "trust" has been shown to be central in wisdom literature and therefore a basic idea to creation theology: so, Zimmerli, "Structure of O. T. Wisdom," 190; and von Rad, *Wisdom in Israel*, 190-206. "Trust" is also a significant term in covenant contexts: so, A. R. Johnson, *Sacral Kingship*, 122-23; and F. C. Fensham, "Ps 21," 197.

Of Josiah, the Dtr writes:

Before him there was no king like him
who turned to the Lord
    with all his heart and
    with all his soul and
    with all his might,
according to all the law of Moses
nor did any like him arise after him
    (2 Kgs 23:25)

כמהו לא־היה לפניו

ואחריו לא־קם כמהו

The Dtr evaluation of Josiah focuses upon his fidelity to Yahweh in keeping the Torah. When the book of the law was found in the Temple during
the reign of Josiah, Josiah "turned" to the Lord wholly in his response to
the words of the book which were read to him.[140] Josiah lost no time in
following its directives,[141] and in calling the nation to a renewal of
covenant and obedience to the words of the law.[142]

    The formulaic expression is used only in the DtrH and only in these
significant accounts. The Dtr may well be adopting a royal annalistic
formula to carry the characteristic of each of the three kings within the
DtrH. This is another example of the appropriation by the Dtr of a form
from another royal tradition to serve his theological purpose.

    The second evaluative statement consists of a single part:

There has never been any one like you among the kings
לא־היה כמוך איש במלכים (1 Kgs 3:13c).

This statement may be simply a repetition of the fuller formulary used
above for the sake of literary elaboration within the narrative. Notwithstanding this possibility, the sophisticated way in which the Dtr uses
literary balance for theological effect prompts us to suggest another
possibility. The Dtr account of Moses ends with the evaluation:

    On "trust" in both wisdom and covenant, see W. A. Brueggemann, *In
Man We Trust*, 42-45.

    [140]Wolff ("Kerygma of the DtrH," 83-100), has demonstrated that
the term "return" is programmatic for the entire work. Wolff says,
"Because the call to return and thereby also the covenant made with the
fathers were despised, the final judgment upon Israel took place. It is not
the total apostasy which makes the judgment final, but the contemptuous
disregard of the call to return" (p. 91).

    [141]2 Kgs 23:4-24.

    [142]2 Kgs 23:1-3.

there has not arisen a prophet since
in Israel like Moses
לא-קם . . . נביא (Deut 34:10).

We notice that the summarization for the life of Moses is phrased with
the verb לא-קם, which is the normal balance to the verb לא-היה,
used in the case of Solomon.[143] The evaluations of Solomon and Moses,
so phrased, form a literary pair. The Dtr undoubtedly intended to draw a
deliberate comparison between Moses and Solomon.

We may only conjecture about the message hidden in this comparison. Since the dream narrative, as we have so often stated, sets forth
the theology for kings that governs the composition of the accounts of all
kings after Solomon, the comparison of Solomon with Moses would demonstrate the integration between royal tradition and Mosaic traditions which
form the basis of Dtr royal theology. Moreover, the comparison focuses
upon Moses as "prophet" and Solomon as "one of the kings." The Dtr history of kings is composed as a controversy between prophets and the
kings, a dialectic already forecast in the exposition of Moses as prophet
par excellence[144] set in balance with Solomon, one of the unfaithful
kings.

We found that the chiastically phrased formulary is employed in
the accounts of Solomon, Hezekiah and Josiah, and that, in each of the
three uses, the formulary is linked to a statement about each king which
characterizes that king according to the emphasis intended by the Dtr.
Thus, the Dtr highlights three distinct themes which, if investigated for
their theological import in the history, will throw light, we suspect, on the
Dtr intention in each historical account.

The second expression, we noted, is more brief, but based on the
fuller formulary. It serves to tie the dream narrative to the history as a
whole. We suggested that, with this phrase, the Dtr makes a connection
between Solomon and Moses. This link exemplifies the integration between the royal traditions and Torah effected in the dream and programmatic for the history of the kings, as well as the dialectic between the
prophets and kings upon which the history of the kings beginning with
Solomon is based.

---

[143]Cf. the verbs לא-היה and לא-קם in the formularies applied
to Solomon, Hezekiah, and Josiah, above.

[144]In Deuteronomic law, the prophets are compared with Moses:
Deut 18:15-22, esp. vv 16-18.

VI

Content of the Framework in
Verses 4-5a and 15

In our study, we have demonstrated that the body of the dream narrative is composed out of traditional elements deriving from royal traditions and from traditions of Yahwism. We have observed that these traditional components were combined with deuteronomistic elements that fill out and give precision to the various dimensions of a Dtr design for kingship.

In the present chapter, we will consider the content of the framework to the narrative so that the Dtr purpose in the formulation of the framework may become obvious to us.

DREAM AS THE MEDIA FOR DIALOGUE

Like the Königsnovelle model, the narrative is set in a dream. The dream takes place in one sanctuary, and like the events in the ancient Egyptian text, after the dream the king goes to another, the shrine of the deity he had encountered, where he offers sacrifice in thanksgiving.[1] Although the elements in the framework parallel the ancient source remarkably, we must not assume that the Dtr simply emulated that piece of literature so that the form would be complete. The fact of the matter is that the content in the framework reflects specifically Israelite tradition which has been rhetorically expressed by the Dtr according to the established mold, but this content is also pregnant with theological meaning that characterizes the new era of kingship as this is understood by the Dtr.

---

[1]See the discussion on the comparison of Solomon's dream with the Königsnovelle in Chap. II, pp. 27-32.

The "frame" of the narrative, of course, does precisely what the term suggests: it makes a boundary about the dialogue thus setting clear limits to the narrative.[2]   On account of the precision with which the framework has been composed, there is little room for argument about the extent of the narrative.

As we have noted, the framework to the narrative consists of two distinct parts which stand parallel to each other. In each is mentioned a specific place at which sacrifice is offered by the king, and in each there is a formulary that marks either the beginning or the closing of the dream.

> a) And the king went to Gibeon to sacrifice there,
>   for that was the great high place;
>   a thousand burnt offerings did Solomon offer
>   upon that altar (v 4).
>
> b) At Gibeon, Yahweh appeared to Solomon
>   in a dream by night (v 5a).
>
> c) And Solomon awoke, and behold,
>   it was a dream (v 15a).
>
> d) And he came to Jerusalem,
>   and he stood before the Ark of the Covenant of the Lord
>   and offered burnt offerings and made peace offerings,
>   and prepared a feast for all his servants (v 15b).

The formularies which announce the beginning and the conclusion to the dream form an inclusio that directly encircles the dialogue content (b and c). Surrounding this and making another inclusio are the parallel statements about Solomon's sacrificial activity at the two sacred places (a and d).

Because the components of the framework are separable into two distinct divisions, we will discuss the content of each section accordingly. First, we direct our attention to the dream formularies that are used to create the occasion for Solomon's theophanic experience.

A dream was adopted by the Dtr to vehicle the dialogue between Yahweh and Solomon. A typical mode for divine communication in royal ideology, a dream was the appropriate means for the transmission of the divine message. The Dtr shows remarkable acumen in selecting from royal tradition a most dramatic form of communication and one that makes the narrative represent most convincingly the setting of the early

---

[2]See the discussion on the use of the framework in the structure of the text in Chap. III, pp. 41-43.

monarchy.[3] This was the intention of the Dtr that the text reflect the era of Solomon though the content that is presented there is the view of kingship which is the ideal of the author.

The dream introduction formulary must have existed as a literary form in the ancient Near Eastern world over an extended period, as we learn from the evidence of the Memphis Stela. This inscription preserves the announcement of a dream in words that correspond remarkably with the formulary used by the Dtr in the dream of Solomon.[4] The Egyptian version tells of the dream of Amen-hotep II:

> The majesty of his august god, Amon . . .
> came before his majesty in a dream (*ANET*, 246, l. 22).

With this introduction we compare the formulary used by the Dtr in the biblical text:

> Yahweh appeared to Solomon in a dream by night
> (1 Kgs 3:5a).

The similarity between these statements is transparent. Both name the deity; each records the action of the deity in manifestation; each declares that the king is the receiver of the divine visitation and that the mode is that of a dream.

---

[3]We find in extra-biblical literature that a king was divinely nominated in a dream: e.g. the divine oracle addressed to Thut-mose IV (*ANET*, 449). The dream was the mode through which instructions and encouragement could be spoken to the king: e.g. the instructions given to Amen-em-het I (*ANET*, 418); and the protection promised to Amen-hotep II (*ANET*, 246b). Through the dream, kings usually sought the will of the deity: e.g. the Canaanite tales of Keret (*Canaanite Myths*, 29, ll. 35-51); and Aqhat (*Canaanite Myths*, 51, ll. 5-23). The Yahwist narrator who composed his work in the environment of the fledgling monarchy employed the dream as the medium for Yahweh to reiterate his promise of land and descendants to the patriarchs: Gen 26:24-25; 28:11-16. The dream was also the manner of God's communication with the prophet: Num 12:6.

[4]For a survey of dream texts and discussion of the dream form and its content, see, A. L. Oppenheim, *The Interpretation of Dreams*; H. and H. A. Frankfort, Thorkild Jacobsen, et al., *The Intellectual Adventure of Ancient Man* (Chicago: University of Chicago, 1946) 11-12, 189-91; Ernst L. Ehrlich, *Der Traum im Alten Testament* (BZAW 73; Berlin: Alfred Töpelmann, 1953) 56-57.

The Dtr undoubtedly used a familiar formulary from tradition. But we must not accept too readily that the Dtr drew upon this Egyptian source or a source from any other culture in the ancient Near East. As was the Dtr methodology in the use of traditional elements in the body of the narrative, the Dtr depended upon the formulaic elements that existed in the early Israelite literature for the material for his work.

There is ample evidence in the biblical literature to affirm that the introduction to a dream was a traditional formulary. The dream of Abimelech is announced with the words:

But God came to Abimelech in a dream by night (Gen 20:3).

The Hebrew text reads ויבא אלהים--בחלום הלילה. Another example is the divine visitation to Laban. The biblical account states that:

God came to Laban the Aramean in a dream by night
(Gen 31:24).

and in Hebrew the reading is ויבא אלהים--בחלם הלילה.

Both these texts like the Dtr narrative in 1 Kings 3 are expressed with the phrase "in a dream by night" (בחלום הלילה).

Another biblical illustration of a nocturnal visit is present in the Balaam narrative. That dream is announced with the formulary:

And God came to Balaam at night

(Num 22:20).[5] ויבא אלהים--לילה

The phrase בחלום (in a dream) is lacking in the formulaic expression of this particular dream announcement. With the evidence from the texts we have already quoted, there can be no doubt that the writer is making use of the commonly known formulary for the announcement of a dream and that "in a dream" is simply implied in this case. When a formulary has become so common we cannot expect that the author would use every word but rather, in the manner of a skilled traditionist, there is ease and freedom in the employment of traditional elements.

The texts we are quoting here differ from the statement introducing Solomon's dream only in the naming of the divine visitor. Each of the above texts reads: "God came . . . (ויבא אלהים)"; whereas the statement as it was written by the Dtr reads: "Yahweh appeared . . . (יהוה

---

[5]Cf. Num 22:9 and 13. In this latter, there is also the intimation of a dream. V 9 reads, "And God came to Balaam and said. . . ." In v 13, we learn that "Balaam rose in the morning. . . ."

נראה)." At first sight the difference between these statements may seem dramatic and therefore exclude possibilities for comparison. We have already established the formulaic nature of בחלום הלילה (in a dream at night). There remains the need to account for the Dtr deviation from the expected pattern.

The disparity in the choice of subject and verb on the part of the Dtr reflects, we suspect, a rather precise reliance upon traditional usage. Throughout the literature of the Tetrateuch, there is an uncanny consistency in the way a divine visitation is expressed. When the deity is termed by the general name *Elohim*, the verb that follows is always בא.[6] On the other hand, when the divine name *Yahweh* is used, the verb that describes the action is always נראה.[7]

The Dtr chose to use the particular name for the God of Israel, and therefore, he used the verb that tradition suggested. Together with the traditional "Yahweh appeared," the Dtr joined the formulaic expression for the beginning of a dream. The Dtr not only used the particular name *Yahweh* but he used the verb that is generally found in traditional language together with *Yahweh* to describe the self-revelation of God. There is no surprise in this precision, for this is what is expected from one who is familiar with the traditional language of Israel and who is consciously drawing upon that language for the articulation of a wholly new statement. In the precise selection of expressions, the Dtr proves that he is using the acceptable Israelite tradition and not some source from another ancient oriental culture.

It is necessary that we reiterate our conviction that the choice of *Yahweh* is quite deliberate for this context of the dream introduction formulation. The name *Yahweh* links the dream narrative to the three verses that precede the dream.[8] These verses, which are the work of the Dtr as an introduction not simply to the history of Solomon but to the Dtr history of kings, name the special God of Israel. The use of *Yahweh* as the subject of the dream would function to weld the narrative to the introduction.

---

[6] Exod 20:20, 24; Num 22:9.

[7] Exod 3:16; 4:1, 5; 6:3; Lev 9:4; Deut 31:15; 1 Kgs 9:2; 11:9.

[8] Vv 1-3 which precede the dream of Solomon are the work of the Dtr also, but these verses are entirely distinct from the narrative. They were so composed to be an introduction to the Dtr interpretation of Israelite kingship. For a discussion about the function of these verses in the history, see below, n. 30.

But more importantly, the God who showed himself to Solomon and who was addressed by Solomon in vv 6-9 was the particular God of Israelite history. The Dtr is quite precise in identifying the divine visitor. This is the God of covenant who bound himself by promise to David. This is the God who chose the people Israel to be his own and special people. This is the God who revealed himself to the Patriarchs, to Moses, to David and now to Solomon. That there might be no question that the God by whose choice Solomon reigns is the God of Israel, the Dtr names *Yahweh* as the deity who appeared to Solomon in the dream.

A formulaic expression also concludes the dream of Solomon. This formulary likewise derives from the store of traditional language that existed in the ancient Orient over an extended period.

Several noteworthy examples from extra-biblical literature warrant consideration for purposes of comparison. The second dream of Gudea, which is recorded in the Gudea cylinder, terminates with the words:

> he awoke with a start, it was a dream![9]

In the Ugaritic literature, there is a record of a dream during which Keret was promised a son. This dream ends with the announcement:

> Keret looked, and it was a dream.
> krt . yḫt . wḥlm[10]

The conclusion to the dream of Solomon compares remarkably with the above formulations to announce the ending of the dream. The biblical text reads:

> And Solomon awoke, and behold it was a dream
> ריקץ שלמה והנה חלום (1 Kgs 3:15a).

Within the biblical tradition, the ending of a dream is less often expressed than is the announcement of the dream's inception. We have noted that when the dream is formally announced, the formulation is traditional to extra-biblical as well as biblical literature. Usually the conclusion of the dream is simply presumed to have occurred, for none of the examples we have noted mentions the termination of the dream.

---

[9]Cyl A XIII: 12; translated in Oppenheim, *The Interpretation of Dreams*, 191a. Cf. F. Thureau-Dangin, *Die Sumerischen und Akkadischen Königsinschriften* (Leipzig: J. C. Hinrichs, 1907) 103.

[10]Keret I: iii, 50, in *Canaanite Myths*, 32-33.

There is, however, an example of a formal dream conclusion within the Joseph Story. At the end of one of the records of Pharaoh's dream, there is an announcement that the dream had come to an end. The formulation is precisely the expression used also to announce the end of Solomon's dream. It reads:

And Pharaoh awoke, and behold, it was a dream

וייקץ פרעה והנה חלום (Gen 41:7b).

One would think that both these biblical texts come from the same hand. Such a conclusion is not necessarily appropriate. The Dtr is responsible for the formulation of Solomon's dream, and as overwhelming evidence presented in this study attests, the Dtr employed a traditional formulation for the conclusion of a dream in the manner that the Dtr used traditional language throughout the narrative.

We have observed that both the formal introduction and the conclusion to the dream of Solomon occur elsewhere in biblical literature. We have indicated that these formulations have extra-biblical roots as well. The dream form belongs to the sphere of influence of the Dtr. It is part of the intellectual heritage of the author, an example of the expressions known from traditional language.

We see no reason to assume with Weinfeld,[11] that the "original

---

[11]Moshe Weinfeld, *Deuteronomy*, 248-54. Weinfeld assumes that because the content of the dream in the cylinder of Gudea and in certain other extra-biblical texts concerns approval for the building of a temple, the same message must have originally been conveyed in the dream of Solomon. Weinfeld's argument is based on the fact that the greater portion of the Solomon history focuses upon the execution of the building projects. That the content was ever other than what is currently available to the reader is, of course, beyond proof and therefore highly questionable.

The burden of Weinfeld's argument is made to demonstrate that the content of the dream is the contribution of the Dtr. The substituted material, Weinfeld argues, reflects a view of wisdom that is judicial and moral in contrast to an earlier wisdom which meant "cunning, pragmatic talent, and the possession of extraordinary knowledge" (p. 255).

The intention in the present study is also to demonstrate Dtr authorship of the dream narrative. Having worked through the text, we vehemently disagree with Weinfeld's line of reasoning. We have found the text to be coherent and integral, the masterful work of a perceptive and learned theologian. There is no apparent reason to assume that the Dtr was not the author of the entire work, the dream form as well as the dream of Solomon at Gibeon was a prophetic vision whose purpose was to grant approval for the construction of a sanctuary. . . .[12] Nor do we concur with Ehrlich and others[13] that Solomon was practicing the ritual incubatio so frequently attested in later Near Eastern and Greek practice. Nor do we admit of historicity of any kind, such as the explanation that Solomon went to Gibeon in an attempt to meet with the northern tribes to gain cooperation.[14] There was neither an original experience of a dream *per se* nor a dream which served as the model for Solomon's dream. The Dtr simply employed the dream form which was a wholly acceptable means for theophany as the rhetorical frame for the content of the dream. The specific formularies employed to express the inception and the termination of the dream belong to the store of traditional expressions available to the Dtr.

THE SETTING FOR THE EVENTS

The final text for discussion is the outermost framework of the narrative. This pair of texts is made up of parallel summary passages that set the limits of the narrative and that convey a sense of passage in place and time. In each summary statement there is mention of a cultic place, the naming of a significant feature of that place according to tradition, and an account of the sacrifice offered there. We quote the two texts:

---

content of the dialogue between Yahweh and Solomon. Every part of the narrative was expressed out of the building blocks of the Dtr literature, i.e., out of the traditional phrases, expressions and words which the Dtr was wont to use. We are showing in this study that the narrative was composed out of formulaic expressions to present a design for kingship which was meant to be programmatic for the whole of the Dtr interpretation of kings.

[12]Ibid., 248.

[13]According to Ehrlich (*Der Traum*, 20): "We are dealing with a genuine incubation scene, the basis of which was probably a local tradition at the shrine of Gibeon. Solomon goes to Gibeon, which apparently even in Solomon's time, held a leading place among the Israelite shrines, in spite of the existence of the altar in Jerusalem which David had built." So, also, Oppenheim, *The Interpretation of Dreams*, 187-88; J. Gray, *The Legacy of Canaan: The Ras Shamra Texts and Their Relevance to the Old Testament* (2d rev. ed.; Leiden: E. J. Brill, 1965) 210; and *I and II Kings*, 124; Fichtner, *Das erste Buch*, 72; and Weinfeld, *Deuteronomy*, 246.

[14]So, Fichtner, *Das erste Buch*, 71; and Wifall, *Court History*, 44.

And the king went to Gibeon to sacrifice there,
>   for that was the great high place;
Solomon used to offer a thousand burnt offerings
>   upon that altar (v 4).

Then he came to Jerusalem,
and stood before the Ark of the covenant of Adonai,
and offered burnt offerings and made peace offerings,
and prepared a feast for all his servants (v 15b).

By design the religious center Gibeon is mentioned at the beginning of the narrative and Jerusalem at the close. We will demonstrate that the transition from Gibeon to Jerusalem carries a significant theological meaning. And we will show that precisely in this transition, it becomes clear that the narrative was designed as a programmatic statement about the reign of Solomon and as an introduction to the deuteronomistic interpretation of kings.

We recall at this point that in the genre of Königsnovelle, there is the text that describes the movement of Thutmose IV who went to the central sanctuary in the city to worship after having received a divine communication in a dream at another sacred place.[15] While we mention this comparison, we are certain that the Dtr did not intend simply that Solomon should be presented sacrificing at Jerusalem in thanksgiving after the revelation in the dream at Gibeon. Nor does the Dtr intend only to emulate the Königsnovelle in its particular aspects. The purpose of the Dtr, to be sure, will become perceptible as we investigate the significance of the places Gibeon and Jerusalem.

Significantly, the place Gibeon is never mentioned in the biblical narratives of the Tetrateuch. On the other hand, Gibeon or the Gibeonites are mentioned no less than twenty-eight times within the DtrH. Gibeon is mentioned three times as the sacred place where Yahweh spoke with Solomon in a dream.[16] Gibeon is named as the city that sought peace with the people of Yahweh;[17] it is distinguishable as one of the cities in the territory of Benjamin;[18] it is also one of the cities given to the descendants of Aaron.[19] Though these references are numerous, they shed no light on the reason why Gibeon would be the place where God

---

[15]This text is quoted in Chap. III, p. 42.
[16]1 Kgs 3:4, 5; 9:2.
[17]Josh 9:3, 17; 10:1, 2, 4, 5, 6, 10, 12, 41.
[18]Josh 18:25.
[19]Josh 21:17.

would reveal himself to Solomon. The heavy interest in Gibeon noted here indicates only that the Dtr held Gibeon and its environs in high regard.[20]

Gibeon, on the other hand, plays an important role as the place where the conflict between the family of Saul and the followers of David was resolved. The hostilities between the Saulites and the Davidids were brought to a close at Gibeon with the murder there of Abner, commander of Saul's army, by Joab who was the commander of David's army.[21] At Gibeon, Joab also assassinated Amasa, a leader in David's army who deserted to the support of Sheba a Benjaminite in his revolution against David.[22]

Tradition tells us that Gibeon was "a great city like one of the royal cities."[23] Relying upon this epitaph for the city, the suggestion has been introduced that Gibeon was made the royal city of Saul, the capital being transferred to that location from Gibeah in the later years of Saul's reign.[24]

The hypothesis has been introduced, also, that Gibeon was the location for the ark during the years just prior to its transfer to the city of David.[25] So little is known about the residence of the ark during this time, and attempts to reconstruct historical circumstances on the basis of the information offered in the DtrH prove so problematic, that the conjecture is purely hypothetical. We must say, however, that Gibeon as the site of the ark offers attractive possibilities for speculating about the motivation of the Dtr with respect to the ark. It might be possible to claim that the Dtr meant to portray the transfer of the ark from its place at Gibeon before the temple construction to its place in the Jerusalem sanctuary after the temple construction.

Since the biblical tradition offers only very limited information concerning the ark and Gibeon, we will not depend upon mere speculation

---

[20]On the basis of the Dtr's interest in this territory, Jepsen (*Quellen*, 96-100), argues that the DtrH was drafted in the region of Benjamin. So also, Noth, *Ü St.*, 9, 110, n. 1; and Fichtner, *Das erste Buch*, 26-27.

[21]Cf. 2 Sam 2:12ff; 3:1, 30.

[22]Cf. 2 Sam 20:8.

[23]Josh 10:2.

[24]So, Joseph Blenkinsopp, *Gibeon and Israel: The Role of Gibeon and the Gibeonites in the Political and Religious History of Early Israel* (Cambridge: University Press, 1972) 63-64; and "Did Saul Make Gibeon His Capital?" *VT* 24 (1974) 1-7.

[25]For the arguments set forth to establish this hypothesis, see Blenkinsopp, *Gibeon and Israel*, 65-83.

for the material of our insight. Instead, we will look to that information given to us by the Dtr himself in the framework passages to shed light on the meaning of Gibeon in this context. We will consider the description of the place given by the Dtr and determine what meaning, if any, this description may have within Dtr theology.

The Dtr designates Gibeon as "the great high place" (הבמה הגדולה); he indicates that the king went there "to sacrifice upon the altar" that was at that place.[26] From this description, we can surmise that Gibeon was a place of worship where there was an altar for sacrifice. However, we must rely upon the evidence given within biblical tradition to support this description. The Chronicler preserves the tradition that the tabernacle built by Moses and the altar of burnt offerings were at Gibeon.[27] In the mind of the Chronicler, there is no distinction between the ancient tabernacle tradition and the tradition of the tent of meeting, for the Chronicler states that Gibeon was the place where one went to inquire of God.[28]

On account of this tradition, which obviously was known by the Dtr, Gibeon was named as the site where Solomon met with God and where he sacrificed upon the altar that was at that place. However, for the Dtr, it is not the place Gibeon itself which is central. It is rather that Gibeon was the "great high place" that matters for Dtr interpretation.

A perusal of the uses of "high place" (במה) within the DtrH will confirm that this term carries a distinct theological significance. There is clearly a *before* and *after* for the use of the "high place" as places for worship in Dtr thought. According to Dtr evaluation, the "high place" was the legitimate place for sacrifice prior to the building of the temple. Once the temple has been dedicated, however, worship at the "high places" is interpreted as an act of apostasy.

The "high places" are of no concern during the periods of Joshua and Judges; indeed, a "high place" is never mentioned either in the source material or in Dtr comment within these books. In the book of Samuel, however, the "high place" is the location for Samuel's activities. For the composition of the Samuel narratives, the Dtr made use of an early

---

[26]On "high places," see W. F. Albright, "The High Place in Ancient Palestine," in *Volume du Congrès* (VTSup 4; Leiden: E. J. Brill, 1957) 242-58; and Patrick H. Vaughn, *The Meaning of 'Bāmâ' in the Old Testament: A Study of Etymological, Textual and Archeological Evidence* (SOTSMS 3; New York and London: Cambridge University, 1974).

[27]1 Chr 21:29. Cf. Exodus 25.

[28]1 Chr 21:30. Cf. Exodus 33:7-11.

pro-monarchical source[29] which cites the "high place" as the place around which the event of Saul's designation for kingship and anointing was accomplished. According to this information, the "high place" was the site for offering of sacrifice (1 Sam 9:12, 14), where the prophet and the people shared the sacrificial meal (1 Sam 9:13). Samuel and Saul ate together at the "high place" (1 Sam 9:19, 24-25). Moreover, the "high place" is significant in the experience of Saul. The band of prophets among whom Saul prophesied are presented "coming down from the 'high place' with harp, tambourine, flute, and lyre before them, prophesying" (1 Sam 10:5). Saul prophesied among the band of propehts (1 Sam 10:10-11), and when he had finished prophesying, "he came to the high place" (1 Sam 10:13).

The source appropriated by the Dtr reveals that the "high place" was the usual and legitimate place for worship in the time prior to the construction of the temple. There is, in fact, no evident attempt on the part of the Dtr to adumbrate the significance of the "high place" for worship in this era. The case is, rather, that the Dtr consciously makes the distinction between the "high place" as the appropriate place for worshipping Yahweh before the building of the temple, and the illegitimacy of worshipping at the "high places" after the temple construction.

An indication that our interpretation of the use of "high place" within the DtrH is correct is affirmed by the Dtr himself. In a programmatic statement that is typically deuteronomistic, the author states:

> The people were sacrificing at the *high places,* however, because no house had yet been built for the name of the Lord (1 Kgs 3:2).[30]

---

[29]The source is located in 1 Sam 9:1-10:16; 11. On the composition of these narratives that describe the inauguration of the monarchy and a discussion of the sources used there, see: Rolf Knierim, "The Messianic Concept in the First Book of Samuel," in *Jesus and the Historian. Written in Honor of E. C. Colwell* (ed. F. T. Trotter; Philadelphia: Westminster, 1968) 20-51; Dennis J. McCarthy, "The Inauguration of Monarchy in Israel. A Form-Critical Study of 1 Samuel 8-12," *Int* 27 (1973) 401-12; Bruce C. Birch, "The Development of the Tradition on the Anointing of Saul in I Sam 9:1-10:16," *JBL* 90 (1971) 55-68; and *The Rise of the Israelite Monarchy: The Growth and Development of I Samuel 7-15* (SBLDS 27; Missoula: Scholars, 1976) 29-42, 54-63.

[30]This statement as well as the statements in vv 1 and 3 provide a *mise-en-scène* for the Dtr view of the Solomonic reign. Vv 1-3, which introduce the whole of the History of Solomon, are programmatic, for

This statement functions to mark the transition from the time before the temple to the time after the temple. In the era before Solomon, the Dtr recognizes the practice of worship at the high places without censure.

---

they set the stage upon which the indictment against Solomon and the people will be pronounced. If we compare 1 Kgs 3:1-3 with 1 Kings 11, the conclusion to the History of Solomon, we notice that what has been introduced in the programmatic introduction is brought to completion in the final chapter. It is worthy of notice that, for the sake of emphasis, the same interests are summarized at a climactic point within the history at 9:24-25 in anticipation of the conclusion.

Solomon's marriage to the daughter of Pharaoh and her presence in the city of David (3:1a), alluded to again in 9:24, introduces Solomon's departure from following Yahweh (11:1-6). The statement about Solomon's achievements in building (3:1b), anticipates the completion of these projects (6:14, 38; 7:1, 51; 9:1, 25b), and foreshadows Solomon's further building enterprises (11:7) which are dedicated not to Yahweh but to the gods of his foreign wives. A most emphatic note of contrast is struck in the presentation of Solomon's love for Yahweh in 3:3, and his love for the women who drew his heart away from loving Yahweh (11:1-6). The movement is from Solomon's love ($^{\flat}hb$) for Yahweh (3:3a) to his love ($^{\flat}hb$) for the foreign women (11:1a) to whom he cleaved (dbq) in love (11:2c). The formulaic "loving" and "cleaving" to Yahweh is typical deuteronomic language (cf. Deut 10:20; 11:22; 13:3-4; 30:20). These expressions, however, were made thematic for the structure of the entire DtrH. The motif of marriage with foreigners as the way of separating from Yahweh is presented in commandment form in Deut 7:3-5. It is reiterated in Josh 22:5 and 23:7-8. Solomon is portrayed as paradigmatic of this type of infidelity (1 Kgs 11:1-2); and he is contrasted with Hezekiah who is the model of fidelity to Yahweh by cleaving to Him (1 Kgs 18:6).

The reference to the people worshipping at the "high places" in v 2 foreshadows the great evil during the new era of the temple. The participation of the people and the king in sacrifice at the high places in the pre-temple era (1 Kgs 3:2 and 4) points to the corporate responsibility of king and people for the consequences of this activity in the new era. The history of Solomon itself represents the new era of the temple with a narration about the building and dedication of the temple (1 Kings 6-8). The consequences for infidelity are stated, however, immediately afterward in 1 Kgs 9:6-9 and 11:10-13; for, this very house will be destroyed and this land will be lost on account of the evil of the people and the king for worshipping at places other than the central sanctuary. The remainder of the history of the kings is devoted to a narration of the fulfillment of these events--the apostasy of the king and the people and the consequent destruction of the temple and loss of the land.

This statement also foreshadows the era after the temple which the Dtr evaluates with the judgment:

> Judah did what was evil in the sight of the Lord . . . they built
> for themselves *high places* (1 Kgs 14:22-23. Cf. 2 Kgs 17:9-
> 22).

Within the time after the temple construction, each king of Judah is evaluated accordingly because

> the *high places* were not taken away and the people still
> sacrificed and burned incense on the *high places.*[31]

Only the kings Hezekiah and Josiah meet with the approval of the Dtr precisely because these kings "removed the high places."[32]

There is a careful delineation of the time before the temple and the time after projected by the Dtr through the use of the term "high places." Whereas the "high place" was suitable and appropriate as a place for worship prior to the temple, the "high place" is looked upon negatively as a place for the practice of idolatry after the temple was built. The Dtr attack upon the "high places," we have seen, is reserved solely to this new era. Thus the programmatic statement at the beginning of the Solomon History provides the clue to the Dtr intention in his reference to the "high place" at Gibeon: the people sacrifice at the high places because the house for the name of the Lord is not yet built (1 Kgs 3:2).

Likewise when the Dtr mentions that Solomon went to Gibeon the great high place to sacrifice upon the altar there, the concern is not that the place is Gibeon though tradition holds that this is the site of the ancient tent of meeting and tabernacle from the wilderness era. The Dtr intends, rather, to contrast worship at a high place as a legitimate situation before the time of Solomon and worship at the high place as an act of apostasy after that time.[33]

According to the Dtr, the cultic practice for Israel radically changed from worship at various shrines to the worship of Yahweh at the

---

[31] 1 Kgs 22:44 (Eng 22:43); 2 Kgs 12:4 (Eng 12:3); 14:4; 15:4, 35.

[32] 2 Kgs 18:4, 11; cf. 23:8, 13, 15, 19. Cf. W. Boyd Barrick, "On the Removal of the 'High Places' in 1-2 Kings," *Bib* 55 (1974) 257-59.

[33] Cf. Peter J. Kearney, "The Role of the Gibeonites in the Deuteronomic History," *CBQ* 35 (1973) 13-16. Kearney argues that the Dtr intends to contrast Gibeon unfavorably with Jerusalem by presenting Gibeon as a scene of violence and deception, particularly in the Dtr composition in Joshua 9.

shrine exclusively designated for this purpose in Jerusalem in the reign of Solomon.[34] The construction of the temple, the transfer of the ark to the temple, and the consecration of the temple represent the great achievement of Solomon. The Dtr intends in no way to obscure these events which, in the Dtr perspective, mark the turning point to a new moment in Israelite life with Yahweh. Indeed, the Dtr appropriated sources relative to the temple construction as the principal content for the composition of the Solomon History. Virtually all of chapters 5-8 focus upon the building activity and the crowning event of the building, the dedication of the temple with the transfer there of the ark.

The locus for the great contribution of Solomon is, to be sure, Jerusalem which is the place named in the concluding half of the framework. It is the solemn event of the temple dedication at Jerusalem which is the focus of the history of Solomon. Let us consider the Dtr report of that event. The Dtr tells us that when the temple had been completed, Solomon assembled the elders of Israel, the heads of the tribes, and the leaders of the fathers' houses "to bring up the ark of the covenant of the Lord out of the city of David, which is Zion" (1 Kgs 8:1b). Thereupon, the Dtr recounts that "the priests took up the ark, and they brought up the ark of YHWH . . . /the ark of the covenant of YHWH to its place, underneath the wings of the cherubim" (1 Kgs 8:3b-4a). Thus Yahweh came to dwell in Jerusalem, the city chosen by him where a house would be built,[35] that He might have "a place to dwell in forever" (1 Kgs 8:13b). The events of the day when the ark was transferred from the city of David to its place in the temple culminated with the offering of sacrifice and with a great feast. The Dtr narrates these events:

> Then the king and all Israel with him offered sacrifice before the Lord.
> Solomon offered as peace offerings to the Lord twenty-two thousand oxen . . . (1 Kgs 8:62-63a).

---

[34] There are critics who argue that the report of Solomon's sacrifice at Jerusalem was a deuteronomic addition introduced to exonerate Solomon, the builder of the temple, for his illegitimate ritual involvement at the Gibeon shrine. So, Noth, *Ü St.*, 68; James A Montgomery, Henry S. Gehman, ed., *A Critical and Exegetical Commentary on the Books of Kings* (ICC; New York: Scribner's, 1951) 104; James Robinson, *The First Book of Kings* (The Cambridge Bible Commentary; Cambridge: University Press, 1972) 53; and Gray, *I and II Kings*, 127.

[35] 1 Kgs 8:16, 20-21, 29, 42b, 43b, 48.

So Solomon held the feast at that time and all Israel with him
    (1 Kgs 8:65a).

The image obtained from this description is that of a solemn ritual. The
king is the leader in the enactment. He stands before the ark in the sanctuary at Jerusalem and he offers sacrifice, specifically burnt offerings
and peace offerings.[36]

With the event of ritual celebration that took place in the temple
at the time of the transfer of the ark, we compare the activity of Solomon at the termination of the dream. The Dtr relates that:

Solomon came to Jerusalem
and stood before the ark of the covenant of the Lord
and offered burnt offerings and made peace offerings
and prepared a feast for all his servants (1 Kgs 3:15b).

Here too the king is presented in the stance of the leader in a solemn
celebration. There is the offering of sacrifice before the ark and participation in a great feast.

It could be argued that the Dtr summary of ritual action and
solemn celebration presented at the conclusion to the dream was meant to
reflect the event of the temple dedication. But this is not the case, in the
opinion of the writer. We have in both presentations, rather, the use of
common material. As the source for these presentations, both of which
are the work of the Dtr, there is undoubtedly a cult of the Jerusalem
sanctuary.[37] It is beyond our interest to attempt to reconstruct such a

---

[36]See Rolf Rendtorff, *Studien zur Geschichte des Opfers im Alten
Israel* (WMANT; Neukirchen-Vluyn: Neukirchener, 1967) 42-45, 78-79,
123-26. Rendtorff concludes that these are the required offerings for a
king at special circumstances such as the dedication of an altar or a
sanctuary.

[37]Efforts have been made to reconstruct the official cult of the
Jerusalem temple. Some argue that the cult was the feast of Yahweh's
enthronement. So, S. Mowinckel, "Das Thronbesteigungsfest Jahwä's," in
Psalmenstudien II (Amsterdam: P. Schippers, 1961) 44-145; and *The
Psalms in Israel's Worship*, 15-22, 106-92; R. E. Clements, *God and Temple*
(Philadelphia: Fortress, 1965) 63-78. Others argue that the cult was the
Royal Zion Festival which recalled the bringing of the ark into Jerusalem
and the founding of the Davidic dynasty. So, Hans-Joachim Kraus, *Worship in Israel*, 208-22; and *Psalmen I*, 197-205, 342-45; Keith Crim, *Royal
Psalms*, 40-51. The feast could be the celebration of the enthronement of
both Yahweh as King and the Davidid as the vice-regent of Yahweh on
earth. So, A. R. Johnson, *Sacral Kingship*.

Jerusalem cult. Nonetheless, we presume that such a cult existed on the basis of the consistency with which the Dtr presents the kings in a stance of worship. Knowing that the Dtr typically made use of such traditional material, we are encouraged in our assumption that such a source was available to the Dtr.

Besides the occasion of the temple dedication and the termination of the dream, both of which involve Solomon, the same ritual seems to be the source for the presentation of David in an act of solemn worship. In 2 Samuel 6, the Dtr reports the transfer of the ark by David from its resting place to the city of David. On that day, the Dtr tells us, David involved himself in what appears to be a ritual activity. David

> offered burnt offerings and peace offerings
>   before the Lord . . .
> he blessed the people in the name of the Lord,
> and distributed among all the people, the whole
>   multitude of Israel, both men and women, to
>   each a cake of bread, a portion of meat, and
>   a cake of raisins (2 Sam 6:17-19).[38]

The scene obvious in this portrayal of David is that of a solemn ritual celebration. The king blesses the assembly; he offers a suitable offering; and the event climaxes with a feast in which everyone present participates. This presentation like the two that concern Solomon was composed by the Dtr on the basis of a known Jerusalem cult. The pattern of that celebration was utilized by the Dtr and became for him the building blocks out of which he was enabled to portray the king in solemn ritual each time such a scene served the purpose of the narrative.

What we have discovered in this review of these three separate biblical texts is a pattern for ritual that we suggest was a cult of the Jerusalem temple. This cult was used by the Dtr as the pattern for those instances when the king was to be shown in a stance of worship. He used the pattern for the cult in the way that he usually used formulaic language for his compositional work.

It becomes clear that the scene of Solomon at the conclusion of the dream, is the scene of the king involved in the ritual that was appropriate to the king in the setting of the temple. For the Dtr, the stress is upon the fact that this is temple worship and therefore, worship in the new era --the era of Yahweh's presence in the temple.

---

[38]Cf. 1 Chr 15:25-28. The sharing of the food suggests participation in a feast: Lev 7:12-13; Num 6:15; Exod 29:23; Hos 3:1.

It is this new era that is contrasted with the time conveyed in the parallel statement that introduces the dream narrative. While the two framework passages, 1 Kgs 3:4 and 15b are certainly meant to be parallel in structure, their content marks two distinct eras that the Dtr consciously intended to contrast. In the time before the temple, the high places were acceptable places for worship. We have noted that the Dtr makes this fact quite clear in the manner that he uses the term "high place" for theological issue. Once the temple was completed, the temple alone was the legitimate place for worship, in the mind of the Dtr. It is therefore necessary that Solomon be presented giving thanks in Jerusalem and that the thanks be expressed in the manner of the Jerusalem cult.

There is one curiosity in the second half of the framework that remains to be discussed. That is the designation of the ark as the "Ark of the covenant of Adonai." Nowhere else in the biblical tradition is the Ark precisely so designated.[39] In the few instances when the word "covenant" is used with ark, the designation is "the ark of the covenant of Yahweh."[40] Usually the ark is simply "the ark of Yahweh"[41] or "the ark of Elohim."[42]

Having already discussed the deliberateness by which the Dtr made use of the variety of titles for God to serve his theological purpose, are we not to suspect that the Dtr also intentionally used *Adonai* in connection with the expression "ark of the covenant" in the context of the dream to serve his theological purpose? We must ask ourselves the question:

_____

[39]In Josh 3:11, the designation is Ark of the covenant of the Lord (Adonai) of all the earth; to which should be compared the designation in v 12: the Ark of Yahweh Lord (Adonai) of all the earth. On account of the additional clause "of all the earth," the emphasis here is quite different from the emphasis in the Solomon dream text. In 1 Kgs 2:26, the desigation is "the ark of the Lord God (Adonai Yahweh)." This latter is a typical address that occurs in a wide range of literature: in the DtrH, Deut 3:24; 9:26; Josh 7:7; Judg 6:22; 16:28; 2 Sam 7:18, 19, 20, 22, 28, 29; 1 Kgs 8:53; in the Psalms, 69:7; 109:21; 140:8; 141:8; in the closing formulae in Amos, 1:8; 3:13; 4:5 and passim; in Jeremiah, 1:6; 2:19, 22; 4:10; 14:13; 32:17, 25; and frequently in Ezekiel.

[40]So, Num 10:33; 14:44; Deut 10:8; 31:9, 25, 26; Josh 3:3, 17; 4:7, 18; 6:8; 8:33; 1 Sam 4:3, 5, 4 (Lord of Hosts); 1 Kgs 6:19; 8:1, 6; Jer 3:16.

[41]So, Josh 3:13; 4:5, 11; 6:6, 7, 11, 12, 13; 7:6; 1 Sam 5:3, 4; 6:1, 2, 8, 11, 15, 18, 19, 21; 7:1; 2 Sam 6:9, 10, 11, 13, 15, 16, 17; 1 Kgs 8:4.

[42]So, 1 Sam 3:3; 4:11, 13, 17, 18, 19, 21, 22; 5:1, 2, 10; 14:18; 2 Sam 6:2, 3, 4, 6, 7, 12; 7:2; 15:24, 25, 29.

what would be the theological impact of the title *Adonai* in conjunction
with the "ark of the covenant"?

Reflecting back to our discussion on *Adonai*,[43] we pointed out that
this title implies a covenant relationship between unequal parties. The
burden of responsibility for the endurance of the covenant falls upon the
vassal who must demonstrate loyalty or bear the consequences for having
violated the treaty stipulation. Indeed, such a covenant is conditional.

We have been arguing that the transition from Gibeon to Jerusalem
intended to convey the transition from the pre-temple to the temple era.
In order that we might understand the Dtr purpose in the introduction of
the title *Adonai* in conjunction with the ark, we must consider the function of the ark in the temple era.

Again, we look at the Dtr text in 1 Kings 8. Prior to the consecration of the temple, "the ark of the covenant of Yahweh" is dramatically
brought "out of the city of David" (1 Kgs 8:1b). The ark, the tent, and all
the vessels were brought up by the priests and Levites (1 Kgs 8:4). They
brought the "ark of the covenant of Yahweh" into "the inner sanctuary of
the house, in the most holy place underneath the wings of the cherubim"
(1 Kgs 8:6).

The ark which is brought to the temple is the ark of tradition--the
ark that had accompanied the Israelite armies to battle,[44] and the ark
that was the divine presence among the people.[45] The divine presence
was brought into the "house of the Lord."[46]

When the ark had been placed in the temple, the Dtr makes the
comment:

---

[43]See above, Chap. V, 124-27.

[44]Cf. Num 10:35-36; 14:44; 1 Sam 4:3-5.

[45]Cf. Num 10:35; Josh 3:3, 17; 4:7, 18.

[46]According to the Dtr, the divine presence was in the "cloud" that
"filled the house of the Lord," and in the "glory of the Lord" that "filled
the house of the Lord"; and in "thick darkness" (1 Kgs 8:10-12).

As the Dtr has recounted the history of the pre-temple era, Yahweh
was present with his people in this variety of ways: he visited his people
in the pillar of cloud and the tent of meeting (Deut 31:14-15); he spoke to
them through the cloud and the thick darkness (Deut 4:11; 5:19 [Eng
5:22]); his glory was present in the Ark (1 Sam 4:21-22; 2 Samuel 6); his
words were written on the tables of stone (Deut 4:13; 5:19 [Eng 5:22]; 9:9-
12; 10:1-5). These various modes of divine presence culminate in the
temple (1 Kgs 8:4, 6, 9-13). With the temple a new era is inaugurated; the
temple is the place of the divine presence among the people.

> there was nothing in the ark except the two tables of stone
> which Moses put there at Horeb, where Yahweh made a
> covenant with the people of Israel . . . (1 Kgs 8:19).

This is the last reference to the ark in the DtrH. The ark has been transformed by the Dtr from being the throne for the God of Israel to being a receptacle for the Torah.

The picture of Solomon standing before the ark and offering sacrifice does not make sense, according to our interpretation; for, we have argued that the Jerusalem setting indicates the temple era. In the temple era, the ark contained the words of Torah. Yahweh's presence filled the temple; he was not present on the ark. We aver that the Dtr made the distinction exact by calling the ark the "ark of the covenant of Adonai," implying that in the temple era the ark was no longer the seat of Yahweh's presence; it was the place for keeping the tablets on which were written the Torah.

If our interpretation is correct and we submit that it is, then *Solomon standing before the ark of the covenant of Adonai* projects an image of the king that is commensurate with the image that has been presented throughout the narrative. The image is that of *the king under torah*:

> . . . keeping all the words of the law and these statutes, and
> doing them; that his heart may not be lifted up above his
> brethren, and that he may not turn aside from the command-
> ment . . . so that he may continue long in his kingdom . . .
> (Deut 17:19b-20).

We conclude that the framework was composed to indicate a definite movement in time and place. By the use of the places, Gibeon and Jerusalem, the Dtr intended to depict the era prior to the construction of the temple in contrast with the time when Jerusalem was established as the national center for worship; he intended to differentiate between worship at the altar at the high place and worship in the sanctuary of the temple where Yahweh was present. The Dtr also fittingly climaxed the narrative with an image of the king standing before the ark which, at that time, was the container for the Torah. This is the completion of the Dtr design for kingship--the "king under Torah."

Before concluding the discussion, we must take note of another instance when the Dtr sets the sanctuaries at Gibeon and Jerusalem in parallel construct. This is observable within the DtrH in the section that interrupts the Succession Narrative at 2 Samuel 21 and 24.[47]

The narrative in 2 Samuel 21 tells of a famine in Israel which King David learns is the result of Saul's guilt on account of the death of the Gibeonites. To expiate this blood-guilt, the Gibeonites ask that "seven of (Saul's) sons be given to (them), so that (they) may hang them up before the Lord at Gibeon on the mountain of the Lord."[48] The sacred place where David "sought the face of the Lord"[49] that he might know the cause of the famine may have been Gibeon also, for there was at Gibeon according to the Chronicler, "the tent of meeting of God."[50] A reconstruction of the place, time, and circumstances of the event, however, is impossible with the information provided in the biblical material. We are concerned, nonetheless, that the basic components of the narrative be recognized that a comparison may be made with the narrative in 2 Samuel 24.

The incidents told in 2 Samuel 24 are also concentrated in a catastrophe, in this case, a pestilence. The cause of the disaster is the transgression of David, whereas in 2 Samuel 21, the sin was attributed to Saul. To make expiation, David purchases a threshing floor from a Jebusite, that on it, he may build an altar to the Lord and offer burnt offerings and peace offerings,[51] that the Lord may heed his supplication and avert the plague.

According to tradition, the threshing floor purchased by David was the site of the future sanctuary. The Chronicler whose interest is the temple elaborates this point perceptively, making certain that from that

---

[47] R. A. Carlson (*David, the Chosen King. A Traditio-Historical Approach to the Second Book of Samuel* [Uppsala: Almqvist & Wiksell, 1964] 194-259, and esp. 219-21) argues that the Succession Narrative is a "deuteronomized" history of David, and suggests that the unit 2 Samuel 21 and 24 determined the character of the Dtr composition of 1 Kings 3-11. Cf. P. J. Kearney, "Gibeonites in the Deuteronomic History," 16-17. Most critics assume that 2 Samuel 21-24 is an intrusion into the DtrH. So, Noth, *Ü St.*, 62, n. 3; Eissfeldt, *The Old Testament*, 324; and Blenkinsopp, *Gibeon and Israel*, 89.

[48] 2 Sam 21:6; cf. vv 9 and 11.

[49] 2 Sam 21:1b.

[50] 2 Chr 1:3. Cf. 1 Chr 21:29-30.

[51] The ritual suggested here noticeably reflects that which we have described above as the material used by the Dtr for his work in 1 Kings 8, 2 Samuel 6, and 1 Kgs 3:15.

time on the legitimate place for worship would be upon this altar and not in Gibeon. The Chronicler states that the site was designated by God himself to be the center for worship:

> And David built there an altar to the Lord and presented burnt offerings and peace offerings, and called upon the Lord, and he answered him with fire from heaven upon the altar of burnt offering . . . but David could not go before it to inquire of God for he was afraid of the sword of the angel of the Lord. Then David said, "Here shall be the house of the Lord God and here the altar of burnt offering for Israel" (1 Chr 21:26-22:1).

A sanctuary is the site for the expiation in each of these narratives. But the places Gibeon and Jerusalem are not as crucial for the intention of the Dtr as are the persons involved at these places.

The first of the narratives (2 Samuel 21) looks back to the time of Saul. It brings the pre-monarchic era to closure by the expiation of Saul's blood-guilt. The events recorded in this narrative are not intrusions; they are rather events that are presupposed in the preceding report of the accession of David.[52]

Generally, the narrative is perceived to be placed without reason. The fact is that the narrative is precisely positioned as an interruption to the Succession Narrative, at the end of the struggle between the houses of Saul and David and just prior to the designation of Solomon. The narrative in 2 Sam 21:1-14 was intended to put closure upon the conflict between the two houses and to end the infliction brought upon the people because of Saul. The narrative thus reflects backward to the events of the struggle and of Saul's transgression that had been related in the accession and succession narratives.

The narrative also focuses upon David, as do the intervening lists and poetic sections. The present time in history is being represented. David is King; on the reigning monarch the psalms and lists concerning the army of David are focused.

As a conclusion to the masterly literary construct in 2 Samuel 21-24, a collector whether of the Dtr school or later, understanding fully the

---

[52]With 2 Sam 21:7 compare 2 Samuel 9. Mephibosheth alone of the sons of Saul was spared that David might keep his covenant with Jonathan.

The sons who were hung had been mentioned in 1 Sam 3:7-8 and 18:17-19.

Dtr theology as we have shown, positioned the narrative that looks forward to the future. 2 Samuel 24 centers upon the site for the temple,
thus having ready the place for the sanctuary for the son who will build
it. Just after this narrative is the section of the Succession Narrative
that tells of Solomon being named as the co-regent and heir to David.
The narrative in 2 Samuel 24 with content that concentrates upon the site
for the temple is positioned just prior to the introduction of Solomon
whose achievement will be the construction of the temple.

      We may conclude with the observation that we have unlocked a
significant feature in Dtr methodology. In this study we have been looking at a narrative composed out of traditional formulae. The narrative so
composed marks a transition from the time prior to Solomon and the
temple to the era after Solomon and the temple. But we find in the case
of 2 Samuel 21-24 that the writer achieved such a transition through the
structuring of larger literary blocks. This supposedly problematic literary
sequence functions in the DtrH as do the Dtr compositions. It marks the
transition from Saul to Solomon without naming either. David is the actor
and object of interest throughout, since the historical period under consideration is that of David. David brings the era of Saul to a close by
ordering that the blood-guilt be expiated. David inaugurates the era of
Solomon by purchasing the site for the temple. By literary structuring
such as is evident in the unit 2 Samuel 21-24 which had been positioned as
an intrusion into the Succession Narrative at a precise point, a statement
is being made about the progression of events within the history.

VII

Dtr Methodology and Theology
A Summary

The Dtr narrative technique proves to be creative, indeed, and entirely predictable. So much of the text is expressed in the style of speeches that it is a wonder that the peculiar Dtr methodology in composition has not long ago been recognized. As the DtrH is written, the setting in the traditions of the people (Deuteronomy 1-4) is established in a public oral address spoken by Moses to the people. Several key passages throughout the history are designed as speeches and put in the mouth of principal characters. Besides these, speeches in the form of a prophetic word interrupt the otherwise continuous narrative and annalistic materials. The pronounced rhetorical style of the DtrH has been noted and commented upon. Explanations for this move no further than to point out that this rhetorical style was prevalent in the court writings of the 8th-7th centuries. It has not been noted, however, that the rhetorical style was itself key for understanding the content and message of these speeches.

THE DTR TECHNIQUE OF
"TRADITIONAL COMPOSITION"

Our study has brought to light two principal aspects of the Dtr methodology of composition: (1) the Dtr appropriated a literary genre which was used as the rhetorical mold for the content of his choosing; (2) the content is expressed out of traditional elements that function as building blocks for the presentation of a specific theological focus.

The Dtr emulated the Königsnovelle genre which in Egyptian royal ideology contained a number of forms that provided expression for the attribution of royal deeds, victories, and significant events to the will of the king's patron-god. The Dtr copied the formal dimensions of the Königsnovelle, but within the confines of its forms, the Dtr skillfully structured and precisely articulated a content that was uniquely a contribution of his own.

The selection of the Königsnovelle as the rhetorical device proved to be significant in itself. It was borrowed from the royal sphere and used in the narrative to create the semblance of a royal setting. It is no wonder that until now critics have unquestioningly admitted that the dream narrative was originally a ceremonial text for the king's coronation.

We have identified the adaptation of the formal structure of a genre as a technique of Dtr methodology in composition. The appropriation of the treaty form, which had been demonstrated by Dennis J. McCarthy,[1] to be a rhetorical device for the composition of the book of Deuteronomy and other texts within the DtrH, provides another example of this aspect of the Dtr technique of narrative composition. In addition to the Königsnovelle and the treaty, there are other literary forms employed for rhetorical effect yet to be discovered in the history.

Using the pattern of the Königsnovelle as a rhetorical device, the Dtr linked together traditional elements within the limits of the formal structure. The traditional elements were drawn from Israel's own tradition--traditions deriving from various royal ideologies, and traditions reflecting various dimensions of Yahwism, as well as elements reflective of the Dtr's own interests. These traditional elements in the shape of formulae, technical terms, phrases, motifs, and words, were systematically linked together in a style reminiscent of oral composition. Most significant is the fact that the traditional elements had been precisely selected and creatively combined to articulate a theology of kingship that is the Dtr design for kingship. The selection of the traditional components as well as their arrangement served the single purpose of presenting a kingship that is limited by Torah.

To express this, the Dtr outlined a schema of kingship that included each of the essential dimensions--the king related to God and the king related to the people in his kingdom; the duties of the king and the limits of kingship; the benefits of kingship and the obligations incumbent upon the king. Each aspect was presented in its fullest possible description out of components taken from royal traditions and traditions of Yahwism, and effectively colored by elements reflective of the Dtr interest in Torah.

---

[1]*Treaty and Covenant.*

By the skillful conjoining of this diversity of elements, the Dtr set forth the design for kingship which was his intention and his contribution: the king under Torah.

We generalize that the Dtr methodology in composition emulates the technique of oral composition, i.e., the conjoining of traditional elements, that are structured into a traditional form which also is borrowed for rhetorical purposes. We call the Dtr technique a methodology of "traditional composition."

CRITERIA OF DTR-COMPOSED TEXTS

The basic assumption upon which we have grounded our study is that Noth is correct in his hypothesis that the DtrH is a unified and coherent document written in the time of the exile. Noth had argued that the Dtr selected blocks of material from a variety of sources and joined these together with summarizing texts composed specifically as transitions. Noth, followed by McCarthy, identified a number of these Dtr-composed texts and showed that each text acted as a transition from what preceded to what followed in the historical recounting.

Our analysis of the dream narrative verifies that 1 Kings 3:4-15 also is one of the Dtr-composed texts which functions in the history to make a transition between sources. The significance of our work lies in the fact that we have identified two criteria for determining Dtr composition. First, the text in question must function in its setting as a summary statement and must make a transition between larger blocks of narrative material. Second, the text must be composed out of traditional elements that can be shown to have been conjoined to present a single theological issue.

We will discuss, first of all, the function of the dream of Solomon as (a) a summarizing text, and (b) as a text that makes a significant link within the history.

There are two features that are highlighted in the Solomonic history--the wisdom of Solomon, and the building of the temple. Both of these features are synthesized in the dream narrative, thereby identifying the dream of Solomon as programmatic for the history of Solomon.

Wisdom receives its legitimation among the traditions of Israel and specifically as a tradition associated with royalty in its being "given" to Solomon by God. Wisdom as it is presented in the Solomon history is an all-encompassing phenomenon embracing the multi-dimensions of human skill and intelligence. The dream narrative itself specifies skill and intelligence for the exercise of authority, be this in administration or in making judgments. The examples presented in the history are illustrative of the possibilities for wisdom. Wisdom is needful for making judgment (1 Kgs 3:16-28), for intellectual acumen (5:9-14 [Eng 4:29-34] and 10:1-10), and for skill in administration (5:15-26[Eng 5:1-12]).[2]

It should be noted that each illustration for the use of wisdom is stated in Dtr's own style of "traditional composition." At the end of the wise judgment, the Dtr comments:

> And all Israel heard of the *judgment* which the king had rendered; and they stood in awe of the king, because they perceived that the *wisdom of God* was in him *to render justice* (1 Kgs 3:28).

The recounting of the display of Solomon's learning is introduced with the Dtr comment:

> And *God gave* Solomon *wisdom and understanding* beyond measure and *largeness of mind* like the sand on the seashore (1 Kgs 5:9 Eng 4:29).

Solomon's negotiations with Hiram for peaceful co-existence provoked the response:

> Blessed be the Lord this day, who has given to David *a wise son* to be *over this great people* (1 Kgs 5:21 [Eng 5:7]).

and the summary statement:

> And the Lord gave Solomon *wisdom,* as he had promised, and there was *peace* between Hiram and Solomon; and the two of them made a treaty (1 Kgs 5:25 [Eng 5:12]).

As a final comment upon the display of Solomon's wisdom in all its aspects, the Queen of Sheba exclaims:

---

[2]See Martin Noth, "Die Bewährung von Salomos 'Göttlicher Weisheit'," in *Wisdom in Israel,* 225-37. Noth correctly argues that each of the elaborations upon wisdom derives from a pre-deut. source which was incorporated into the history by the Dtr and given divine approbation by the Dtr who attributed the giving of wisdom to God. Against this view, Scott argues that the "accounts of Solomon's wisdom and glory are legendary and late; . . . they were not part of the original edition of the Book of Kings" (p. 269). These accounts reflect the "grandiose imagination" of the post-exilic writers, according to Scott. So, "Solomon and the Beginnings of Wisdom in Israel," in *Wisdom in Israel,* 262-79.

> Happy are your men![3]   Happy are these your servants, who
> continuously stand before you and hear your *wisdom*! Blessed
> be the Lord your God who has delighted in you and *set you on
> the throne of Israel*! Because the Lord loved Israel for ever,
> he has *made you king*, that you may *execute justice and
> righteousness* (1 Kgs 10:8-9).

These Dtr speeches and summaries reiterate the dimensions of the wisdom
that had been given to Solomon in the dream. As king, Solomon's wisdom
is displayed in rendering justice, in drawing from the collected experience
of generations, in negotiating peace, and in ruling in a way that insures
life and harmony for the community. All these aspects of kingship are
capsulized within the dream. In this sense the dream is programmatic for
the focus upon wisdom in the Solomonic history. It is a wisdom and intelligence given by God. This point is well made and continually emphasized
by the Dtr: God gives the wisdom and intelligence. The critical issue in
the dream, however, is that the wisdom and intelligence are transformed
by Torah. The abilities displayed by Solomon to render justice, to negoti-
ate peace, to provide for the welfare of the people in the realm are not
simply indications of human capability or having successfully benefitted
from the learned experience of the past; these abilities and successes are
effectual on the basis of having complied with Torah.

The dream narrative is programmatic for the Solomonic history in
a second way that accords with the other focus of the history--the consecration of the temple. A major portion of the content of three chapters
concerns the building activities and a fourth narrates the dedication of
the temple.

We indicated in our study that the frame for the narrative that is
placed introductory to and at the conclusion of the narrative body, contains information pertinent to places of worship. Sacrifice at the great
high place, which was Gibeon, on account of its association with the tent
and ark traditions, was intended by the Dtr as a portrayal of the legitimate place for worship in the pre-temple era. Sacrifice at Jerusalem in
the style peculiar to the temple cult was intended as a portraiture of the
legitimate place for worship in the temple era. Thus, events described in
the frame correspond with ritual practice before and after Solomon's
reign and the construction of the temple. In this sense the narrative is
transitional. It summarizes in itself the translation from worship at the

---

[3]Some versions read "wives" in place of "men."   We prefer the
Hebrew reading which preserves the parallelism with "servants."

shrines to worship at the central shrine in Jerusalem. This latter is of crucial importance to the Dtr for whom there is one legitimate place for the worship of Yahweh. The law for worship, spelled out in Deut 12:1-15, indicates the deuteronomic concern for the abolition of the high places and the centralization of the cult in the place where Yahweh chose to put his name.

We have pointed out that the two texts introductory to the dream narrative, 1 Kgs 3:2-3, were not meant disparagingly but rather reflect the practice prior to the temple era. The people worship at the high places because there was no house for the name of the Lord in those days (v 2). So also did Solomon, who loved Yahweh sacrifice in the high places in this era. Once the temple is completed, the situation is entirely different. Successive kings receive unfavorable evaluation specifically because the high places were not taken away.[4] Only Hezekiah is evaluated favorably, and that because "he removed the high places. . . ."[5] Manasseh is condemned because "he rebuilt the high places which Hezekiah his father had destroyed. . . ."[6]

The Dtr attitude toward the temple is clearly reflected in the formulaic references concerning worship at the high places. The transition from the high place as a legitimate place for worship to its being an abomination takes place in the dream and specifically in the alternate forms of worship presented in the two parts of the narrative frame.

The use of transitional texts or text-complexes to tie together various facets within the history is a significant characteristic of the Dtr. We have demonstrated in this study that 1 Kgs 3:4-15 summarizes the transition from the pre-temple to the temple era. We have also demonstrated in somewhat less detail, but nonetheless compellingly that the narrative complex 2 Samuel 21-24 is also a deliberate Dtr construct which summarizes in itself the events from the demise of the Saulites to the inauguration of Solomon's reign. The function of the ark narrative has been demonstrated independently by two scholars. Timm argued that the narrative, divided as it was, linked together and showed continuity from the era of the judges to that of kings.[7] Campbell demonstrated that the ark narrative functioned in the history to show the inauguration of a new era of Yahweh's presence.[8]

---

[4] 1 Kgs 15:14a; 22:44; 2 Kgs 12:3; 14:4; 15:4, 35; 16:2b, 4a.
[5] 2 Kgs 18:4a, 22//Isa 36:7.
[6] 2 Kgs 21:3a.
[7] "Die Ladeerzählung."
[8] *The Ark Narrative.*

In our study, we have also pointed out a correspondence between Deut 1:9-18 and 1 Kgs 3:4-15, the former introductory to the pre-monarchical era and the latter introductory to the new Dtr-interpreted royal era. In both, the qualities are surprisingly similar and the texts are structured similarly. Deut 1:9-18 makes the transition into the rulership during the pre-monarchical era; 1 Kings 3 makes the transition into the era of kings interpreted by the Dtr.

Because each of these texts--the ark narrative, 2 Samuel 21-24, Deut 1:9-18 and 1 Kgs 3:4-15--fit so precisely into the history as links for the continuity of the narrative account, it would be difficult, indeed to argue other than that these texts were consciously and skillfully written into the history precisely for the purpose of making the transitions we have noted. The composition was done by the Dtr himself, out of formulaic language or out of larger literary sources,[9] to weave together the narrative blocks that describe the historical eras. Among these transitional texts we have examples in Deut 1:9-18 and 1 Kgs 3:4-15 of single-themed narratives fashioned from traditional elements; and in 2 Samuel 21-24 and the ark narrative, we have examples of transitional texts composed out of literary sources that act in the manner of traditional elements.

We have been describing the function of the dream narrative for the Solomonic history and the DtrH. We noted that the body of the narrative, specifically in the qualities for leadership presented there, is programmatic for Solomon's reign. In each dimension of his rulership, Solomon displayed the wisdom that was given by God. The framework of the narrative, however, focuses upon the transition from worship at high places to worship in Jerusalem and thereby encompasses the change that was effected during Solomon's time in the building of the temple. The importance of the temple for the Dtr is evident in the span of references from the deuteronomic law code to the evaluations of the kings on the basis of their attitude toward the high places.

We identified a second criterion for determining Dtr composition: the text must be composed out of traditional components that are structured to make a theological point of concern to the Dtr. We have argued that the Dtr conjoined components, in the shape of formulae, technical

---

[9]Larger literary pieces were combined in the ark narrative and in 2 Samuel 21-24. The larger literary sources used as building blocks have the same effect as the traditional elements that combine into the texts focused upon a single theological issue.

language, phrases, and words, deriving from royal traditions, from traditions of Yahwism, and from deuteronomic theology, to present a Dtr-
design for kingship which is kingship under Torah.

This theological point is made in the selection of motifs from royal
tradition that are suggestive of the subordination and dependence of the
king, and in the skillful use of a conditional statement which has the
effect of transforming the motifs from royal theology to a subordination
of the king to Torah.

The image of the king under Torah is projected also in the framework text in the skillful explicitation of ark theology by the appendage of
the divine title Adonai. The alteration in the theology of the ark had
indeed occurred in the transfer of the ark to the temple. In the context
of temple, the ark is no longer the presence of God; it becomes the receptacle in which the Torah is contained. Solomon standing before "the ark
of the covenant of Adonai," which is understood to be the ark in which is
contained the Torah, the stipulations for covenant loyalty, is the image of
the king subject to Torah.

The design for kingship defined by the Dtr as a kingship under
Torah and made explicit in the dream narrative has a function of its own
with respect to the Dtr history of kings. Every king after Solomon is
evaluated on the basis of obedience to Torah. The deuteronomic law for
kings makes explicit the obligation of the king to keep Torah.[10] This
obligation is fulfilled by only one king, by Josiah, who in the eyes of the
Dtr, is the ideal model of a king under Torah. Of Josiah, the Dtr says:

> he turned to the Lord with all his heart and with all his soul
> and with all his might, according to all the *Torah* of Moses
> (2 Kgs 23:25).

The dream narrative functions in the DtrH as a central and key
theological text. The content regarding the place of the temple in the
religious worship of Israel links the dream and the Solomonic history with
the report of Hezekiah who removed the high places that Yahweh may be
worshipped in the place chosen by him for his name to dwell. The ideal
for kingship that is imaged of Solomon links the kingship of Solomon with
the kingship that is modelled by Josiah who found the Torah in the temple
and who immediately responded to its contents by following Yahweh
obediently. The wisdom and intelligence given by God to Solomon for the
exercise of his authority in accord with Torah links Solomon with the

---

[10]Deut 17:18-20. On this text, see: Kurt Galling, "Das Königsgesetz
im Deuteronomium," *TLZ* 3 (1951) cols. 133-138.

leaders for Israel in the era during the pre-monarchy, and also with the people in his kingdom who are described as having wisdom and intelligence because they keep and do Torah which is "their wisdom and understanding in the sight of the people" (Deut 4:6a). Solomon, as leader and as one among the people, is charged with keeping all the words of the law and these statutes, and doing them; that his heart may not be lifted up above his brethren. . . ." (Deut 17:19b-20a). Thus, the Dtr king is a *King under Torah.*

Bibliography

Ackroyd, Peter R. "The Historians and Theologians of the Exilic Age, the Deuteronomic History." In *Exile and Restoration: A Study of Hebrew Thought of the Sixth Century B.C.* Philadelphia: Westminster, 1968. 62-83.

Ahlström, Gösta W. "Solomon, the Chosen One." *HR* 8 (1968) 93-100.

Albright, William F. "The High Place in Ancient Palestine." In *Volume du Congrès.* VTSup 4; Leiden: E. J. Brill, 1957. 242-58.

Alt, Albrecht. "Josua." *Werden und Wesen des Alten Testaments.* Ed. F. Stummer and J. Hempel. BZAW 66; Berlin: Alfred Töpelmann, 1936. 13-29. Reprinted in *Kleine Schriften zur Geschichte des Volkes Israel.* Munich: C. J. Beck, 1953. 1. 176-92.

_____. "Das Grossreich Davids." *Kleine Schriften zur Geschichte des Volkes Israel.* Munich: C. H. Beck, 1953. 2. 66-75.

_____. "Die Weisheit Salomos." *TLZ* 76 (1951) 139-44. Reprinted in *Kleine Schriften zur Geschichte des Volkes Israel.* Munich: C. H. Beck, 1959. 2. 90-99; and as "Solomonic Wisdom." In *Studies in Ancient Israelite Wisdom.* Selected, with a Prolegomenon by James L. Crenshaw. The Library of Biblical Studies; New York: KTAV, 1976. 102-12.

Anderson, Bernhard W. *Understanding the Old Testament.* 2d ed. Englewood Cliffs, NJ: Prentice-Hall, 1966.

Baltzer, Klaus, "Considerations Regarding the Office and Calling of the Prophet." *HTR* 61 (1968) 567-81.

_____. *The Covenant Formulary in Old Testament, Jewish, and Early Christian Writings.* Trans. David E. Green. Philadelphia: Fortress, 1971.

_____. *Die Biographie der Propheten.* Neukirchen-Vluyn: Neukirchener, 1975.

Barr, James. "Covenant." In *Dictionary of the Bible.* 2d ed. Original edition by James Hastings, revised by Frederick C. Grant and H. H. Rowley. New York: Scribner's, 1965. 183b-185.

Barrick, W. Boyd. "On the (Removal of the 'High Places') in 1-2 Kings." *Bib* 55 (1974) 257-59.

Bauer-Kayatz, Christa. *Studien zu Proverbien 1-9*. WMANT 22; Neu-kirchen-Vluyn: Neukirchener, 1966.

Begrich, Joachim. "Sōfēr und Mazkīr: ein Beitrag zur inneren Geschichte des davidisch-salomonischen Grossreiches und des Königsreiches Juda." *ZAW* 58 (1940-1941) 1-29.

Benzinger, Immanuel. *Jahvist und Elohist in den Königsbuchern*. BWANT 27; Stuttgart: W. Kohlhammer, 1921.

Birch, Bruce C. "The Development of the Tradition on the Anointing of Saul in I Sam 9:1-10:16." *JBL* 90 (1971) 55-68.

_____. *The Rise of the Israelite Monarchy: The Growth and Development of I Samuel 7-15*. SBLDS 27; Missoula: Scholars, 1976.

Blenkinsopp, Joseph. *Gibeon and Israel: The Role of Gibeon and the Gibeonites in the Political and Religious History of Early Israel*. Cambridge: University Press, 1972.

_____. "Did Saul Make Gibeon His Capital?" *VT* 24 (1974) 1-7.

Braulik, Georg. "Die Ausdrücke für 'Gesetz' im Buch Deuteronomium." *Bib* 51 (1970) 39-66.

Brekelmans, C. H. W. "Die sogenannten deuteronomischen Elements in Genesis bis Numeri. Ein Beitrag zur Vorgeschichte des Deuteronomiums." In *Volume du Congres Genève 1965*. VTSup 15; Leiden: E. J. Brill, 1966. 90-96.

Bright, John. *Jeremiah*. AB 21; New York: Doubleday, 1965.

Brownlee, W. H. "Psalms 1-2 as a Coronation Liturgy." *Bib* 52 (1971) 321-36.

Brueggemann, Walter. "David and His Theologian." *CBQ* 30 (1968) 156-81.

_____. "The Kerygma of the Deuteronomistic Historian." *Int* 22 (1968) 387-402.

_____. "Israel's Moment of Freedom." *TBT* (April 1969) 2917-2925.

_____. "Amos' Intercessory Formula." *VT* 19 (1969) 385-90.

_____. "Scripture and an Ecumenical Life-Style: A Study in Wisdom Theology." *Int* 24 (1970) 3-19.

_____. "Kingship and Chaos (A Study in Tenth Century Theology)." *CBQ* 33 (1971) 317-32.

_____. "On Trust and Freedom: A Study of Faith in the Succession Narrative." *Int* 26 (1972) 3-19.

_____. "From Dust to Kingship." *ZAW* 84 (1972) 1-18.

_____. "Life and Death in Tenth Century Israel." *JAAR* 40 (1972) 96-109.

_____. *In Man We Trust: The Neglected Side of Biblical Faith.* Richmond, VA: John Knox, 1972.

_____, and Wolff, Hans Walter. *The Vitality of Old Testament Traditions.* Atlanta: John Knox, 1975.

_____. *The Land.* Overtures to Biblical Theology; Philadelphia: Fortress, 1977.

Brunner, H. "Das hörende Herz." *TLZ* 79 (1954) 697-700.

Burney, C. F. *Notes on the Hebrew Text of the Books of Kings.* New York: KTAV, 1970.

Buss, Martin J. "The Study of Forms." In *Old Testament Criticism.* Ed. John H. Hayes. San Antonio: Trinity University, 1974. 1-56.

Calderone, Philip J. *Dynastic Oracle and Suzerainty Treaty.* Logos I; Manila: Ateneo de Manila University, 1966.

Campbell, Antony F. *The Ark Narrative (I Sam 4-6; 2 Sam 6): A Form-Critical and Traditio-Historical Study.* SBLDS 16; Missoula: Scholars, 1975.

Campbell, Edward F. "Sovereign God." *McCQ* 20 (1967) 173-86.

_____. "Moses and the Foundations of Israel." *Int* 29 (1975) 141-54.

Carlson, R. A. *David, the Chosen King: A Traditio-Historical Approach to the Second Book of Samuel.* Uppsala: Almqvist & Wiksell, 1964.

Carmichael, C. M. "Deuteronomic Laws, Wisdom, and Historical Traditions." *JSS* 12 (1967) 198-206.

Cazelles, Henri. "Institutions et Terminologie en Deut. I 6-17." In *Volume du Congres Genève 1965.* VTSup 15; Leiden: E. J. Brill, 1966. 97-112.

Chadwick, Hector M. and Chadwick, N. K. *The Growth of Literature.* 1932-1940, 3 vols. Cambridge: University Press, 1968.

Childs, Brevard S. "Deuteronomic Formulae of the Exodus Traditions." In *Hebräische Wortforschung.* Fs. W. Baumgartner. VTSup 16; Leiden: E. J. Brill, 1967. 30-39.

_____. *The Book of Exodus: A Critical Theological Commentary.* Philadelphia: Westminster, 1974.

Clements, Ronald E. *God and Temple.* Philadelphia: Fortress, 1965.

_____. *Abraham and David: Genesis 15 and its Meaning for Israelite Tradition.* SBT, Second Series 5; London: SCM, 1967.

Coats, George W. "The Joseph Story and Ancient Wisdom: A Reappraisal." *CBQ* 35 (1973) 285-97.

_____. "Redactional Unity in Genesis 37-50." *JBL* 93 (1974) 15-21.

_____. *From Canaan to Egypt: Structural and Theological Context for the Joseph Story.* CBQMS 4; Washington, DC: The Catholic Biblical Association of America, 1976.

Crenshaw, James and Willis, John T., eds. *Essays in Old Testament Ethics.* Fs. J. Philip Hyatt. New York: KTAV, 1974.

Crenshaw, James L., ed. *Studies in Ancient Israelite Wisdom.* Selected, with a Prolegomenon by James L. Crenshaw. The Library of Biblical Studies; New York: KTAV, 1976.

Crim, Keith R. *The Royal Psalms.* Richmond, VA: John Knox, 1962.

Cross, Frank M. and Freedman, D. N. "A Royal Song of Thanksgiving: II Samuel 22-Psalm 18." *JBL* 72 (1953) 15-34. Now appearing in *Studies in Ancient Yahwistic Poetry.* SBLDS 21; Missoula: Scholars, 1975. 125-58.

Cross, Frank Moore. "Yahweh and the God of the Patriarchs." *HTR* 55 (1962) 225-59.

_____. *Canaanite Myth and Hebrew Epic: Essays in the History of the Religion of Israel.* Cambridge: Harvard University, 1973.

Culley, Robert C. "An Approach to the Problem of Oral Tradition." *VT* 13 (1963) 114-25.

_____. *Oral Formulaic Language in the Biblical Psalms.* Near and Middle East Series 4; Toronto: University of Toronto, 1967.

_____, ed. *Oral Tradition and Old Testament Studies.* Semeia 5; Missoula: Scholars, 1976.

_____. *Studies in the Structure of Hebrew Narrative.* Philadelphia: Fortress, 1976.

Dahood, Mitchell. *Psalms I:1-50; Psalms II:51-100; Psalms III: 101-150.* AB 16, 17, 17a; Garden City: Doubleday, 1966-70.

Delekat, Lienhard. "Tendenz und Theologie der David-Salomo-Erzählung." In *Das ferne und nahe Wort.* Ed. Fritz Maass. BZAW 105; Berlin: Alfred Töpelmann, 1967. 26-36.

Diepold, Peter. *Israels Land.* BWANT 95; Stuttgart: W. Kohlhammer, 1972.

Dietrich, Walter. *Prophetie und Geschichte: Eine redaktionsgeschichtliche Untersuchung zum deuteronomistischen Geschichtswerk.* FRLANT 108; Göttingen: Vandenhoeck & Ruprecht, 1972.

Driver, G. R. and Miles, John C. *The Babylonian Laws,* Vol I: *Legal Commentary.* Oxford: Clarendon, 1952.

Driver, G. R. *Canaanite Myths and Legends.* Old Testament Studies 3; Edinburgh: T. & T. Clark, 1956.

Eaton, J. H. *Kingship and the Psalms.* SBT, Second Series 32; London: SCM, 1976.

Ehrlich, Ernst Ludwig. *Der Traum im Alten Testament.* BZAW 73; Berlin: Alfred Töpelmann, 1953.

Eissfeldt, Otto. *The Old Testament: An Introduction. The History of the Formation of the Old Testament.* Trans. Peter R. Ackroyd. New York: Harper & Row, 1965.

Ellis, Peter F. "1-2 Kings." In *JBC.* Ed. R. A. Brown et al. Englewood Cliffs: Prentice-Hall, 1968. 179-209.

_____. *The Yahwist: The Bible's First Theologian.* Collegeville, MN: Liturgical, 1968.

Engnell, Ivan. *Gamla Testamentet. En traditionshistorisk inledning.* I. Stockholm: Svenska Kyrkans Diakonistyrelses Bokförlag, 1945.

_____. *Studies in Divine Kingship in the Ancient Near East.* Oxford: Basil Blackwell, 1967.

_____. "The Pentateuch." In *A Rigid Scrutiny: Critical Essays on the Old Testament.* Ed. and trans. John T. Willis. Nashville: Vanderbilt University, 1969. 50-67.

Fensham, F. Charles. "The Judges and Ancient Israelite Jurisprudence." *Die Ou Testamentiese Werkgemeenskap in Suid-Afrika.* Papers read at the 2nd meeting held at Potchefstroom, 2-5 February, 1959.

_____. "Ps 21--A Covenant Song?" *ZAW* 77 (1965) 193-202.

_____. "Father and Son as Terminology for Treaty and Covenant."
In *Near Eastern Studies in Honor of William Foxwell Albright*. Ed.
Hans Goedicke. Baltimore and London: Johns Hopkins, 1971. 121-35.

Fichtner, Johannes. *Die altorientalische Weisheit in Ihrer israelitisch-
judischen Ausprägung*. BZAW 62; Giessen: Alfred Töpelmann, 1933.

_____. "Jesaja unter den Weisen." *TLZ* 74 (1949) 75-80. Also
appearing in *Gottes Weisheit. Gesammelte Studien zur Alten Testament*. Ed. Klaus Dietrich Fricke. Stuttgart: Calwer, 1965.

_____. *Das erste Buch von den Königen*. Die Botschaft des Alten
Testament 12/1; Stuttgart: Calwer, 1964.

Finnegan, Ruth. "How Oral is Oral Literature?" *BSO(A)S* 37 (1974) 52-64.

Flanagan, James W. "Court History or Succession Document? A Study of
2 Samuel 9-20 and 1 Kings 1-2." *JBL* 91 (1972) 172-81.

Fohrer, Georg. "Der Vertrag zwischen König und Volk in Israel." *ZAW* 71
(1959) 1-22.

_____. *Introduction to the Old Testament*. Trans. David E. Green.
Nashville: Abingdon, 1965.

_____. *History of Israelite Religion*. Trans. David E. Green. Nash-
ville: Abingdon, 1972.

Frankfort, Henri and H. A., et al. *The Intellectual Adventure of Ancient
Man: An Essay on Speculative Thought in the Ancient Near East*.
Chicago: University of Chicago, 1946.

Frankfort, Henri. *Kingship and the Gods: A Study of Ancient Near
Eastern Religion as the Integration of Society and Nature*.
Chicago: University of Chicago, 1948.

Freedman, David N. "Divine Commitment and Human Obligation." *Int* 18
(1964) 419-31.

_____. "The Deuteronomic History." In *IDB Sup*. Ed. George
Buttrick. Nashville: Abingdon, 1976. 226-28.

Gadd, C. J. *Ideas of Divine Rule in the Ancient East*. The Schweich
Lectures on Biblical Archaeology, 1945. London: Oxford University,
1948.

Galling, Kurt. *Die Erwählungstraditionen Israels*. BZAW 48; Giessen:
Alfred Töpelmann, 1928.

_____. "Das Königsgesetz in Deuteronomium." *TLZ* 3 (1951) 133-38.

Gammie, John G. "The Theology of Retribution in the Book of Deuteronomy." *CBQ* 32 (1970) 1-12.

Gerstenberger, E. "Covenant and Commandment." *JBL* 84 (1965) 38-51.

_____. *Wesen und Herkunft des "apodiktischen Rechts."* WMANT 20; Neukirchen-Vluyn: Neukirchener, 1965.

Gervitz, Stanley. *Patterns in the Early Poetry of Israel.* Studies in Ancient Oriental Civilization 32; Chicago: University of Chicago, 1963.

Gese, H. *Lehre und Wirklichkeit in der alten Weisheit. Studien zu den Sprüchen Salomos und zu dem Buche Hiob.* Tübingen: J. C. B. Mohr (Paul Siebeck), 1958.

Gilmer, Harry W. *The If-You Form in Israelite Law.* SBLDS 15; Missoula: Scholars, 1975.

Glueck, Nelson. *Ḥesed in the Bible.* Cincinnati: Hebrew Union College, 1967.

Goldsworthy, Graeme Lister. "Empirical Wisdom in Relation to Salvation History in the Psalms." Diss. Union Theological Seminary in Virginia, 1973.

Gordis, Robert. "Knowledge of Good and Evil in the Old Testament and the Dead Sea Scrolls." In *Poets, Prophets and Sages: Essays in Biblical Interpretation.* Bloomington: Indiana University, 1971. 198-216.

Görg, Manfred. *Gott-König-Reden in Israel und Ägypten.* BWANT 105; Stuttgart: W. Kohlhammer, 1975.

Goetze, Albrecht. "Ḫattušiliš. Der Bericht über seine Thronbesteigung nebst den Paralleltexten." In *Hethitische Texte in Umschrift mit Übersetzung und Erläuterungen.* Ed. Ferdinand Sommer. Leipzig: J. C. Hinrichs'sche Buchhandlung, 1925.

Gottlieb, H. "El und Krt--Jahwe und David." *VT* 24 (1974) 159-67.

Graesser, Carl. "The Message of the Deuteronomic Historian." *CTM* 39 (1968) 542-51.

Gray, Bennison. "Repetition in Oral Literature." *Journal of American Folklore* 84 (1971) 289-303.

Gray, John. *The Legacy of Canaan: The Ras Shamra Texts and their Relevance to the Old Testament.* 2d rev. ed. Leiden: E. J. Brill, 1965.

_____. *I & II Kings. A Commentary.* 2d rev. ed.. Philadelphia: Westminster, 1970.

Gurney, O. R. *The Hittites.* Baltimore: Penguin, 1954.

Habel, Norman. "The Form and Significance of the Call Narratives." *ZAW* 77 (1965) 297-323.

Harrelson, Walter. "Life, Faith, and the Emergence of Tradition." In *Tradition and Theology in the Old Testament.* Ed. Douglas A. Knight. Philadelphia: Fortress, 1977. 11-30.

Hayes, John H., ed. *Old Testament Form Criticism.* San Antonio: Trinity University, 1974.

Hermann, Alfred. *Die ägyptische Königsnovelle.* Leipziger Ägyptologische Studien 10; Glückstadt-Hamburg-New York: J. J. Augustin, 1938.

Hermisson, Hans-Jürgen. *Studien zur israelitischen Spruchweisheit.* WMANT 28; Neukirchen-Vluyn: Neukirchener, 1968.

Herrmann, Siegfried. "Die Königsnovelle in Ägypten und Israel." *Wissenschaftliche Zeitschrift der Karl-Marx-Universität.* Leipzig: Gesellschafts- und Sprachwissenschaftliche Reihe 3, 1953-4. 51-62.

Hertzberg, Hans Wilhelm. "Die Entwicklung des Begriffes משפט im AT." *ZAW* 40 (1922) 256-87; 41 (1923) 16-76.

_____. *I and II Samuel: A Commentary.* Philadelphia: Westminster, 1964.

_____. *Die Bücher Josua, Richter, Ruth.* ATD 9; Göttingen: Vandenhoeck & Ruprecht, 1965.

Hillers, Delbert. "A Note on Some Treaty Terminology in the O.T." *BASOR* 176 (1964) 46-47.

Hölscher, Gustav. "Das Buch der Könige, seine Quellen und seine Redaktion." In *Eucharisterion.* Fs. Hermann Gunkel. FRLANT 36/1; Göttingen: Vandenhoeck, 1923. 158-213.

_____. *Die Anfänge der hebräischen Geschichtsschreibung.* Sitzungberichte der Akademie, Heidelberg, Philos.-hist. Klasse, 1942.

_____. *Geschichtsschreibung in Israel: Untersuchungen zum Jahvisten und Elohisten.* Lund: Gleerup, 1952.

Hooke, S. H. ed. *Myth, Ritual and Kingship. Essays on the Theory and Practice of Kingship in the Ancient Near East and in Israel.* Oxford: Clarendon, 1958.

Humphreys, W. Lee. "The Motif of the Wise Courtier in the Old Testament." Diss. Union Theological Seminary, 1970.

Ishida, T. "The Leaders of the Tribal Leagues 'Israel' in the Premonarchic Period." *RB* 80 (1973) 514-30.

Jenni, Ernst. "Zwei Jahrzehnte Forschung an den Büchern Josua bis Könige." *TRu* 27 (1961) 1-32, 97-164.

Jepsen, Alfred. *Die Quellen des Königsbuches.* 2d ed. rev. Halle (Saale): Max Niemeyer, 1956.

_____. "צדק und צדקה im Alten Testament." In *Gottes Wort und Gottes Land.* Ed. Henning Graf Reventlow. Göttingen: Vandenhoeck & Ruprecht, 1965. 78-89.

_____. *Sacral Kingship in Ancient Israel.* 2d ed. Cardiff: University of Wales, 1967.

Johnson, Aubrey R. "The Rôle of the King in the Jerusalem Cultus." In *The Labyrinth. Further Studies in the Relation between Myth and Ritual in the Ancient World.* Ed. S. H. Hooke. New York: Macmillan, 1935. 71-111.

_____. "Hebrew Conceptions of Kingship." In *Myth, Ritual, and Kingship.* Ed. S. H. Hooke. Oxford: Clarendon, 1958. 204-35.

_____. *Sacral Kingship in Ancient Israel.* 2d ed. Cardiff: University of Wales, 1967.

Kapelrud, A. S. "Temple Building, a Task for Gods and Kings." *Or* 32 (1963) 56-62.

Kearney, Peter J. "The Role of the Gibeonites in the Deuteronomic History." *CBQ* 35 (1973) 1-19.

Kellogg, Robert. "Oral Literature." *New Literary History* 5 (1973) 55-66.

Kenik, Helen A. "Code of Conduct for a King: Psalm 101." *JBL* 95 (1976) 391-403.

Knierim, Rolf. "The Messianic Concept in the First Book of Samuel." In *Jesus and the Historian. Written in Honor of E. C. Colwell.* Ed. F. T. Trotter. Philadelphia: Westminster, 1968. 20-51.

_____. "Old Testament Form Criticism Reconsidered." *Int* 27 (1973) 435-68.

Knight, Douglas A. "The Understanding of 'Sitz im Leben' in Form Criticism." In *SBLASP*, 1974. Ed. George MacRae. Massachusetts: Society of Biblical Literature. 1. 105-18.

_____. *Rediscovering the Traditions of Israel.* SBLDS 9; Missoula: Scholars, 1975.

_____, ed. *Tradition and Theology in the Old Testament.* Philadelphia: Fortress, 1977.

Koch, Klaus. "Gibt es ein Vergeltungsdogma im Alten Testament." *ZTK* 52 (1955) 1-42.

_____. "Zur Geschichte der Erwählungsvorstellung in Israel." *ZAW* 67 (1955) 205-26.

_____. *The Growth of the Biblical Tradition: The Form-Critical Method.* Trans. S. M. Cupitt. New York: Scribner's, 1969.

Koch, Walter A. "Recurrent Units in Written and Oral Texts." *Linguistics* 73 (1971) 62-89.

Köhler, Ludwig. *Hebrew Man.* London: SCM, 1956.

_____. "Problems in the Study of the Language of the Old Testament." *JSS* 1 (1956) 3-24.

Kramer, Samuel N. *Sumerian Mythology: A Study of Spiritual and Literary Achievement in the Third Millennium B.C.* Philadelphia: The American Philosophical Society, 1944.

_____. *The Sumerians: Their History, Culture and Character.* Chicago: University of Chicago, 1963.

Kraus, Hans-Joachim. *Worship in Israel: A Cultic History of the Old Testament.* Trans. Geoffrey Buswell. Richmond, VA: John Knox, 1963.

_____. *Psalmen I.* Neukirchen-Vluyn: Neukirchener, 1966.

_____. *Geschichte der historisch-kritischen Erforschung des Alten Testaments.* 2d ed. rev. Neukirchen-Vluyn: Neukirchener, 1969.

Kutsch, Ernst. *Salbung als Rechtsakt im Alten Testament und im Alten Orient.* BZAW 87; Berlin: Alfred Töpelmann, 1963.

_____. "Gesetz und Gnade: Probleme des alttestamentlichen Bundesbegriffs." *ZAW* 79 (1967) 18-35.

_____. "Der Begriff ברית in vordeuteronomischer Zeit." In *Das ferne und nahe Wort.* Ed. Fritz Maass. Berlin: Alfred Töpelmann, 1967. 133-43.

Labat, Rene. *Le Caractère religieux de la royauté assyro-babylonienne.* Paris, 1939.

Lindars, Barnabas. "Torah and Deuteronomy." In *Words and Meanings: Essays presented to David Winton Thomas.* Eds. Peter R. Ackroyd and B. Lindars. Cambridge: University Press, 1968. 117-36.

Lindhagen, Curt. *The Servant Motif in the Old Testament.* Uppsala: Lundequistska Bokhandeln, 1950.

Lohfink, Norbert. "Die deuteronomistische Darstellung des Übergangs der Führung Israels von Moses auf Josue." *Scholastik* 37 (1962) 32-44.

_____. "Die Bundesurkunde des Königs Josias." *Bib* 44 (1963) 261-88, 461-98.

_____. "Hate and Love in Osee 9, 15." *CBQ* 25 (1963) 417.

_____. "Bilanz nach der Katastrophe. Das deuteronomistische Geschichtswerk." In *Wort und Botschaft: Eine theologische und kritische Einführung in die Probleme des Alten Testaments.* Ed. Josef Schreiner. Wurzburg: Echter, 1967. 196-208.

Lord, Albert B. *The Singer of Tales.* New York: Atheneum, 1974.

_____. "Perspectives on Recent Work on Oral Literature." *Forum for Modern Language Studies* 10 (1974) 187-200.

Luckenbill, Daniel D. *Ancient Records of Assyria and Babylonia.* Vol. II: *Historical Records of Assyria.* Chicago: University of Chicago, 1927.

Malchow, Bruce Virgil. "The Roots of Israel's Wisdom in Sacral Kingship." Diss. Marquette University, 1972.

Malfroy, J. "Sagesse et Loi dans le Deuteronome." *VT* 15 (1965) 49-65.

Mendenhall, George E. "Covenant Forms in Israelite Tradition." *BA* 17 (1954) 50-76. Now appearing in *BAR* 3. 25-53.

_____. "Covenant." In *IDB.* Ed. George Buttrick. Nashville: Abingdon, 1962. 1.714-723.

_____. "Election." In *IDB.* Ed. George Buttrick. Nashville: Abingdon, 1962. 2.76-82.

_____. *The Tenth Generation. The Origin of the Biblical Tradition.* Baltimore: Johns Hopkins University, 1973.

Mettinger, Tryggve N. D. *Solomonic State Officials: A Study of the Civil Government Officials of the Israelite Monarchy.* Lund: CWK Gleerups, 1971.

Miller, Patrick D. "The Blessing of God." *Int* 29 (1975) 240-51.

Miller, Patrick D. and Roberts, J. J. M. *The Hand of the Lord: A Reassessment of the "Ark Narrative" of 1 Samuel.* Baltimore/London: Johns Hopkins University, 1977.

Montgomery, James A. *A Critical and Exegetical Commentary on the Books of Kings.* Ed. Henry S. Gehman. ICC; New York: Scribner's, 1951.

Moran, William L. "The Ancient Near Eastern Background of the Love of God in Deuteronomy." *CBQ* 25 (1963) 77-87.

_____. "A Note on the Treaty Terminology of the Sefîre Stelas." *JNES* 22 (1963) 173-76.

_____. "A Study of the Deuteronomic History." *Bib* 46 (1965) 223-28.

Mowinckel, Sigmund. *He That Cometh. The Messiah Concept in the Old Testament and Later Judaism.* Trans. G. W. Anderson. Nashville: Abingdon, 1954.

_____. "Das Thronbesteigungsfest Jahwä's." In *Psalmenstudien II.* Amsterdam: P. Schippers, 1961. 44-145.

_____. "Israelite Historiography." *ASTI.* Ed. Hans Kosmala. Leiden: E. J. Brill, 1963. 2. 4-26.

_____. *Tetrateuch-Pentateuch-Hexateuch. Die Berichte über die Landnahme in den drei altisraelitischen Geschichtswerken.* BZAW 90; Berlin: Alfred Töpelmann, 1964.

_____. *The Psalms in Israel's Worship.* Vol. 1-2. Trans. D. R. Ap-Thomas. Nashville: Abingdon, 1967.

Muffs, Yochanan. *Studies in the Aramaic Legal Papyri from Elephantine.* Studia et Documenta 8; Leiden: E. J. Brill, 1969.

Muilenburg, James. "The Form and Structure of the Covenantal Formulations." *VT* 9 (1959) 347-65.

Murphy, Roland E. "The Wisdom Literature of the Old Testament." In *The Human Reality of Sacred Scripture.* Concilium I/10; New York: Paulist, 1965. 126-40.

_____. "Assumptions and Problems in O. T. Wisdom Research." *CBQ* 29 (1967) 407-18.

_____. "Form Criticism and Wisdom Literature." *CBQ* 31 (1969) 475-85.

_____. "Wisdom and Yahwism." In *No Famine in the Land. Studies in Honor of John L. McKenzie*. Eds. James W. Flanagan and Anita Weisbrod Robinson. Missoula: Scholars Press for the Institute for Antiquities and Christianity--Claremont, 1975. 117-26.

McCarthy, Dennis J. "Three Covenants in Genesis." *CBQ* 26 (1964) 179-89.

_____. "Covenant in the O. T.: The Present State of Inquiry." *CBQ* 27 (1965) 217-40.

_____. "II Samuel 7 and the Structure of the Deuteronomic History." *JBL* 84 (1965) 131-38.

_____. "Notes on the Love of God in Deuteronomy and the Father-Son Relationship between Yahweh and Israel." *CBQ* 27 (1965) 144-47.

_____. "Theology and Covenant in the Old Testament." *TBT* (April 1969) 2904-2908.

_____. "An Installation Genre?" *JBL* 90 (1971) 31-41.

_____. "The Theology of Leadership in Joshua 1-9." *Bib* 52 (1971) 165-75.

_____. "B^{e}rît and Covenant in the Deuteronomistic History." In *Studies in the Religion of Ancient Israel*. VTSup 23; Leiden: E. J. Brill, 1972. 65-85.

_____. "b^{e}rît in Old Testament History and Theology." *Bib* 53 (1972) 110-21.

_____. "The Inauguration of Monarchy in Israel. A Form-Critical Study of I Samuel 8-12." *Int* 27 (1973) 401-12.

_____. "Review of *Deuteronomy and the Deuteronomic School* by Moshe Weinfeld." *Bib* 54 (1973) 448-52.

_____. "Covenant Relationships." In *Bibliotheca Ephéméridum theologicarum lovaniensium XXXIII. Questions disputées d'Ancien Testament: Méthode et Théologie*. Ed. C. Brekelmans. XXII session des *Journées Bibliques de Louvain*, 1974. 91-103.

_____. "The Wrath of Yahweh and the Structural Unity of the Deuteronomistic History." In *Essays in Old Testament Ethics*. Eds. James Crenshaw and John T. Willis. New York: KTAV, 1974. 97-110.

_____. *Treaty and Covenant: A Study in Form in the Ancient Oriental Documents and in the Old Testament*. New edition completely rewritten. AnOr 21A; Rome: Biblical Institute, 1977.

McKane, William. *Prophets and Wise Men.* SBT 44; London: SCM, 1965.

_____. *Proverbs: A New Approach.* OTL; Philadelphia: Westminster, 1970.

McKay, J. W. "Man's Love for God in Deuteronomy and the Father/ Teacher--Son/Pupil Relationship." *VT* 22 (1972) 426-35.

McKenzie, Donald A. "Judicial Procedure at the Town Gate." *VT* 14 (1964) 100-104.

McKenzie, John L. "The Dynastic Oracle: II Sam 7." *TS* 8 (1947) 187-218.

_____. "Royal Messianism." *CBQ* 19 (1957) 25-52. Reprinted in *Myths and Realities: Studies in Biblical Theology.* Milwaukee: Bruce, 1963. 203-31.

_____. "Reflections on Wisdom." *JBL* 86 (1967) 1-9.

Nelson, Richard D. "The Redactional Duality of the Deuteronomistic History." Diss. Union Theological Seminary in Virginia, 1973.

_____. "Dynastic Oracle in DTR: A Workshop in Recent Trends." In *SBLASP*, 1976. Ed. George MacRae. Missoula: Scholars, 1976. 1-14.

Nicholson, E. W. *Preaching to the Exiles. A Study of the Prose Tradition in the Book of Jeremiah.* New York: Schocken, 1971.

North, Christopher R. *The Old Testament Interpretation of History.* London: Epworth, 1946.

Noth, Martin. *Das Buch Josua.* 2d ed. HAT 1/7; Tübingen: J. C. B. Mohr, 1953.

_____. "Zur deuteronomistischen Geschichtsauffassung." In *Proceedings XXII Congress of Orientalists, Istanbul, 1957.* Leiden: E. J. Brill, 1957. 2. 558-66.

_____. *The History of Israel.* Rev. ed. New York: Harper & Row, 1960.

_____. *Überlieferungsgeschichtliche Studien: Die Sammelnden und Bearbeitenden Geschichtswerke im Alten Testament.* 3rd ed. Tübingen: Max Niemeyer, 1967.

_____. *The Laws in the Pentateuch and Other Studies.* Philadelphia: Fortress, 1967.

_____. *Könige.* BKAT 9/1; Neukirchen-Vluyn: Neukirchener, 1968.

_____. "Die Bewährung von Salomos 'Göttlicher Weisheit'." In *Wisdom in Israel and in the Ancient Near East.* Eds. M. Noth and D. Winton Thomas. VTSup 3; Leiden: E. J. Brill, 1969. 225-37.

_____. *A History of the Pentateuchal Traditions.* Trans. B. W. Anderson. Englewood Cliffs: Prentice-Hall, 1972.

Oppenheim, A. Leo. *The Interpretation of Dreams in the Ancient Near East.* Transactions of the American Philosophical Society, N.S. Vol. 46, Part 3; Philadelphia: The American Philosophical Society, 1956.

Patton, John Hastings. *Canaanite Parallels in the Book of Psalms.* Baltimore: Johns Hopkins, 1944.

Pederson, John. *Israel Its Life and Culture.* London: Geoffrey Cumberlege, 1-2: 1926, 3-4: 1940.

Perlitt, Lothar. *Bundestheologie im Alten Testament.* WMANT 36; Neukirchen-Vluyn: Neukirchener, 1969.

Porteous, Norman W. "Royal Wisdom." In *Wisdom in Israel and in the Ancient Near East.* Eds. Martin Noth and D. Winton Thomas. VTSup 3; Leiden: E. J. Brill, 1969. 245-61.

Postgate, J. N. *Neo-Assyrian Grants and Decrees.* Studia Pohl: Series Maior I, Pontifical Biblical Institute, 1969.

Pritchard, James B., ed. *Ancient Near Eastern Texts Relating to the Old Testament.* 3rd ed. with Supplement. New Jersey: Princeton University, 1969.

Quell, Gottfried. "The O T Term בְּרִית." In *TDNT.* Ed. G. Kittel. Grand Rapids: Eerdmans, 1965. 2. 106-24.

Rad, Gerhard von. *Studies in Deuteronomy.* Trans. David Stalker. SBT 9; London: SCM, 1953.

_____. *Deuteronomy: A Commentary.* Trans. Dorothea Barton. Philadelphia: Westminster, 1966.

_____. *The Problem of the Hexateuch and Other Essays.* Trans. E. W. Trueman Dicken. New York: McGraw-Hill, 1966.

_____. *Old Testament Theology: The Theology of Israel's Historical Traditions.* Trans. D. M. G. Stalker. New York: Harper & Row, 1962.

_____. *Genesis: A Commentary.* Rev. ed. Philadelphia: Westminster, 1972.

_____. *Wisdom in Israel.* Trans. James D. Martin. Nashville: Abingdon, 1972.

Randolph, Wm. Pierce. "The Development of History Writing in the Scribal Wisdom of Judah." Diss. Emory University, 1970.

Redford, D. B. *A Study of the Biblical Story of Joseph (Gen. 37-50).* VTSup 20; Leiden: E. J. Brill, 1970.

Reventlow, Henning Graf. "Sein Blut komme über sein Haupt." *VT* 10 (1960) 311-27.

Richter, Wolfgang. "Traum und Traumdeutung im AT: Ihre Form und Verwendung." *BZ* 7 (1963) 204-20.

_____. *Die Bearbeitungen des "Retterbuches" in der deuteronomischen Epoche.* BBB 21; Bonn: Peter Hanstein, 1964.

_____. "Zu den 'Richtern Israels'." *ZAW* 77 (1965) 40-72.

_____. "Urgeschichte und Hoftheologie." *BZ* 10 (1966) 96-105.

_____. *Die sogenannten vorprophetischen Berufungsberichte: Eine literaturwissenschaftliche Studie zu 1 Sam 9.1-10,16 Ex 3f. und Ri 6,11b-17.* FRLANT 101; Göttingen: Vandenhoeck & Ruprecht, 1970.

Ringgren, Helmer. *The Messiah in the Old Testament.* SBT 18; London: SCM, 1956.

Robinson, J. *The First Book of Kings.* The Cambridge Bible Commentary; Cambridge: University Press, 1972.

Ross, J. F. "The Prophets as Yahweh's Messenger." In *Israel's Prophetic Heritage. Essays in Honor of James Muilenburg.* Eds. B. W. Anderson and W. Harrelson. New York: Harper & Brothers, 1962. 98-107.

Rost, Leonhard. *Das kleine Credo und andere Studien zum Alten Testament.* Heidelberg: Quelle & Meyer, 1965.

Rowley, H. H. *The Biblical Doctrine of Election.* London: Lutterworth, 1953.

Ruppert, L. *Die Josepherzählung: Ein Beitrag zur Theologie der Pentateuchquellen.* Munich: Kösel, 1965.

Rylaarsdam, J. Coert, ed. *Transitions in Biblical Scholarship.* Chicago: University of Chicago, 1968.

Salmon, John M. "Judicial Authority in Early Israel: An Historical Investigation of Old Testament Institutions." Diss. Princeton Theological Seminary, 1968.

Sanders, James A. *Torah and Canon.* Philadelphia: Fortress, 1972.

Schmid, Hans Heinrich. *Wesen und Geschichte der Weisheit: Eine Untersuchung zur Altorientalischer und Israelitischen Weisheitsliteratur.* BZAW 101; Berlin: Alfred Töpelmann, 1966.

_____. *Gerechtigkeit als Weltordnung. Hintergrund und Geschichte des alttestamentlichen Gerechtigkeitsbegriffes.* BHT 40; Tübingen: J. C. B. Mohr (Paul Siebeck), 1968.

_____. "Schöpfung, Gerechtigkeit und Heil." *ZTK* 70 (1973) 1-19.

Scott, R. B. Y. *Proverbs, Ecclesiastes.* AB 18; Garden City: Doubleday, 1965.

_____. "Solomon and the Beginnings of Wisdom in Israel." In *Wisdom in Israel and in the Ancient Near East.* VTSup 3; Leiden: E. J. Brill, 1969. 262-79. Now appearing in *Studies in Ancient Israelite Wisdom.* New York: KTAV, 1975. 84-101.

Shafer, Byron. "The Root bḥr and Pre-Exilic Concepts of Chosenness in the Hebrew Bible," *ZAW* 89 (1977) 20-42.

Simpson, Cuthbert A. *The Early Traditions of Israel: A Critical Analysis of the Pre-deuteronomic Narrative of the Hexateuch.* Oxford: Blackwell, 1948.

_____. "The Growth of the Hexateuch." In *IB.* Ed. George Buttrick. Nashville: Abingdon, 1952. 1. 185-200.

_____. *Composition of the Book of Judges.* Oxford: Blackwell, 1957.

Skladny, Udo. *Die ältesten Spruchsammlungen in Israel.* Göttingen: Vandenhoeck & Ruprecht, 1962.

Smend, Rudolf. "JE in den geschichtlichen Büchern des AT." *ZAW* 39 (1921) 181-217.

_____. "Das Gesetz und die Völker: Ein Beitrag zur deuteronomistischen Redaktionsgeschichte." In *Probleme biblischer Theologie.* Ed. Hans W. Wolff. Munich: Chr. Kaiser, 1971. 494-509.

_____. "Tradition and History: A Complex Relation." In *Tradition and Theology in the Old Testament.* Ed. Douglas A. Knight. Philadelphia: Fortress, 1977. 49-68.

Snaith, Norman H. "The Historical Books." In *The Old Testament and Modern Study.* Ed. H. H. Rowley. Oxford: Clarendon, 1951. 84-107.

_____. "I-II Kings." In *IB.* Ed. George Buttrick. New York: Abingdon, 1954. 3. 1-338.

Soggin, Alberto. "Deuteronomistische Geschichtsauslegung während des babylonischen Exils." In *Oikonomia: Heilsgeschichte als Thema der Theologie*. Ed. Felix Christ. Hamburg-Bergstedt: Herbert Reich, 1967. 11-17.

Speiser, E. A. "Authority and Law in Mesopotamia." *Supplement to the Journal of the American Oriental Society* 17 (1954) 8-15.

Steck, Odil Hannes. *Israel und das gewaltsame Geschick der Propheten. Zur Überlieferung des deuteronomistischen Geschichtsbildes im Alten Testament, Judentum und Urchristentum*. WMANT 23; Neukirchen-Vluyn: Neukirchener, 1967.

Sturtevant, Edgar H. and Bechtel, George. *A Hittite Chrestomathy*. William Dwight Whitney Linguistic Series; Philadelphia: Linguistic Society of America, University of Pennsylvania, 1935.

Szikszai, S. "Kings, I and II." In *IDB*. Ed. George Buttrick. New York: Abingdon, 1962. 3. 26-35.

Thompson, Thomas L. *The Historicity of the Patriarchal Narratives: The Quest for the Historical Abraham*. BZAW 133; New York: Walter de Gruyter, 1974.

Thureau-Dangin, F. *Die sumerischen und akkadischen Königsinschriften*. Voderasiatische Bibliothek 1; Leipzig: J. C. Hinrichs, 1907.

de Tillesse, G. Minette. "Sections 'tu' et sections 'vous' dans le Deuteronome." *VT* 12 (1962) 29-87.

Timm, Hermann. "Die Ladeerzählung (I Sam. 4-6; II Sam. 6) und das Kerygma des deuteronomistischen Geschichtswerkes." *EvT* 26 (1966) 509-26.

Tucker, Gene M. *Form Criticism of the Old Testament*. Guides to Biblical Scholarship, O T Series; Philadelphia: Fortress, 1971.

Van Selms, A. "The Title 'Judge'." In *Die Ou Testamentiese Werkgemeenskap in Suid-Afrika*. Papers read at the 2nd Meeting held at Potchefstroom, 2-5 February, 1959. 41-50.

Van Seters, John. *Abraham in History and Tradition*. New Haven: Yale University, 1975.

Vaughn, Patrick H. *The Meaning of 'Bāmā' in the Old Testament: A Study of Etymological, Textual and Archaeological Evidence*. SOTSMS 3; New York/London: Cambridge University, 1974.

de Vaux, Roland. "Titres et fonctionnaires égyptiens a la cour de David et de Salomon." *RB* 48 (1939) 394-405.

_____. "Le Roi d'Israël, Vassal de Yahvé." In *Mélanges Eugène Tisserant*. Vol. I: *Écriture Sainte-Ancien Orient*. Studi e Testi 231; Città del Vaticano: Biblioteca Apostolica Vaticana, 1964. 119-33.

_____. *Ancient Israel*. Vol. I: *Social Institutions*. New York: McGraw-Hill, 1965.

_____. *The Bible and the Ancient Near East*. Trans. Damian McHugh. New York: Doubleday, 1971.

Vriezen, Th. C. *Die Erwählung Israels nach dem Alten Testament*. ATANT 24; Zürich: Zwingli, 1953.

Wagner, Norman E. "Abraham and David?" In *Studies on the Ancient Palestinian World*. Eds. J. W. Wevers and D. B. Redford. Toronto: University of Toronto, 1972. 117-40.

Weinfeld, Moshe. "The Origin of Humanism in Deuteronomy." *JBL* 80 (1961) 241-47.

_____. "The Covenant of Grant in the Old Testament and in the Ancient Near East." *JAOS* 90 (1970) 184-203.

_____. *Deuteronomy and the Deuteronomic School*. Oxford: Clarendon, 1972.

Weippert, Helga. "Die 'deuteronomischen' Beurteilung der Könige von Israel und Judah und das Problem der Redaktion der Königsbücher." *Bib* 53 (1972) 301-39.

Weiser, Artur. *The Old Testament: Its Formation and Development*. New York: Association, 1961.

_____. *The Psalms: A Commentary*. Philadelphia: Westminster, 1962.

Weisman, Z. "Anointing as a Motif in the Making of the Charismatic King." *Bib* 57 (1976) 378-98.

Wellhausen, Julius. *Prolegomena to the History of Ancient Israel*. New York: Meridian, 1957.

_____. *Die Composition des Hexateuchs und der historischen Bücher des Alten Testaments*. Berlin: Walter de Gruyter, 1963.

Westermann, Claus. "Die Begriffe für Fragen und Suchen im Alten Testament." *KD* 6 (1960) 2-30.

_____. "The Way of Promise through the Old Testament." In *The Old Testament and Christian Faith*. Ed. B. W. Anderson. New York: Harper & Row, 1963. 200-224.

_____. *Basic Forms of Prophetic Speech.* Philadelphia: West-minster, 1967.

_____. *Der Segen in der Bibel und im Handeln der Kirche.* Munich: Chr. Kaiser, 1968.

_____. "Die Joseph-Erzählung." In *Calwer Predigthilfen V.* Stutt-gart: Calwer, 1970. 11-118.

_____. "Creation and History in the Old Testament." In *The Gospel and Human Destiny.* Ed. Vilmos Vajta. Minneapolis: Augsburg, 1972. 11-38.

Whallon, William. "Formulaic Poetry in the Old Testament." *Comparative Literature* 15 (1965) 1-14.

Whybray, R. N. *Wisdom in Proverbs: The Concept of Wisdom in Proverbs 1-9.45.* SBT 45; London: SCM, 1965.

_____. *The Succession Narrative: A Study of II Samuel 9-20; I Kings 1 and 2.* SBT, Second Series 9; Naperville, IL: Alec R. Allenson, 1968.

_____. *The Intellectual Tradition in the Old Testament.* BZAW 135; New York: Walter de Gruyter, 1974.

Widengren, Geo. *Sakrales Königtum im Alten Testament und im Juden-tum.* Stuttgart: W. Kohlhammer, 1955.

Wifall, Walter. *The Court History of Israel.* St. Louis: Clayton, 1975.

Wilcoxen, Jay A. "Narrative Structure and Cult Legend: A Study of Joshua 1-6." In *Transitions in Biblical Scholarship.* Ed. J. Coert Rylaarsdam. Chicago: University of Chicago, 1968. 43-70.

_____. "Narrative." In *Old Testament Form Criticism.* Ed. John H. Hayes. San Antonio: Trinity University, 1974. 57-98.

Wolff, Hans Walter. "The Kerygma of the Yahwist." *Int* 20 (1966) 131-58. Now appearing in *The Vitality of Old Testament Traditions* by W. A. Brueggemann and H. W. Wolff. Atlanta: John Knox, 1975. 41-66.

_____. "The Kerygma of the Deuteronomic Historical Work." In *The Vitality of Old Testament Traditions.* Atlanta: John Knox, 1975. 83-100. Translated from "Das Kerygma des deuteronomistischen Geschichtswerks." *ZAW* 73 (1961) 171-86.

_____. *Hosea. A Commentary on the Book of the Prophet Hosea.* Trans. Gary Stansell. Hermeneia Series; Philadelphia: Fortress, 1974.

Wright, G. Ernest. "Israel in the Promised Land: History Interpreted by Covenant Faith." *Encounter* 35 (1974) 318-34.

Würthwein, Ernst. *Die Weisheit Ägyptens und das Alte Testament.* Schriften der Philipps-Universität Marburg 6. Marburg: N. G. Elwert, 1960. Now appearing as "Egyptian Wisdom and the Old Testament." Trans. Brian Kovacs. In *Studies in Ancient Israelite Wisdom.* Selected, with a Prolegomenon by J. L. Crenshaw. New York: KTAV, 1975. 113-33.

Zenger, Erich. "Die deuteronomistische Interpretation der Rehabilitierung Jojachins." *BZ* 12 (1968) 16-30.

Zimmerli, Walther. "Zur Struktur der alttestamentlichen Weisheit." *ZAW* 51 (1933) 177-204. Trans. Brian W. Kovacs and appearing as "Concerning the Structure of Old Testament Wisdom." In *Studies in Ancient Israelite Wisdom.* Selected, with a Prolegomenon by J. L. Crenshaw. New York: KTAV, 1975. 175-207.

_____. "The Place and Limit of the Wisdom in the Framework of the Old Testament Theology." *SJT* 17 (1964) 146-58. Now appearing in *Studies in Ancient Israelite Wisdom.* Selected, with a Prolegomenon by J. L. Crenshaw. New York: KTAV, 1975. 314-26.

Indexes

SCRIPTURE REFERENCES

MODERN AUTHORS

SUBJECTS